# CHRISTIAN
# FRATRICIDE

*Why Christians Continue
to be Divided Politically*

FRANK S. KACER

Printed in the United States of America

ISBN 9781498462525

www.xulonpress.com

# Dedication

I t's with deep gratitude that I dedicate this book to Lynn, my loving, godly wife of 42 years. Not only has she been patient during the untold number of hours required to research and develop this material, but she has been a constant source of encouragement for me to equip Christians in our political battles for the sake of the gospel.

Thank you honey, and thank you for being a Proverbs 31 woman by my side.

# Acknowledgements

Drawing from experience gained over 20 years, it's hard to identify just a few individuals that had the greatest impact on the material presented in this book. Besides local Christian activist groups, literally hundreds if not thousands of church members, ministry leaders and pastors have influenced and refined my understanding of our role as Christians in the political arena.

Given that caveat, I would like to acknowledge the insights and recommendations of Lori Arnold, who went through the entire transcript and made innumerable and much needed corrections and suggestions to improve its content and readability. In addition, I'd like to thank my fellow Elders at Grace Bible Church who were patient with me as I ministered to other churches and Christian groups throughout the Southern California region, and who provided godly counsel and biblical balance to my understanding of a Christian's role in our nation.

# Preface

*"Faith apart from works is dead"* – **James 2:26**

Most Christians know faith brings glory to God when it activates us to do good works, both within the body of Christ and to those that are lost and needy in the world.

What most Christians don't realize is that the unbelieving world also understands this. Prevent the good works, and the faith is no longer credible. To do this, those in darkness are willing to use every tool at their disposal to remove any Christian influence that would bring credit upon the Lord and ultimately the gospel of Jesus Christ.

The ungodliness polluting our society's fabric hasn't stopped with capturing college campuses, the entertainment industry or the mainstream news media. Its proponents now exercise incredible political power through unceasing, creative and deceitful tactics the Christian community is unable or unwilling to challenge in a united way.

Why remove Christian influence from politics? Because our adversaries know if government can co-opt the Christian's Matthew 22:39 and 5:13-16 mandates, then eventually Matthew 28:19-20 will be relegated to the dark corners of a locked closet. In effect: remove the tangible "works" we're called to do and the "faith" is dead.

Our generation is witnessing the takeover of government by worldviews that despise our values and our source of hope. Although there are reasons why the nation's largest demographic group has so little influence, there's hope if we stop removing politics from the list of "good works" we're called to do.

To help do just that, this book identifies three interrelated problem areas: pastoral leadership, Christian divisiveness, and ineffective political engagement. It then gives practical advice on how to do kingdom work in political minefields for our personal good, the common good and ultimately for the sake of the gospel.

# Table of Contents

## Part 3: Fratricide Between Believers and the World

# Introduction

*"If even lifeless instruments, such as the flute or the harp, do not give distinct notes, how will anyone know what is played? And if the bugle gives an indistinct sound, who will get ready for battle?"*
**– 1 Corinthians 14:7-8**

*"I became all things to all people, that by all means I might save some. I do it all for the sake of the gospel"*
**– 1 Corinthians 9: 22-23**

### The Awakening

I don't know exactly when I became politically "aware"; but it was in the early 1990's during our children's teenage years as they became influenced by the cultural/political debates raging all around them. I do vividly remember, however, when I asked fellow elders if we had a responsibility to equip church members to be godly citizens and politically involved. The response around the table was the classic deer-in-the-headlights look. After an awkward silence, someone finally said "What's that have to do with what we do here?" I was embarrassed and a bit taken aback to see my question met with a mixture of amusement and indifference.

That elder board question started a private journey to understand if spiritual leaders in a local church had any biblical duty to educate and exhort members to actively engage in the politics of the day. Clearly, Christians are to set an example of righteousness in sharp contrast to the ungodly cultural wasteland around us, but were we to aggressively hold government accountable and reverse its growing disdain of anything Christian? Answering this question wasn't easy for me. Our children weren't yet adults, church ministry consumed incredible time and energy, and I had a demanding secular job. But over time I arrived at an answer by searching the Scriptures, stumbling onto materials readily available at the time[1], and naively engaging in local politics.

It wasn't long before I ran into a conundrum. How could Christians holding the very words of God in their hands, who believe in the sufficiency of Scripture for all of faith, life, and practice become so ineffective and non-credible in our nation's participative political realm? On the other hand, how could much smaller demographic groups such as African-Americans, Muslims, Jews, or homosexuals have such an inordinate impact on our nation? Clearly there was a gap between what Christians believe to be true, and what we think applies to governing our country.

Even more troubling for me was recognizing that Christian faith and biblical principles in any realm of government were becoming ever more irrelevant and unwelcome. The trend line is obvious: our freedom to openly preach the full counsel of God, worship, exercise church discipline, hire and fire, and to make personal and business decisions consistent with our faith are daily becoming a matter of government caprice and not legally protected rights.[2] Clearly, what's ultimately at stake in this spiritual war is not just the marginalization of Christians in the public square, but the silencing of the proclamation of the gospel of Jesus Christ!

---

[1]   Besides material produced by Pro-Life groups (Operation Rescue), sermons and writings of Jerry Falwell (Moral Majority), there were excellent materials by Dr. D. James Kennedy who promoted vigorous evangelism (Evangelism Explosion) and a cultural mandate through the Center for Reclaiming America.

[2]   Examples of these very things will be found throughout this book.

## *The Root Issue*

Scripture says we should expect opposition from an unbelieving world (1 Peter 5:8-9) that has little, if any, ability to understand spiritual truths (1 Corinthians 2:11-13). But even in the face of hostility and unbelief Christianity has made incredible impacts throughout history by preaching the gospel, nurturing regenerated lives, and applying scriptural principles in a discerning way to man's burdens and labors in a fallen world.[3]

But something else is going on in our nation.

The Christian community has become dysfunctional when it comes to the political realities of how to influence our nation in a biblical, reasonably coherent manner. Indeed, precious time, energy and influence are squandered by arguing among ourselves about whether a biblical worldview even applies to a secular, civil realm.

It's not that the Christian community is being "triangulated"[4] by its opponents; it's a self-inflicted fragmentation and hostility amongst Christians on major moral issues and approaches to them. This type of "fratricide" can easily be seen when fellow believers become at odds, or even demeaned, for holding a different position on some piece of legislation or the worthiness of a particular candidate. When this happens, and it does quite often, the predictable result is a divided and politically ineffective community.[5]

---

[3]    A short list includes: primacy of education and scientific endeavor; equal human dignity independent of gender, social class or age; hospitals and compassionate care giving to those in need; and a coherent moral code for all of mankind.

[4]    Triangulation is a political tactic popularized by Dick Morris to weaken opposition to Bill Clinton's re-election. It claims some of your political opponent's ideas as your own to divide the opposition while remaining above the fray. The apostle Paul used a form of triangulation by pitting the Sadducees against the Pharisees on the issue of the resurrection, resulting in them fighting amongst themselves instead of united to do away with him (Acts 22:30-23:11).

[5]    In fact, I've personally had my faith in Christ challenged solely because I questioned the worth of a voter initiative. This level of attack is not only ungracious; it is unworthy of the Body of Christ.

I'm not advocating for a theocratic "Christian Nation", or trying to "Restore the Nation for Christ".[6] I am, however, concerned about our inability to articulate and infuse God's biblical truths and insights in an influential way towards our government and our elected leaders. Without a clear and balanced understanding of our moral imperative to be salt-and-light, infused with practical wisdom and accountability from strong spiritual leadership, the larger Christian community will continue to find itself internally disjointed, marginalized by society, and unwelcome in any governmental sphere. I've personally come to the conclusion that since this battle is clearly spiritual in nature, it's not far-fetched to predict the end game the worldly powers around us want to achieve: sufficient hostility towards all things Christian that the laws of the land will become an incredibly powerful weapon to legally end our freedom to practice the tenets and truths of our faith and openly proclaim the gospel.[7] Is this threat far-fetched? Consider a simple example of how weak we already are to standing against the tide.

### *A Personal Example*

Several years ago I was asked to teach a Sunday School series on Christian citizenship at a Baptist church near a major university. In discussing topics with the associate pastor he became more and more nervous. I was warned that half of the membership were registered Democrats. When I asked what difference that made, he said it wouldn't be acceptable to say anything that may be controversial. He agreed that biblical principles could be explained and related to moral issues but there was an unwillingness to go anywhere near the practical implications of

---

[6]    There are different biblical roles for the "church" and "state". History shows if Christianity took over government that it would only be a matter of time before justice would morph into revenge towards the non-orthodox. The proper roles of church and state towards each other are treated in Chapters 4 and 5.

[7]    For any who think this is far-fetched, consider the fact that preaching or speaking out publically against homosexuality is already considered hate speech and punishable in much of Europe and Canada.

a biblical worldview in political discourse. In effect, stick with the Bible but not its consequences for the common good. "Politics" became the dividing line no matter how delicately it would be covered – and this in a series entitled Christian Citizenship! Needless to say, the series was never taught.

This one example has all the key factors addressed in this book: lapses in pastoral leadership to fully equip a flock for every good work (2 Timothy 3:16-17); the resultant confusion and contention among the flock over what (if any) role they play in the political realm; the unavoidable confusion and disunity among the flock on important issues of the day; and a predictably ineffective response to countering the government's continuing plunge into unwise and ungodly exercising of power.

It was true in Christ's time, and its true today: darkness can't stand any light to be around, and in spiritual warfare there's no such thing as peaceful co-existence. When concerned Christians are not properly led, they end up fighting each other and giving mixed responses to spiritual attacks. When Christians remove themselves from politics, government will not just rot, it will also become an active enemy and antagonist to everything we hold of value.

### The Bottom Line

This book attempts to pastorally address the fault lines in modern evangelicalism and the wider Christian community concerning involvement in political issues and to correct them in practical ways to build unity and increase effectiveness. This isn't an easy task, but it's an important one.

For many these will be unfamiliar waters. But clearly scripture provides illumination on every issue our government concerns itself with and that we have an opportunity, yes, even an obligation to influence (2 Timothy 3:16-17). Though Satan may be the prince of this age, we need to be reminded that we serve the ruler of the universe, the King of kings and Lord of lords; so who are we to fear (Romans 8:37-39)?

Is this battlefield to take precedence over our ministry to each other (John 13:34-35), our commitment to worship and fellowship (Acts 2:42), or our acts of mercy and compassion to those in need (Matthew 22:39)? Of course not. But are the political battles of our day to be trivialized or ignored? I believe that would be dangerous. Our challenge is to rise as one people (Judges 20:8), work together; and strive for the unity of the Spirit and fruitful labor against the darkness trying to eradicate our Christian witness and transformational influence. In doing so we must never forget to treat each other with the knowledge that we share much more together through faith in Jesus Christ than we'll ever share in politics.[8]

## Book Structure

In the following pages I've divided the material into three sections. The first covers leadership and the pastor's role with his flock; the second deals with issues amongst believers; and the third addresses practical issues with the Christian community engaging the world around us. Virtually all of the material is based on personal experiences that came from ministering with sincere believers trying to do what they thought was right, but many times by the wrong means.

May the Lord grant His favor on His bride, and her kingdom labor in this world to bring Him glory!

Jude 24, 25.

---

[8]    Clearly, I'm referring to those that are truly Christians, those that have accepted Jesus Christ as both Lord and Savior, and not to those that are Christian in name only (social Christians) that have no regard for biblical authority and for all intents and purposes are part of the unbelieving society we live in.

# Part 1

# Fratricide Between
# The Pastor and His Flock

# Chapter 1

# Making the Case

*"The hottest places in hell are reserved for those who,*
*in a time of moral crisis, maintain their neutrality."*
**– Dante Alighieri (1265-1321)**

### The Elephant In the Room

Typically, Christians only think of abortion or homosexual activism as the primary political hot buttons with any moral implications. But government control of our lives, our businesses, the economy, public education, international affairs, who or what will be taxed, even whether a special surcharge should be applied to Christmas trees[9] are all moral decisions based on a value

---

[9]  In 2011 Congress, through the Department of the Agriculture seriously considered a $0.15 surcharge on the sale of all Christmas trees in order to raise money to promote the Christmas tree industry. But what would actually promote business better: raising the cost of buying trees, creating additional administrative burdens, and opening the door for higher future taxes; or deregulating businesses to reduce unnecessary administrative costs currently imposed by the government?

system of some kind. In fact, the prevalent government attitude is that there's very little that shouldn't be under its direct control, or at least influence.[10]

Many people will argue, "That's the nature of government. Obviously it's ineffective and corrupt. Why should I be surprised?" On one level I absolutely agree. The problem is that in just one generation the government has become a colossal, perhaps the largest, stumbling block to our freely exercising biblical faith and influence in this nation. In fact, if government is left unchecked our future Christian witness across America and around the world could be dramatically and needlessly burdened.

The following explains why I believe this is true, several of the key reasons we've become ineffective as a community of believers, and why pastors are one of the keys to turn back this dark tide.

### Is Government Really Our Enemy?

Let's do a quick mental survey. During the entire waking day think of anything you see, touch, eat, use, or throw away that a law, regulation, policy or government agency doesn't regulate, standardize, subsidize, tax, incentivize, legalize, criminalize, protect, destroy, interfere with or in some other way show interest in.

Look at public schools and the thousands upon thousands of pages of state education codes that mandate behavior, attitudes and social engineering to the detriment of academic learning and reasoning excellence.[11] What about the environment and pollution control, species protection, recycling, hiring and firing practices, disciplining of children, treatment of pets, labeling on

---

[10]    The exception is gratefully found in Galatians 5:22-23; "But the fruit of the Spirit is love, joy, peace, patience, kindness, goodness, faithfulness, gentleness, self-control; against such things there is no law" (or tax, yet).

[11]    For one of the most extensive, convoluted, and difficult to understand examples, go to the official California State web-site and access the full text of the "California Education Code".

toothpaste, or even what constitutes a legitimate marriage?[12] The reach of government knows few, if any, bounds.

But wait, these laws and regulations may be annoyances but do they have anything to do with worship, preaching, teaching, shepherding the flock, and evangelism? Obviously, government abuses can provide a laughable, target-rich environment for sermon illustrations; and we can be thankful for the sanctifying process of patience development when dealing with entities like the Department of Motor Vehicles. But there's a more dangerous impact coming from such government growth in power and interference. That impact is full on spiritual warfare against all that we hold dear.

Without being melodramatic, government is no longer willing to remain neutral or benevolent toward churches or public expressions of the Christian faith whether our founders gave us constitutional protections or not.[13] It goes far beyond the removal of prayer from schools, or not being able to mention the name of Christ when giving the invocation at a city council meeting,[14] or the IRS targeting "conservative" groups for harassment leading up to a national election, or having a crèche or cross on public property.[15] Government also forces churches to make major investments in dubious building code improvements; it zones churches out of prominent locations in order to preserve greater property

---

[12]   For a little perspective, the National Conference of State Legislatures (NCSL) reported in December 2011 that 40,000 new state laws would take effect in 2012, while John Stossel reported on Fox news that the Federal government passed more than 80,000 pages of new regulations in 2011 alone. I readily admit, I've not independently verified the accuracy of these counts, nor do I want to.

[13]   First Amendment to the Constitution: "Congress shall make no law respecting an establishment of religion, or prohibiting the free exercise thereof; or abridging the freedom of speech, or of the press; or the right of the people peaceably to assemble, and to petition the Government for a redress of grievances."

[14]   Although the U.S. Supreme Court upheld this practice in a May 2014 decision.

[15]   A classic example of these never ending legal challenges is the Mount Soledad Cross War Memorial in San Diego (my home town). The legal battle has spanned over 20 years and involved: two local votes by the citizens; state courts all the way to the California Supreme Court; federal courts all the way to the U.S. Supreme Court (twice); as well as Congressional legislation – still without resolution.

tax revenues despite federal protections against such actions; it threatens to fine home Bible study groups if they don't obtain a special use permit;[16] and even threatens to revoke a 501(c)3 religious tax exemption if a pastor dares to publicly condemn a particularly vile candidate for elective office.

As government continues to grow and exercise "sovereign" power over every aspect of our lives, why would anyone think it won't come after the open proclamation of biblical truth through preaching and teaching and writing,[17] or street evangelism, or church discipline, or use of church facilities, or hiring practices, or the handing out of Christian literature in shopping malls, or helping homosexuals overcome their same-sex attraction through biblical counseling? Government is rapidly forcing secular, humanistic, relativistic morals on the entire nation, even though this country still has a significant Christian legacy and presence. In fact, government has demonstrated over and over again that our values should be in line with those of the world or be kept in our own homes (more accurately, in our own closets!).[18] To put it even more bluntly, inclusiveness, tolerance, and values-free secularism - not truth and justice - comprise

---

[16] This was dramatically illustrated in the Pastor Jones home Bible study case in 2010 where an overzealous county employee cited a small group home Bible study for not having a Conditional Use Permit. If they continued in non-compliance, they would be subject to stiff daily fines. Through the aid of the National Center for Law & Policy (formerly Western Center for Law & Policy) the county admitted to violating the religious and assembly rights of this group. If this was an isolated case, it may be understandable, but unfortunately it's representative of a growing pattern across our nation.

[17] If you think this is not going to happen, think again. Hate Crime legislation already treats the same crime in a discriminatory manner depending on the presence of a protected class of victim and the perceived motivation of the criminal. Hate Speech will be the next criminal act; claiming a hate crime was motivated by a sermon (hate speech) directed toward sinful behavior (e.g. homosexuality) or by taking extreme offense which resulted in "justifiable" retaliation; or being offended to the point of deep psychological damage. In California, because of SB 48, any discussions that reflect negatively on homosexuality are already banned from the classroom

[18] Though examples would be legion, remember the Roman Catholic church being forced out of providing adoption services in Massachusetts because they wouldn't place children in the homes of same-sex partners; or the violation of conscience issues for health-care professionals who refuse to perform or even assist in abortions because of a belief in the sanctity of life from conception to natural death.

the new state religion independent of how vile the consequences may be to lives and souls.

The recent Supreme Court decision concerning same-sex-marriage[19] is a particularly glaring example of government abuse of authority and a willingness to impose legal recognition of Biblically condemned sexual behaviors across the entire nation. Not only was this decision contrary to reason, biology, and historical-traditional marriage patterns around the world for millennia, it sets up the inevitable clash with any institution, whether religious or not, that openly takes a stand against it.

The bottom line is that when government goes outside its swim lanes of biblical responsibility it's no longer our friend; it becomes a powerful and determined adversary.

### *Benign Neglect*

Most Americans would agree that we've enjoyed incredible freedoms since our nation came into being. But there's a common phrase that applies to freedoms: either "use 'em, or lose 'em." We have a choice, either we continue to exercise and aggressively protect our freedom to proclaim the gospel and perform the good works we're called to do (Ephesians 2:10), or we can "curse the darkness" and wait for the inevitable to happen.[20] Unfortunately, many have decided this is not a battle in which the church should actively engage.

---

[19]   United States Supreme Court decision: *Obergefell v. Hodges*; 26 June 2015

[20]   In the secular realm an analogy would be trademark infringement. A company must challenge every encroachment, no matter how small or trivial. If it fails to do so, their exclusive rights to that trademark will become weakened and maybe eventually lost. For our freedoms to remain intact, we must intentionally protect against each incursion or risk losing them all.

It's common for many pastors to believe it's illegal[21], un-biblical; or non-biblical[22] to address moral issues from the pulpit once they're thought to be "political". In fact, there's often great resistance to allowing the formation of any church-based citizenship or action-based ministry, no matter how benign. The implication seems to be that church members are expected to independently figure out how to effectively apply biblical principles to the sophisticated spiritual warfare in which our government is engaged.[23] But what would happen if this same abstract approach was taken with any other type of church ministry – such as counseling, marriage, parenting, finances, hospitality, evangelism, or even mercy and compassion?

Obviously, if leadership consistently overlooks or actively belittles political involvement, then the message is loud and clear: politics, deliberative legislation, and even election campaigns are either not important or they're unworthy of our time and energy. All too often when something is actually mentioned from the pulpit the pastor seems to breathe a sigh of relief that the duty is done and now he can get back to what's really important.

This mindset doesn't stop at the pulpit. Consider a leadership self test: does political engagement (citizenship) ever come to mind when future ministries are being strategized and resourced? Are talented young adults ever encouraged and mentored to seek elective office or public service as a rewarding but difficult ministry? Have we refined our understanding of the Matthew 5:13-16 salt-and-light mandate so narrowly that it excludes anything to do with the political or governmental realm? Can it possibly be that our reluctance

---

[21]  The legal aspects of what a church (or pastor) can and cannot do legally is addressed in Chapter 10: Common Myths as well as Chapter 18 where reference tools are provided.

[22]  Chapter 3: Do We Have a Cultural Mandate?; addresses this in detail. It's a complex issue that needs to be addressed with wisdom and with sound application of biblical principles without going to extremes.

[23]  Government interest includes our personal lives, our families, our schools, our places of work, and even our places of worship.

to engage government with a biblical worldview may be contributing to the growth of its abusive power?

Like it or not, the biggest threat to our religious liberties and Christian witness isn't radical Islam, or the church down the street with contemporary worship services, it's an uncontrolled government with values anathema to our faith (Colossians 2:8; Ephesians 6:12). In league with government's increasing hostility are activist groups and legal organizations that are trying to convince the public that politics is off-limits for Christians and the church. This obviously plays well for those who see us as a threat to their bankrupt, soul-destroying philosophies. Unwittingly, we actually help their cause if we buy into the lie that God's Word isn't relevant, or we have no role or legal right to directly influence government to remain within its proper biblical role (Romans 13:1-7; 1 Peter 2:13-14).[24]

The Christian community didn't go from its historical role as our nation's moral authority and conscience to its current position of virtual irrelevancy overnight. Some of the causes were self-inflicted while others were pressures from the world. In either case it's instructive to understand the dynamics that resulted in where we are today – a sincere, disparate, somewhat isolated community that may be far more concerned with numerical church growth than impacting our nation for the common good and the preservation of our freedom to proclaim God's truths to all of life.

### *What Have We Done to Ourselves?*

That the visible church in America is fragmented is an understatement. It brings to mind the famous 1971 Pogo cartoon by Walt Kelly that said: "We have met the enemy and he is us." Though biblical truth has been challenged for

---

[24] For a more detailed discussion on the practical relationships between the state and the church, go to Chapter 4: Separation of Church *from* State and Chapter 5: Separation of State *from* Church.

millennia, it was the advent of higher criticism (Historical – Critical methodology) in the 1800's that dramatically challenged the doctrine of inerrancy and infallibility for wide swaths of Christianity. This weakened the resolve to rely on the sufficiency and trustworthiness of Scripture for all matters of faith and practice. This wasn't the start of selective acceptance of biblical truths, or the adding of extra-biblical sources as equally authoritative, but it accelerated the use of worldly reasoning and science as a judge over scripture and its relevancy.[25] All too often, with that weakening came outright rejection of God's Word when in conflict with modern "enlightened" worldviews (Colossians 2:8).

Though well-meaning, attempts to yoke together the sacred (church) and secular (state)[26] for a greater good has also resulted in an incredible increase in reliance on government instead of turning to an almighty God for our earthly needs.[27] Ultimately, an unchecked government begins to see itself as the source of rights and blessings and bestows them on whoever it will in an attempt to reverse the effects of unacknowledged sin.[28] Jim Wallis and the Sojourners organization is a clear example of co-joining the realms of church with state for supposed higher purposes of social justice. This capitulation is the "social gospel" re-invented, but this time making big government appear all powerful, and Almighty God seem small by comparison.[29] Instead of the

---

[25]   My first awareness of this destructive trend was when I read the classic book: "The Battle for the Bible" by Harold Lindsell (1976).

[26]   Numerous Christian authors have pointed out that the church is failing to evangelize (and transform) the world, and instead the world has successfully been evangelizing (and transforming) the church.

[27]   An outstanding treatment of the history behind the development of our governments co-opting the church's Biblical compassion and mercy imperative is Marvin Olasky's "The Tragedy of American Compassion" (1992).

[28]   One way this is done is by redefining what's good or evil, with abortion and homosexuality being prominent examples (Isaiah 5:20; Proverbs 17:15). Another way is when government is looked to for solutions to life's problems and the source of a paradise on earth (entitlements; utopianism).

[29]   This isn't to say that the life-giving and transforming gospel truth of Jesus Christ isn't present; only that using the tools of government to bring about social justice and the improvement of

church holding the government accountable to stay within its biblical realm of responsibilities, many church leaders have become "useful idiots" to justify government co-opting the church's rightful place as the only true salt-and-light. This development over many years has had devastating effects on proclaiming the gospel as people turn to government as their new idol and not the true and living God to which they will ultimately be accountable.

Obviously the fight for what constitutes proper biblical orthodoxy has continued in every generation since the Apostles (Galatians 1:8-9; 1 John 1:1-4). However, the growth of the fundamentalist movement since the early 1900's has also had an impact on our perceived relevancy in the political realm. Rightfully, the movement's focus was on Christ the Redeemer, however, what tended to be overlooked was any substantive emphasis on our role beyond the clear command to evangelize (Matthew 28:19-20; Acts 1:6-8). A full-orbed development of the salt-and-light mandate (Matthew 5:13-16) and the second greatest commandment to love our neighbor (Matthew 22:39) weren't necessarily being ignored, but the impression could too easily be given that they're only discretionary actions and not imperatives for Christians to diligently pursue.

Likewise, the resurgent reformed movement has stressed the primacy of preaching Christ, but the emphasis has been to build up of the Body of Christ, and not so much (if ever) for equipping and sending of these same believers back into the decaying world around us (Ephesians 4:11-16).[30]

An opposite development has been pietism: stressing withdrawal from the outside world and a concentration on personal holiness untainted by surrounding

---

mankind's condition can be misplaced. Government will never point a person to Christ, but it will attempt to co-opt the biblical role of the Body of Christ to the world (Matthew 22:39)

[30]    It's not without some justification that Reformed (Calvinistic) churches are known pejoratively to outsiders as the "frozen chosen". The introspective, inward focus of the preaching and teaching often concentrates exclusively on the believing member and not the Lord's imperatives to go into the world to evangelize and influence. As a consequence, the hearer may then be left to figure out how to go about engaging wickedness and darkness all on their own.

evil. This desire, though commendable to a certain level, may see the world and its systems as beyond reforming in any meaningful sense, with minimal interaction the way to build a strong, direct relationship with the Lord. In this view, politics is seen as corrupting and not worthy of the attention of God's people.[31]

One other development worthy of note is the tremendous growth of the seeker-friendly church movement. Though there are exceptions, the tendency is to not offend visitors that may be curious about Christianity (Romans 10:2) by avoiding inflammatory language such as sin, evil and hell, and steering clear of controversial "political" issues such as abortion, same-sex marriage or the dangers of the public school system. This approach can produce a zeal for evangelism, but also a tendency to trivialize or ignore solid biblical truths (Romans 10:2) that include our wider duty toward the culture, the state, and the spiritual threats facing us.

Finally, the small but influential Theonomic movement seeks to instill the Lordship of Christ and the authority of Scripture directly over all the worlds' institutions (Psalm 24:1). This has caused many evangelical pastors to become wary of political involvement since they don't want to be painted with the same doctrinal brush.[32] Seeing these views as extreme, a typical reaction is to overcompensate by ignoring political involvement altogether. Interestingly, the political left uses the "threat" of Christian Theonomy as a weapon to impugn broader Christian motives and minimize influence by trying to draw an analogy between Christianity and radical Islam.[33]

---

[31]  I personally know several families that have removed themselves from cities and are raising their children in mountainous, semi-isolation to protect them. I have to wonder, however, if this little "city on the hill" is actually touching any lives for the Lord beyond family.

[32]  Whether it's Theonomy, Triumphalism, reclaiming or restoring America for Christ, or Reconstructionism, the underlying principle is to win and/or impose biblical law on the world's institutions and governments while Christianizing the world - in effect, the combining of church and state until the Lord returns.

[33]  Radical Islam makes no distinction between religion and state; they're one and the same under Sharia law.

When the gospel itself is under attack within the visible church, when God's all-sufficient inerrant Word is being watered down and compromised, then the biblically distinct roles of church and state can become easily confused. Seminaries will focus on what they believe are the most significant spiritual battles and turn out the next generation of pastors and theologians in response. Unfortunately, many now see the world as co-laborers (social liberal adherents), or have become disinterested in the power of the worlds institutions (various reformed adherents), and hence insensitive to the threat unchecked government poses to the body of Christ. The later viewpoint is exemplified by some of the current debate surrounding Two Kingdom theology, where civil affairs are acknowledged as a necessary part of our lives but with little emphasis on engaging it in a transformational manner for the glory of God .[34]

Rest assured, the primary purpose of the church gathered is to worship God in spirit and truth; preach and teach the fullness and sufficiency of the Bible; edify and encourage believers; and to lovingly serve one another (Ephesians 4:11-16; Galatians 6:10). Where we've atrophied spiritually is in matters understood to be secondary (yet very important): providing wise counsel to our nation; restraining government from promoting ungodliness; and protecting our religious freedoms in all our endeavors in this still remarkable nation (Galatians 6:10a).

### *The Curse of Prosperity*

Following World War II our nation experienced the world's greatest growth in prosperity since the days of Solomon. The Christian legacy inherited from our nation's forefathers still provided a moral foundation to our society and helped keep open promotion of wickedness in check.

---

[34] For one treatment of this theology see Dr. David Van Drunen's "Living in God's Two Kingdoms". For a scathing critique of much of this viewpoint see Dr. John Frame's "Escondido Theology"

But prosperity can easily create laziness regarding deep spiritual matters, compromise with the delights of the world, and a sarcastic indifference toward any threat from government. Many may have even seen our prosperity as subtly validating our standing before God, and as a result, allowed apathy to quench any clear imperative to engage the wicked heart or the corrupting influence of our societal environment. Sadly, in many quarters the church began to accommodate a people having an appearance of godliness without its transforming power (2 Timothy 3:5).

When materialism begins to govern our daily lives, when our churches are growing, when we see ourselves as the cowboy with the white hat, it becomes easy to ignore the gathering storm clouds of a distant enemy. Focusing internally on the flock, enjoying God's economic blessings, and becoming less sensitive toward spiritual warfare was a prime setup for a fall. As materialism invaded our lives and churches, the Christian community showed its weakness to counter the sexual, drug and radical feminist revolutions, the rebellious anti-authoritarian sentiment or the much touted generation gap. Add to this the ill-fated Vietnam War, destructive judicial activism, and an inability to articulate a clear Christian position on what was wreaking havoc on every aspect of our nation and it quickly became clear how our relevancy outside the church walls was rapidly disappearing. These and other waves of change quickly built a formidable barrier to our witness and purpose to engage the world around us.

### The Ill-fated 1980's "Resurgence"

The "Jesus Movement" of the 1960's and 1970's had a major impact on many aspects of church life, music and even evangelistic outreach, but little direct, long-lasting influence on the politics of the day. Major of our nation's youth that were raised in a Christian environment in that era turned away from what they perceived as a church that was irrelevant to the political and societal conflicts of the day. A notable exception was the Moral Majority movement led by Jerry Fallwell in the 1980's. This was an exhilarating time for many Christian activists that were able to help shape national policy and return moral roots back to national exposure. Not only did Christians factor heavily in the election of Ronald Reagan to the presidency, but also in shaping legislation and policy decisions on economic, domestic and international affairs. Like Old Testament Israel, the leader of a nation can profoundly impact its conscience and values (Proverbs 29:2). Our nation is no different as we saw with President Ronald Reagan, who embodied many conservative values often aligned with biblical values. In fact, his 1983 essay, "Abortion and the Conscience of the Nation" is still an oft-cited pro-life manifesto.

But the conservative political movement of the 1980's was short-lived. The heavy work to educate, equip and send the next generation of Christians into societal warfare and government service was rarely attempted, and more often completely overlooked or dismissed.[35] Obviously, spiritual warfare is a continual battle until the Lord returns. If the generational aspect of Kingdom labors are ignored and Christians are only mobilized for political "quick fixes" at election times, why would we expect our influence to be better than the useless seed that fell on the rock or among the thorns (Luke 8:9-15)? With a few exceptions,[36] it appeared that much of the legacy conservative Christian movement of the 1980's went back to sleep in the 1990's, resulting in a fragmented understanding of the church's rightful role in politics and caretaker of the soul of our nation.

---

[35]     It's revealing to see popular columnist Cal Thomas' views of what happened in the 1980's. His book "Blinded by Might" claims that the Christian church's direct involvement in government is wrongly placed, and that we should get back to the basics of ministering to each other and to the world. In reading his book, however, it appears to me that his expectations concerning the Moral Majority's impact upon government were entirely misplaced. Government will never be the answer to our nation's problems, it's not a church and it doesn't embrace the gospel. Government is instituted for the common good, but it becomes a harsh taskmaster if allowed to go beyond its proper roles. As Christians we need to constrain it, and keep it focused on exercising justice and protecting our freedoms.

[36]     These include the writings and activism of Dr. D. James Kennedy and many Pro-Life groups.

The rise of Neo-Conservatism,[37] the "dot-com" bubble, economic upheavals, and the collapse of a consistent, articulate, mature public Christian influence only exasperated the difficulty Christians had in engaging the political environment.[38] Without prominent spiritual leadership,[39] and with individuals focused on economic security, government was well poised to grow in power and control over our lives.

## *What the World Is Doing to Us*

The destructive influence of an ungodly culture on the health of the church are far too numerous to recount. However, the fact that so much of the Christian community is compromised and weak shouldn't be a surprise since evil will not rest, using every tool at its disposal to eradicate our testimony to the world and extinguish the light we are commissioned to carry (Ephesians 6:11-12).

Let's take the entertainment industry. How often can we go to a movie and watch an uplifting, edifying story that doesn't contain gratuitous sex, horrific violence, or foul language? When's the last time you saw a major film release or TV show that contained a positive portrayal of a pastor, priest or "spiritual leader?"[40]

---

[37] Neo-Conservatism is a general term covering a broad political movement that advocates the active use of government power in pursuing domestic and foreign conservative policies.

[38] An exception to fading Christian influence is the election of President George W. Bush in 2000 and 2004. After Bill Clinton, Christians were motivated to restore honor and a credible evangelical witness to the presidency. As a matter of fact, the Bush campaign's "Compassionate Conservatism" was based on many biblical principles. However, this was a grassroots movement for the most part, not led by pastors.

[39] Again, a prominent exception was the ministry of the late Dr. D. James Kennedy and his Center for Reclaiming America and related efforts. Dr. Kennedy was widely respected for his commitment to evangelistic and cultural/governmental engagement. Unfortunately, while this mobilized many Christians as individuals, similar results among pastoral leadership never materialized.

[40] . To get a sense of the stark contrast between how today's spiritual truths and leaders are treated and those of the 1930s and 40s, one only needs to watch the TCM movie channel. Those "oldies" offer routine cultural glimpses into the respect, honor and biblical knowledge that were sprinkled throughout films from that era.

How often is a traditional family seen as key to establishing a stable society and a responsible next generation?[41] Over the last several decades, how many films have realistically portrayed the destructiveness of the homosexual lifestyle or its blatant activism to literally destroy any opposition or rationale debate? What about their portrayal of sanctity of life issues, free enterprise (capitalism), sincere and articulate Christian faith, sexual purity and fidelity, and on and on? Clearly the worldview behind the majority of the mass entertainment media is not compatible with historic, biblical truth and values. Valiant efforts are underway to try to grow a counter-entertainment media that upholds values consistent with our beliefs[42], but most of the country (as well as many Christians) are still influenced by open vileness that's corrosive to souls and presents a perverted view of Christianity and its values.[43]

The same can be said for the mainstream news media[44] and many Internet and hardcopy periodicals. When belligerent atheism is given a place at the table of credible "journalistic" insight and opinion, while supposed credible news commentary denigrates and vilifies anything of true faith, how can conservative biblical principles be expected to be treated as credible and welcomed? In fact, many of the values we hold dear are routinely painted as radical in the more liberal media and at times not so subtlety equated to religious zealotry normally equated with terrorism.[45]

---

[41]   Just take one comparison, "Father Knows Best" of the 1960's compared to "Married With Children" of the 1990's. Need I give other examples?

[42]   Good examples are "Courageous," "Amazing Grace," "Machine Gun Preacher," "Luther," and blockbusters such as "The Chronicles of Narnia" and "Lord of the Rings."

[43]   Obviously, the Internet and all kinds of social media outlets only perpetuate this situation and make access to destructive influences more readily available and mainstream.

[44]   By mainstream media I'm referring to national broadcast channels such as ABC, CBS and NBC, but I also include MSNBC on the Internet and the Public Broadcasting System, CNN etc.

[45]   Not convinced. Go to MediaMatters.com and track how it reports anything conservative or representing credible faith.

Obviously, the nation's highest judicial body, the U.S. Supreme Court, has also played a role. Its activist nature of legislating from the bench resulted in one of the most barbaric and destructive decisions in our nation's history, the removal of all legal rights from the unborn.[46] Add to this the government's protection of Internet access to sexual wickedness in public libraries, rejection of conscience provisions for health-care providers, removal of prayer from public schools or the censoring of the name of Christ in official public settings, and the situation becomes quite clear – our values and the truths of our faith have no place in the free-and-open marketplace of ideas. Left unchallenged, activist judicial attacks on Christian values will continue to have devastating impacts on both our credibility and ability to bridle the powers of government.

This hostility towards biblical values also permeates most of the public education system. This environment is training the next generation of voters, policy makers, public leaders and judges who will decide what will legally constitute right or wrong. In all of these realms our worldview is being rejected or denigrated, often without challenge.

### The Bottom Line

These are very real threats to our Kingdom work: to share Christ and be a godly influence in every legitimate endeavor. Without solid equipping and shepherding by pastors, how will Christians effectively live out what Scripture refers to as a distinct sound (1 Corinthians 14:8)? How will we ever be adequately prepared for spiritual battle in politics (Ephesians 6:10-20)? For that matter, how will we know how to contribute to the societal common good

---

[46] Actually, the U.S. Supreme Court in the infamous Roe v. Wade decision effectively made the unborn child a non-person with no legal rights; for all intents and purposes the child is a piece of property to be done with as the "owner" (the mother) deems fit. This mirrors the worst decision of the 19th century where slaves were deemed nothing more than property in the Dred Scott decision of 1857.

(Jeremiah 29:7), or protect our freedom to fulfill the Great Commission (Matthew 28:19-20), Great Commandment (Matthew 22:39), and especially our Great Challenge (Matthew 5:13-16)?

Because a significant part of the answer to these questions rests with pastors and ministry leaders under their authority, Chapter 2 directly addresses that sensitive area.

# Chapter 2

# Where are the Pastor's?

*Just because you do not take an interest in politics doesn't mean politics won't take an interest in you!*
**– Pericles** (430 B.C.)

*"All scripture is breathed out by God and profitable for teaching, for reproof, for correction, and for training in righteousness, that the man of God may be competent, equipped for every good work"*
**– 2 Timothy 3:16-17**

### Reaching Out For Leadership

"But that's a political issue!", and so the discussion with a pastor friend was supposed to end. The trump card of all trump cards, the *sin quo non* had just been thrown down. Then the second punch: "This is a church; our focus is spiritual, not political." Though he didn't think so, this pastor had just painted himself into a corner. The reality is that almost without exception every significant moral (and hence spiritual) issue we face as Christians is also of political interest. As a matter of fact, every political concern involves moral decisions based on a worldview that's either biblical or anti-biblical.

I didn't come to this realization quickly. I knew that Scripture was clearly authoritative on everything it touched, but for years I didn't understand how to apply a coherent biblical worldview to the often strange world of politics. To better understand this complex arena I dabbled in the political realm for a few years.[47] I naively thought that the larger Christian community could be organized and focused on making a change in the political landscape. But over time it was painfully obvious that it was fragmented to the point of ineffectiveness – both locally and nationally.

But another major weakness became uncomfortably clear during this time: the widespread lack of pastoral leadership in guiding flocks to deal with and engage the ever-changing political minefield all around us.

Let me quickly add, I've found the vast majority of fellow pastors, elders and ministry leaders have a deep love for God's Word. Most spend countless hours studying scripture, relishing every nuance squeezed out by detailed exegesis. They enjoy scriptural debate, love to preach and teach, study theological giants of the past, and sincerely try to rightly apply God's truth (2 Timothy 2:15).

Their second passion is faithfully shepherding their flocks (Hebrews 13:17). As under-shepherds (1 Peter 5:1-4), they nurture the spiritual health of the sheep under their care; equipping, exhorting, correcting, and training them in righteousness so they can be mature, attaining to the fullness of Christ (Ephesians 4:11-16; 2 Timothy 3:16-17). These weighty duties consume every ounce of time and energy available to them.

---

[47]  Full disclosure: I was elected to county party central committees, was a California state party representative, ran community precinct operations, recruited and trained precinct volunteers, recruited candidates, and had an exploratory committee to evaluate running for state legislative office. I'll quickly add, however, that my trust is not centered in politics, a political party or a candidate, but in Christ alone.

Given the primacy of preaching, teaching and shepherding it's not surprising the intricacies of secular politics become alien to scriptural research and unworthy of notice except in a narrow, forensic, theoretical way or as sermon illustrations of the world's corruption.[48] Although voting may be mentioned from the pulpit, my experience is that the average pastor is not interested in openly encouraging or equipping his flock to engage in the realm of political spiritual warfare. In fact, a number consider politics as intrinsically evil and corrupt, and hence beneath Christians being involved with it.

### Flocks Without Political Shepherds

I've yet to meet a sincere believer that isn't troubled by the direction our nation is headed and what the implications may become for their families and the living out of their faith. Many describe what they see as the moral death rattle of a once great nation that has turned itself upside down.[49] They want to do something, anything, to reverse this trend but find it increasingly frustrating. Unfortunately, the biblical foundation to guide their zeal is often a bit weak, but what they lack in theological exactness they made up for in passion to constrain an ever more unrestrained government.

Unfortunately, instead of being thoroughly trained in a biblical worldview to be Christ-honoring salt and light in the political realm, and shepherded to be gracious to one another, they typically received no encouragement at all from their pastors. In effect, they're sheep fending for themselves, figuring out how to apply scriptural principles to complex legal, policy and budgetary issues, how to articulate positions to hostile audiences and how to counter relentless

---

[48]    This situation has been pejoratively referred to as being in a "holy cocoon" or "holy huddle"; hermetically sealed from the political warfare raging all around.

[49]    Our nation has always been both exceptionally great and exceptionally wicked. This may seem like a contradiction, but it depends on what criterion is used to make the evaluation. For a treatment of this topic see Chapter 10 Common Myths.

forces undermining all we hold dear. Predictably, conflict then arises with other believers who are trying to do the same thing, but sometimes with a radically different understanding of what the true problem is, what position would be a biblical one to take, and what approach would be the most effective to correct the situation.

I've personally run into this "friendly fire" many times as a result of articles I wrote under the heading of "Biblical Politics".[50] These articles addressed current news items from a biblical principle standpoint. I expected to be attacked by non-believers and hardcore liberal ideologues, but much of the criticism I received was from self-identified Christians who either thought I had no right to apply the Bible to contemporary "political" concerns (the separation of church and state canard) or I had ignored biblical admonitions to never judge anyone or anything (conflating hypocritical judgment with any and all types of judgment).

Another source of division amongst believers is the question of whether the United States is a "Christian nation".[51] Adherents see our country as uniquely Christianized and God ordained to exist for the glory of God. These individuals have little sympathy for church "pew potatoes"[52] that only want to learn about heavenly matters, care for their family, isolate themselves from the ungodly world around them and be a-political. Not surprisingly, pew potatoes tend to view political activists as naive zealots that have an unhealthy interest in such an ungodly environment such as politics.

---

[50]  For several years I was privileged to author a series of commentaries for the on-line Communities section of the Washington Times. These articles addressed current news items from a biblical principle standpoint.

[51]  Although this is treated more in-depth in Chapter 5: Is this a Christian Nation?; I prefer to say we're a Christianized nation and that a true, Christian nation does not exist in the world apart from the Body of Christ (1 Peter 2:9).

[52]  This is an obvious play on the term "couch potato", those that sit in front of a TV for entertainment and are not challenged to do anything with what they hear or see. In effect, they only take (always learning) and never give (never doing).

Since politics can become so contentious, many pastors see it as something not worthy of our attention and energies. As a result, whether intentional or not, many pastors then indirectly teach through their public example or preaching omissions[53] that political engagement isn't important. Even when a public policy issue such as the obvious definition of marriage was on the ballot,[54] many pastors refused to mention this fact from the pulpit – as if that single statement would somehow result in a loose of their tax exempt status, or violate some absolute biblical warning against doing such a thing. To their credit, however, many did preach sermons on what marriage was from God's perspective; although then left it up to their members to decide about whether they should vote or not.

Bolstering this attitude of non-engagement is the memory of the ill-fated Moral Majority activism of the 1980's and the recent alignment of neo-conservative and nationalistic religious right movements. These two movements have unfortunately confused the role of the church by implying a fictitious, nationwide, Christian "heaven on earth" can be reclaimed at every level of government for the glory of God.

As divisiveness increases, a form of self-fulfilled prophesy emerges. By not equipping the sheep in a Christ-honoring biblical worldview of politics, believers will seek conflicting answers somewhere else, including talk radio, anecdotal e-mails they receive, the mainstream media, or even how they subjectively "feel" about the matter. This in turn gives pastors even more evidence that political involvement is not a healthy topic for a church.[55] Obviously, if

---

[53]   There are many arguments about what the content of formal preaching should be from a biblical perspective. However, the reality is that many application options exist with any given text and a pastor's personal interest will play a heavy hand in what's finally selected.

[54]   For California, this happened twice: once in 2003 with Proposition 22 and in 2011 with Proposition 8.

[55]   I'm not implying the pastor is personally responsible to deeply understand all the issues of our day, or lead citizenship ministries himself. For discussions on how this can be done within

not dealt with in a pro-active and biblical manner this miss-match in level of interest will only create more confusion over time.

Without spiritual leadership, Christians can easily end up fighting fellow believers who don't think the same way they do about every gut-wrenching issue of the day. The result is that politically sensitive Christians will easily become disgruntled towards pastors and others that are more politically passive. Clearly, this type of attitude toward other believers should never be.

### *Pastors Have Families Also*

When I talk with pastors I find they share the same frustrations and concerns their church members do about the growing government antagonism and moral bankruptcy around us. They also have a concern for the affect these changes will have on their children as they leave home and begin their own families. But they're not convinced they have any leadership responsibility to equip their church members in the battle. Politics, they argue, should be the responsibility of individual Christians who need to figure out what action they wish to take and how to apply biblical truths. If a Christian is gifted in political activity, that's fine, they can participate if they feel so compelled. If a Christian votes they're doing well, what more is needed? In effect, they are saying that real church ministry needs to be focused on the here and now within the fellowship (Galatians 6:10), whatever happens in the surrounding world only reflects the ongoing spiritual battle, sometimes hotter than at other times, but it will continue until the Lord returns.[56]

a church see Chapter 6: What About Zealots?; Chapter 7: How to Approach Your Pastor; and Chapter 18: Resources

[56] This view is exemplified by the "Two Kingdom" paradigm, which has a much greater emphasis on biblical indicatives than imperatives. A good summary of how narrow this view sees any significant engagement of the "Redemptive Kingdom" of the church with the "Common Kingdom" of the world is found in Dr. David Van Drunen's "Living in God's Two Kingdom's – A Biblical Vision for Christianity and Culture".

But wait a minute. Aren't pastors trying to equip their own families to be godly citizens, to vote in a biblical manner, to apply a biblical lens to the world around them to properly understand and evaluate its dangers and blessings? Don't pastors want their own children to be a Christ-like influence where ever their career paths take them – including public service if that be the Lord's will? If they're diligent in equipping their own families to be discerning and godly when fulfilling the salt-and-light mandate, why wouldn't they approach their own church membership the same way as they shepherd them to fulfill the great commission (Matthew 28:19-20), the great commandment (Matthew 22:39) and the great challenge (Matthew 5:13-16)?

My personal belief is that this distinction between equipping one's personal family and the church family is not only naive; but it shows how deeply the world has convinced church leadership they have no right to influence anything outside of the chapel walls. What's going to be the ultimate result? Every family will eventually be harmed as a hostile government continues to encroach on our freedoms and the exercise of our faith.

### Where's the Equipping?

If public policy issues and political decisions aren't addressed in the church as the moral issues they are; where will it happen? If spiritual leadership refuses to equip and hold its members accountable while wrestling through political questions in a loving, deferential way (Proverbs 27:17); who will? If gifted teachers within the church are unwilling to help work through the application of God's Truth to the values government should be promoting, then secular sources of opinion, emotional arguments, and selected news will continue to fill that role.

A common excuse is that the church is only concerned about moral issues and not political ones. This artificial distinction, in my view, is downright sophomoric.[57] The crux of this book is centered around a simple truth I've discovered during my protracted journey to understand the role of Christians in politics: *Without exception, every moral issue of any substance is a political issue, and every political issue is a moral issue.*

Is it any wonder that Christians strongly disagree over the role of government and legislation when there's no clear leadership from those entrusted with their care (1 Corinthians 14:8)? Is it really surprising that the forces of evil in our government have become so powerful they can create a public school system not just antagonistic to our values, but openly promoting and normalizing perversion[58]? Are we still shocked that government continues to do all it can to protect abortion at any time for any reason or that a candidate for office can be openly tarred as unqualified solely because they're a sincere believer? If pastors and ministry leaders don't help their flocks apply a Christ-honoring vantage point, who will?

Is there an answer?

My own conviction is that Christians are to have zeal to engage the issues of the day but to ensure that zeal and treatment of others is based on a foundation of biblical understanding. As Paul pointed out, enthusiasm must be tempered and undergirded with knowledge (Romans 10:2). If it isn't, passion by itself will be destructive, and knowledge by itself will only puff up. Spiritual leadership carries that responsibility to train and equip Christians to be godly salt-and-light in every legitimate political endeavor with charity and grace. But to do

---

[57]   How and why this novel distinction came into existence is an entire study unto itself. But consider this: whose interests are served by ensuring any Christian influence is removed from anything to do with politics? In fact, what areas of our lives and activities have not been impacted by government intrusion in one form or another? Unfortunately, large sections of Christianity have either bought into this obvious attempt to silence the influence of God's Word in the public square or accepted the government's lead in anything it decides to involve itself in.

[58]   For a case in point, consider the passage of SB 48 into law in California in July 2011. It mandates the celebration of homosexual, lesbian, bisexual, and transsexual lifestyles in core public school curriculum from grades K-12 throughout the state with no involvement or opt-out rights for parents.

this requires wisdom and a willingness to bridge the denial gap that's grown over decades that ignores our rightful place in the public square.

### But That's Not My Job!

If you're a pastor I know what you're thinking. You're already overwhelmed with ministry demands and don't want another complication on your pastoral plate, particularly something as dicey as politics. I understand your hesitation, and I agree that political activism shouldn't be your focus. I'll quickly add, however, that directly or inadvertently discouraging any ministry associated with politics will only breed membership frustration and play into the hands of those hostile to our values. There is a biblical basis for involvement, but it must be done with wisdom and balance. Christian activism necessitates prudence and godly leadership to ensure our political engagement is done in a Christ-honoring way. Where best to be trained but within the church where we can sharpen each other (Proverbs 27:17) using the talents and teaching skills God has provided, just as we do for every other ministry. And, like every other ministry, the proper level of accountability can be applied to ensure divisiveness doesn't erupt, particularly over minor issues where God's Word may not be as clear as everyone would like.

So why should pastors want to equip their flocks to be godly citizens when they have so many other, more important duties? There are at least two primary reasons. One is to fulfill our salt-and-light mandate toward government to serve the common good, which brings glory to God, and ensures the protection of our religious freedoms (Matthew 5:13-16).[59] The second is to train the flock to know how to maturely apply scriptural principles to the troublesome issues

---

[59] A more through treatment of this topic can be found in Chapter 3: Do We Have a Political Mandate?

of the day so that disunity and resentment amongst the family of God will be avoided.

Most pastors agree that a church's focus is: to bring glory to God; to worship in spirit and truth; to pray and minister together; and to exercise spiritual giftedness through works of service. When we are in the world we are to proclaim the gospel, live exemplary lives, and apply a biblical worldview to everything we do. Where we often fall short, however, is effectively applying biblical teachings directly to the ever more powerful and complex threats to our salt-and-light mandate in the political – read that government – realm. When we fail in this, either through apathy, ignorance or misguided passion we inadvertently facilitate increased influence by ungodly leadership trying to implement broken worldviews.

This withdrawal also feeds the general public's widely held view that biblical truth is not only irrelevant to today's problems and that Christians are ignorant (clueless) on important matters, but anything from the Bible is backward or even destructive. I can't count the times I met someone for the first time, have the conversation turn to the news of the day, and find the other person had never been exposed to a conservative position that could be explained beyond the level of a bumper-sticker. Finding out I was a Christian, the other person would often have a pre-conceived notion I was uninformed, intolerant, homophobic, un-teachable, and for sure not relevant or credible towards any moral problem of significance.

I'm reminded of one particular discussion that had to do with animals. Clearly the other person thought more highly of animals than they did for anything else. Instead of writing them off as "animal rights wackos" I started by saying we shared much in common: a love for creatures that God created; how incredibly complex they are; and how much they teach us about ourselves and about God. This bridge building had the dual effect of opening up a conversation with some level of mutual regard, and also pointing towards spiritual truths relating to the created order around us.[60]

Sure, we should expect a hostile attitude from the non-believing world, but don't we hold the very words of God in our hands, words able to equip us for every good work including defending righteousness (2 Corinthians 10:3-5) and even proclaiming truth to authority (Proverbs 11:14; 15:22; 2 Timothy 3:16)? If the flock isn't encouraged and equipped within the church setting to handle and take advantage of the opportunities we all face to stand for truth, they will look to other sources which will invariably be more man-centered than Christ-centered. If pastors don't example how to wrestle with complicated policy issues using a biblical worldview, what hope will his church members have in finding a better example to follow?

If the above aren't compelling reasons to change how the Body of Christ sees political involvement, there's one more – the gospel itself.

### The Gospel is Ultimately at Stake

Like most evangelicals, I believe true, lasting change comes through the gospel and redeemed lives. I also believe the Bible has the basic truths and principles this nation needs to maintain a just environment for the good of all its citizens and to protect our freedom to proclaim the gospel. God's Word governs all matters of faith and practice, bringing blessings when thoughtfully applied and dire consequences when ignored. It also provides a rich source of practical wisdom and life principles that resonate with man's conscience

---

[60]    Whether the issues are animal rights, environmentalism, global warming, economics, extraterrestrials, hate crimes, near-death experiences, capital punishment, or a myriad of other controversies; understanding both the biblical basis for our position as well as any legitimate concerns or insights of the other side will go a long way to ensuring a more thoughtful conversation leading to opportunities to point to God and spiritual truths. Where better to be equipped for this influence opportunity than within a biblically based, teaching, church environment?

(Romans 2:14-15) and should inform institutions (like government) as it tries to control man's baser nature (Romans 13:4).

The liberties we've enjoyed since our nation formed are clearly dependent upon timeless biblical principles. Why would we ever think they're no longer applicable today?[61] Human nature hasn't changed, and God obviously hasn't changed. But remove this understanding from public discourse and the inevitable consequences will occur. Christianity and its value system will first become immaterial to anything of consequence to the world around it; and eventually, as society continues to collapse, Christianity will become the scapegoat for many of society's self-inflicted troubles.

Tragically, as we lose credibility on the issues of the day, our personal credibility to share the gospel is also compromised. If we think we're immune from the world's downward spiral, we don't understand the resourcefulness of evil to do everything in its power to restrain and ultimately remove our freedom to preach truth and share the gospel. Biblically, the church is called to articulate truth to an unbelieving world (2 Timothy 4:1-5), defend what's right and just (Psalm 82:3-4), and expose evil as necessary (Ephesians 5:11) to bring glory to God and His standard.

I'm not ignoring the fact that a seared conscience can't understand or accept spiritual truths (1 Corinthians 2:14-16). But our new nature in Christ gives us a legitimate concern for relieving unnecessary pain and suffering in the world, much of which is caused by an out-of-control government blinded by its own power (Matthew 22:39; Luke 10:25-37). By engaging in a principled way to constrain government to its rightful role and keep it from co-opting ours (Matthew 5:13-16), our faith is demonstrated (James 2:17), our personal and

---

[61] For extraordinary reference material on the Christian roots of our nation and the impact of the Bible and natural law go to www.wallbuilders.com. Though controversy over the type and depth of faith of our nation's founders will continue, the evidence is overwhelming for the impact the Bible and a common Christian heritage have had on us as a nation.

corporate credibility is enhanced, and our freedom to openly share the gospel will continue (Romans 10:14-17).

### So What's a Pastor to Do?

Given the current inconsistent state of Christian influence and credibility, what are pastors to do? Obviously a church shouldn't become a political action committee or unnecessarily jeopardize a 501(c)3 status.[62] At a minimum, however, members can be publicly and routinely encouraged to understand current events, research all candidates for elective office, and to vote biblically in every election. These are basic, but important citizenship responsibilities.

It's also critical to speak directly to the appalling moral conditions around us – whether it's radical agendas contrary to biblical teachings, sexual perversion and the culture of death in all their manifestations, current legislation that panders to destructive special interests, governmental theft and squandering of the wealth of this nation, or elected officials who are not fulfilling their duties. But just using these as sermon examples of evil without providing encouragement to make a difference for the sake of the church, Christian families and the cause of Christ, overlooks the many scriptural imperatives we have to be salt-and-light.

Likewise, pastors can acknowledge when good legislation is passed that benefits the Christian community and when leaders actually do what they're positions of power were intended to demand of them.

Pastors are trained to rightly handle God's Word, and preach and teach the entire counsel of God. They have the privilege to create and shepherd ministries to equip their members to be involved citizens, neighbors and even to retake their position as counselors to the nation; just as they equip them to be godly spouses, parents, employees, ministry workers, and witnesses for Christ. Besides

---

[62]    I say "unnecessarily" jeopardize a tax exempt status since an argument can be made that churches shouldn't need to have a 501(c)3 status at all. If they do have that status, it shouldn't affect decisions on what ministries to pursue.

the use of preaching opportunities, pastors can ensure solid biblical teaching is provided through special Sunday school series, home fellowship groups, routine discussion groups, invited speakers for special events and other venues. Ultimately, this equipping process will help restore the concept of a Christian citizen ministering to a world desperate for answers; answers found only in God's Word and in the person of Jesus Christ.

I know from experience that most pastors are overburdened with existing ministry concerns. But I can almost guarantee that every church has mature members who are gifted and willing to organize a Christian citizenship type of ministry[63] to help educate and motivate the flock to engage the great cultural, political and legislative issues of our day. Look for them and you will find them.[64] As a shepherd, a pastor is to encourage God-honoring ministries and provide shepherding oversight so all activities will be done in a godly, Christ-centered, non-divisive manner. Pastors don't have to do everything themselves, nor should they, but their maturity, leadership and knowledge will be the key factors in whatever ministry is ultimately created.[65]

Is this recapturing of a biblical privilege going to be easy? No!

But the consequences for continuing to be hermetically sealed from the political realm and ignoring the forces at work to destroy us – and our influence – are becoming more dangerous every year. Without fighting the good fight now, our nation will go the way of so many other nations where an active

---

[63]  The title of these types of ministries, though not critical, is important to convey the fact that they're different than typical life, family, and youth ministries. Examples include: Salt and Light; Public Forum; Biblical Citizenship, Citizens of the Book, Contemporary Issues, and Christian Citizenship ministries.

[64]  The ministry of Pastor Jim Garlow of Skyline Church in La Mesa, California is one clear, outstanding example.

[65]  Several upcoming chapters in this book address how to ensure these types of ministries are done with the right spirit.

proclamation of God's truth in love becomes a criminal offense; unnecessarily making our great commission that much harder to fulfill.[66]

## *Where to Go From Here*

Obviously pastors aren't the sole problem, but when mature spiritual leadership is lacking or non-existent, other problems (such as divisiveness) begin to grow. Are we like men of Issachar who understood the times and knew what to do (1 Chronicles 12:32), or are we going to continue to ignore the gathering storm clouds and hope for the best? The rest of this book attempts to clarify the many sources of conflict and confusion created within the Christian community when trying to be good, influential citizens for the good of all and the next generation. Only when we can properly diagnose the problems will a cure become possible.

To set the table properly, we must begin with Scripture to determine whether we actually have a cultural (or political) mandate of some kind. That is the subject of the next chapter. Following that, other impediments to our becoming engaged in a Christ-honoring, balanced manner are explored. We will also answer some common concerns that pastors and church members have about the church's role, and some practical tips on what can realistically be done.

---

[66] Besides well known cases of bakeries and photographers that have been sued and fined for declining to provide their services to same-sex-marriage or commitment ceremonies due to conscience concerns, a May 2014 Huston Equal Rights Ordinance (HERO) illustrates how far government is willing to go to silence the faith community. The ordinance, dubbed the "bathroom bill", bans discrimination in public and private places and allows people to use the restroom of the opposite gender. When local pastors attempted to put an initiative on the ballot to overturn this ordinance the city subpoenaed "all speeches, presentations, or sermons related to HERO, the petition, Mayor Annise Parker, homosexuality, or gender identity." Besides the obvious disregard for these pastor's First Amendment rights, this legal action has a chilling effect on all church "communication" and is one step removed from declaring anything contrary to politically correctness as hate speech and subject to punishment.

# Chapter 3

# Do We Have
# a Political Mandate?

*"You are the salt of the earth...You are the light of the world."* –
**Matthew 5:13,14**

*"I often hear it said, 'Do not bring religion into politics.' This is precisely where it ought to be brought! We have had enough clever men without conscience. Now let us see what honest, God-fearing men will do."*
**– Charles H. Spurgeon**

### Our Many Mandates

There are several profound reasons why we're still in this world and not yet in the heavenly home Jesus Christ promised to us (John 14:2-3). First, our changed lives (1 Peter 2:12), our devotion to each other (John 13:34-35), and our worship are living testimonies to the world of the active grace and mercy of God. In fact, these priorities are consistent with the Great Commandment to love our God with all our heart, mind, soul and strength (Matthew 22:37). But we've been given a second Great Commandment of similar importance:

to love our neighbors as ourselves (Matthew 22:39). This imperative provides the fundamental mandate for our interaction with the world: to evangelize (Matthew 28:19-20); to extend compassion and mercy to the unworthy and needy (Luke 10:25-37); and to be salt and light in every noble and legitimate activity we undertake (Matthew 5:13-16).

Evangelical Christians have a heart for the lost, those who don't know their need for a Redeemer and the love of Christ. This is the very essence of our faith – a desire to be used by God to bring others to Christ and for those lives to bring glory to God. Since this mandate deals with the everlasting state of souls it should undergird and inform our involvement in the world - no matter what activity we're engaged with, including politics.

Another outworking of Matthew 22:39 is compassion toward those in need. Mercy and love to relieve suffering has been a strong distinctive of Christianity from its beginning. Just as Christ unconditionally demonstrated his love to us while we were unworthy sinners (Romans 5:8), and promises to meet our daily needs (Matthew 6:25-34), so we have the privilege and mandate to model Christ's mercy by loving the unworthy and needy around us (1 John 4:19).

While evangelism and compassionate outreach are clear mandates, what's more controversial is the biblical basis for a political one. This type of mandate extends beyond living a godly life every day (1 Peter 2:12), providing for our families (1 Timothy 5:8) and ministering at church (Galatians 6:10), it encompasses the application of a comprehensive biblical worldview to all legitimate activities. This includes our privilege and duty to positively provide a godly influence in: our neighborhood; community service; schools; the media; the arts and sciences; sports; jobs; businesses, and yes, even the government and its blood sport of politics.[67]

---

[67] Clearly I'm not advocating the use of worldly tactics when engaging in politics, I'm only acknowledging the fact that the political realm can be vicious, ruthless and destructive when ungodly men and women are involved.

These salt-and-light labors become the Great Challenge (Matthew 5:13-16)[68] because of the need to be charitable to one another and wise in how we engage the world to fulfill the commands of Scripture. One reason why so much divisiveness and ineffectiveness permeates the broader Christian "activist" community is because of an incredibly uneven, and in most cases non-existent biblical foundation to deal with the complexities of a politicized nation and society.

When we focus our Great Challenge attention to just political involvement the arguments over Christian activism can quickly become heated. For example, my experience is that most pastors align with one of two views. One group sees political activism as distracting and unnecessary to fulfill our primary purpose as Christians. They have a passive, indifferent attitude towards government unless it impacts them personally. We're expected to be good citizens and vote, but little more. These pastors are rightfully concerned about some Christians seeking only political answers to the problems of our nation and communities. In extreme cases, they may even see any attempt to control or move government as violating biblical injunctions to obey government leaders (Romans 13:1-7; 1 Peter 2:13-15).

The other, much smaller group of pastors tend to see Christianity as a triumphant march to take over all worldly institutions for the glory of God – in effect, bending government and political processes to the Lordship of Jesus Christ. Though this desire holds a high view of the universal rule of Christ (Philippians 2:9-10) and the power and sufficiency of God's Word (2 Timothy 3:16-17), it ignores the long, past history of the Christian church when it's taken political power and inevitably slid into religious tyranny.[69]

---

[68] By using this term I have an easy way to remember the three "Greats" we have by using the letter "C": the Great Commission (proclaiming the gospel); the Great Commandment (loving our neighbor); and the Great Challenge (being salt and light in a hostile world).

[69] For a more comprehensive treatment of the practical and biblical relationships that should exist between Church and State see Chapter 4: Separation of Church *from* State? and Chapter 5: Separation of State *from* Church?

Because so much of political involvement is a wisdom issue within a broad application of Matthew 22:39 and 5:13-16, balance is the critical factor often overlooked. Like the men of Issachar who understood the times and knew what to do (1 Chronicles 12:32), the times we live in are becoming increasingly perilous for the health and safety of the Body of Christ. In one short generation, the incredible expansion of government, aided and abetted by culture and media wars that revile Christianity, has been harnessed to suppress our witness, presence, and influence. The freedom to share the gospel and apply moral restraint to evil in the civil realm is rapidly disappearing through the triumph of political correctness, ideologically driven lawsuits and ungodly judicial activism.

Where will this lead? Obviously, spiritual darkness would love to achieve full-throated legal condemnation and suppression of Christian truth.[70] Those that think this isn't possible have a naive understanding of history and the extent evil will go to in eradicating any light. Think back on changes just over the past several decades and then extrapolate several decades into the future. How fertile do you think the ground will be for God's timeless truths?

For Christians, it's not a matter of taking over government; it's a matter of exercising our freedom and civic duty to return government to its proper biblical role instead of passively allowing it to become an increasingly open enemy.[71] Is there a biblical warrant for this type of involvement? I believe there is, just as there is to protect ourselves and our families from harm.[72]

---

[70]   Although there are important differences, it's instructive to recall what happened with the Lutheran church in Germany leading up to and during the Second World War. For excellent insights into the dynamic and how quickly things can change I recommend reading "*Bonhoeffer: Pastor, Martyr, Prophet, Spy*" by Eric Metaxas (2011).

[71]   Again, for a more detailed treatment of the church's role and responsibilities toward government (and government's role toward us) refer to Chapters 4 and 5.

[72]   An example would be Exodus 22:2 where a thief breaks into a home. Another would be Nehemiah, when he was rebuilding the wall around Jerusalem. The men were armed to fight and to work. This example is actually a great illustration of our role: building a safe environment for our family and church through our salt-and-light mandate, while also doing all we can legally

## *The Original Mandate*

The opening chapters of Genesis set the stage for the rest of man's history. The dominion mandate, first revealed in Genesis 1:28, instructs man to be fruitful, fill the earth, and exercise dominion over it. Although the fall of man resulted in sin corrupting every aspect of this high calling (Jeremiah 17:9; Romans 3:10-18) the noble task wasn't completely done away with as we see in God's covenant with Noah in Genesis 9:1-17. Not surprisingly, as we fast forward through the millennia we find man's record of stewardship of the earth and everything in it rather dismal.

What does this have to do with politics?

Actually, a lot! Take for example the powerful environmentalist and animal rights movements. They have successfully lobbied for enactment of far-reaching endangered species protection laws, international cap-and-trade carbon credit manipulation, greenhouse gas emission regulations, water and energy use restrictions, and literally thousands of other laws and policies to control and limit our impact upon mother "nature" and the environment.

In effect, we've seen our dominion mandate to care for and nurture the earth's biological and mineral kingdoms co-opted by secular and pagan worldviews that place the intrinsic value of the natural world above man. In recent times, government (both legislatively and judicially) has become the tool of choice to force our compliance with belief systems that, in effect, worship the creation rather than the God that created it (Romans 1:25).

We may bemoan the cumulative effect of coercive regulation on our way of life, but where are Christians articulating a proper balance of stewardship, conservation and meeting of man's needs?

---

and within our freedoms to discourage and prevent ungodly government power from being used against us.

Basically, we've become irrelevant in the public debate on the proper role (if any) of government in the management (or nurture) of the environment. I'm not implying the task is easy or that the Bible clearly presents how we're to balance every competing demand on the earth's bounty of life and treasures; but if we ignore our duty to restrain and guide government then we've, in effect, become complicit in the exercise of legislative worship of nature.

Stewardship policies are only one of many issues we face. The question that needs to be asked is whether the Bible provides any insights into our responsibility to influence government for our well being and the common good. To answer that, consider the following when addressing what our political role may rightfully be.

## Old Testament Israel

Christians may differ, but Old Testament Israel provides excellent insight into how God's perfect civil and moral laws may apply to other nations, including our own.[73]

Israel was established as a theocracy – one ruled by the Lord Himself. As we know, the need for a theocratic nation in the world ended with the coming of Christ. Conversely, we as a community of Christians belong to a holy, spiritual nation without national borders (1 Peter 2:9), with our ultimate citizenship residing in heaven (Philippians 3:20).[74] Since we don't live in a national Christian theocracy, directly applying Israel's experience to our present day wouldn't be appropriate. But what we can do is apply what's beneficial to our present situation. This has been the blessing of the American experiment – the

---

[73]  The careful reader will note the clarifier "civil and moral" laws. Sacrificial and ceremonial laws were fulfilled in Christ's death and resurrection, while moral laws apply to mankind and Old Testament civil laws can with wisdom be applied to societies. Though easy to say, the distinctions can be problematic.

[74]  This isn't an argument to justify doing away with all national borders. Individual nations exist as part of God's ultimate plan (Acts 17:2627) and will continue until the Lord returns.

infusion of biblical principles, the Judeo-Christian value system, and natural law reasoning into our national institutions of government and justice. This mixture provided the basis for our history-changing legal rights, liberties, religious freedoms, and even freedoms of conscience.

Unfortunately, the application of the Old Testament Israel experience has suffered from two extremes. One is to directly equate Israel's theocratic era with the understanding that Jesus Christ is King of kings and Lord of lords over all nations (Revelation 19:16), therefore God's entire Word applies here and now as in ancient Israel. The second is to ignore Israel's experience altogether since Christians live under a new covenant of grace through Christ. A more prudent approach for our nation's good would appear to take Old Testament laws that governed Israel and adapt them with wisdom, discernment and mercy.

When it was a theocracy, Israel was ruled directly by God. In our era, the Lord rules over his people, and he provides authorities (government) to rule in the civil realm (Romans 13:1-7). This makes sense, since God knows what's best for all of mankind. He also gave Israel moral and civil laws for both their well being and as a testimony to the world of the mighty God they served (Deuteronomy 4:5-8). The challenge is to figure out how to apply Israel's situation in a balanced, effective way for today.

Let's start with the moral law of God as summarized in the Ten Commandments. These reflect God's holy nature, distinguish good from evil, and provide the moral foundation for all other laws[75]. If these are not recognized and valued, then little basis exists for legal standards to properly judge what's right or wrong. This was well understood by John Adams when he said "Our Constitution was made only for a religious and moral people. It

---

[75] The question of the Sabbath under the New Covenant is still controversial among Christians. Until relatively recent times many states even had "blue laws" that prevented certain activities on Sunday (the Lord's Day). The wisdom of enforcing these types of restrictions for everyone is problematic at best; but for Christians the issue has become more a matter of personal conviction and practice, consistent with their church's teachings.

is wholly inadequate for the government of any other". In other words, without a basic moral fabric, no set of laws or coercive enforcement will be effective in controlling sinful actions. Fortunately, through God's mercy and common grace man's conscience does resonate with the truth of these Commandments whether one's faith is Christian or not (Romans 2:12-15). Take away or suppress God's standard and we'll eventually define our own to replace it, then change it at our convenience.

The natural extensions of God's moral law in Israel were civil laws and what should be appropriate punishment (justice). The closer a nation's laws reflect God's standards the greater the blessings, likewise when they're ignored there's going to eventually be unpleasant consequences. Christians may differ on specifics of application, but in general most governing principles are clear. For instance, consider the following. taking innocent life is condemned (Genesis 9:6, Exodus 20:13) but self defense is justified (Exodus 22:2-3); conviction of a capital offense requires two or more witnesses (Deuteronomy 17:6); personal revenge is condemned (Deuteronomy 32:35); punishment is to be appropriate to the crime (Exodus 21:24); judgment is to be impartial (Proverbs 18:5) and not excessive (Deuteronomy 19:21); false witnesses are to be punished (Deuteronomy 19:18-19); rights of appeal are available (Exodus 18:13-26); innocent victims are owed restitution (Exodus 22:3,9); only a guilty person is to be punished (Deuteronomy 24:16); and even irresponsibility (carelessness) has consequences (Deuteronomy 22:8). These principles may seem obvious, but they're not universally understood or accepted in the world.

The point is clear - the further a government strays from God's standard for civil justice the more evil will be tolerated or even promoted. If we don't instill our values into the laws of the land the values of others will be. Will laws change a person's wicked heart? No, only submitting to Jesus Christ as Lord and Savior will truly change an evil heart (2 Corinthians 5:17). But righteous laws help bring godly order to society, and conviction of wrongdoing (sin) to hearts tenderized by God. Laws are meant to control society in a just manner and protect what's good. If we're not using God's Word to influence laws and justice, we know we won't escape the consequences as others take our place to define them.

## *Old Testament Lives*

Because Israel was a unique theocracy and the United States is not, examples of believers living in foreign nations that worshipped false gods would be more akin to what we face today.

Joseph was a man God brought from slavery to prison to being second only to Pharaoh in power (Genesis chapters 37 through 50). His integrity, purity, and truthfulness brought favor with those over him. He applied his considerable abilities for the good of the entire country of Egypt, for his own family, and to begin the events ultimately leading to the creation of Israel. It's important to note that Joseph neither compromised his faith, nor used governmental power to condemn the false beliefs of the Egyptians. Instead, God had him work within that pagan system, respect its authority, establish prudent laws and planning, and become the premier example of an incredibly influential civil servant. His life was one committed for the good of everyone throughout Egypt, independent of their beliefs.

Daniel was another gifted civil servant (Book of Daniel) who rose to a position of power and authority in Babylon through the intervention of the Lord. He distinguished himself in government service through unquestionable displays of trustworthiness (Daniel 6:3-4) and, like Joseph, demonstrated mercy toward false teachers and astrologers: even interceding for their lives (Daniel 2:24). His personal testimony of faith and example so changed the hearts of Babylonian kings that it speaks to us even today of what godly believers can accomplish when they strive for excellence, desire to please God, and work diligently to do what's right[76]. If you think this was easy, mentally place either Joseph or Daniel in our contemporary world under any current Middle Eastern theocratic government and consider the implications.

Though not a civil servant in the normal sense, remember Ester? Mordecai warned that if she remained silent before the king and didn't intercede for the Jews (political activism), God would bring deliverance through someone else while she and her family may end up perishing (Esther 4:12-14). Again, speaking truth to power changed the king's heart and the course of history.

If nothing else, these lives are examples of the great good that people of faith can accomplish when they trust the Lord and invest their lives for others. Yet how often in church preaching or teaching are young men and women encouraged to apply their talents in the political realm, or in positions of public policy making? By ignoring these legitimate (but difficult) careers, we're effectively saying the work is unworthy of our attention even though we'll never escape the intrusion of government into our lives.

What about common people in difficult times? Consider Jeremiah's letter to the exiles in Babylon (Jeremiah 29:4-9). Speaking for the LORD, Jeremiah exhorted the Jews to seek the peace and prosperity of the city where they were forcibly being taken. How were they to do that? Jeremiah specifically mentions prayer, but the implication is also to be diligent in working to ensure peace and be productive. This not only includes righteous living, but obeying the law, being obedient to rulers, paying taxes, not participating in sedition, and the like. In addition, the exiles were to labor hard and seek prosperity. This productive attitude provided for the common welfare of a society and ultimately benefits everyone.

Even though the ancient Israelites had very little (if any) access to Babylonian rulers, they were told to influence the culture and society around

---

[76] Obviously God gave Daniel the gift of dream interpretation which opened the door for his prominence, yet his personal example of faithfulness to Almighty God continued to have dramatic impact upon the kings of the day (e.g. Daniel 6:1-26)

them in fundamental ways; to basically exercise their cultural (and by extension political) influence (mandate) where they found themselves, within the constraints and freedoms available to them. In our day we have the opportunity and privilege to openly encourage, defend, and vote for representatives that will diligently work to promote proper justice, public policy and moral laws. God's people, of all people, realize that without our example – and sometimes strong pressure – government won't automatically do what's right.

When personal freedoms are more limited, the amount of political activity would necessarily be more limited. But when greater freedoms exist, as we have today to speak out and influence, then wisdom would point to greater involvement as not just desirable but critical to protect our ability to freely pursue the three "Greats"[77] to the glory of God.

### The Book of Proverbs

When looking at biblical justifications for political involvement, the Book of Proverbs is a jewel. Verses encouraging the giving of advice to kings are common (Proverbs 11:14; 24:5-6), as are warnings to wise leaders to seek out godly counselors (Proverbs 12:15; 15:22; 19:20). In our day we have unprecedented opportunity to influence those in power to do what's right. We can lobby, support election campaigns, take out ads, write letters and blogs, meet with our elected officials and their staffs, and we can vote.[78] However, the Book of Proverbs also contains many specific principles to guide our leaders, and provide a standard to judge their competency to rule. Since Proverbs summarizes

---

[77] As mentioned in footnote #2, the three "Great's" are the *Great* Commission (Matthew 28:19-20; the *Great* Commandments (Matthew 22:37-39); and the *Great* Challenge (Matthew 5:13-16).

[78] The list of things a person can do with their time, treasure and talents is unlimited as long as it's moral, ethical, legal and doesn't create ungodly divisiveness.

wisdom for the ages they transcend types of governments and apply to any that have eyes to see and ears to hear. To illustrate, consider the following examples:

First and foremost, elected leaders must recognize they're not only accountable to those they impact, but ultimately to the Lord. As Proverbs 15:3 says: "The eyes of the LORD are everywhere, keeping watch on the wicked and the good". Unlike the general public, the Lord doesn't forget, and can't be fooled by deceptive words or actions. The high calling of leadership is to serve to please God, to rule in a just and moral manner – consistent with God's revealed truths. Leadership bears an awesome responsibility, since those who do so will answer to God for their action or inaction. Without the restraining influence of knowing that ultimate judgment waits, self serving interests can eventually rationalize any manner of corrupt actions.

Proverbs 28:9 says: "If anyone turns a deaf ear to the law, even his prayers are detestable". Obviously, a nation ruled by just laws is a blessed nation. When leaders are above the law, or activist judges invalidate laws intended for the common good, the inevitable consequences will occur. Take the *Roe v. Wade* and *Doe v. Bolton* Supreme Court decisions; they overturned legal protections for the unborn throughout the nation. With abortionists being protected, and pro-lifers trying to save lives being jailed, this a classic example of "Acquitting the guilty and condemning the innocent – the Lord detests them both" (Proverbs 17:15). In like manner the current push to corrupt the natural expression of marriage as well as its underlying purpose through legalized same-sex marriages will eventually lead to criminalizing any dissention.[79] When political

---

[79]   Consider just one example: in April 2015 a judge for the Oregon Bureau of Labor and Industries (BOLI) recommended a lesbian couple should receive $135,000 in damages for their emotional suffering after a bakery called Sweet Cakes by Melissa refused to make them a wedding cake.

correctness confuses right and wrong[80] or just laws are ignored[81] how can God's blessing be expected? Our duty is to diligently work for biblically based justice and not just ignore the mainstreaming of evil and the condemnation of what we know to be the good (Proverbs 18:5).

How about different standards? Proverbs 20:23 says: "The Lord detests differing weights, and dishonest scales do not please Him". Not only do hate crimes come to mind, but one judge may be vastly more lenient than another for the same crime. Tax laws are "progressive", extracting a far greater percentage from the rich and thus punishing their success. Congress routinely exempts themselves from the very laws they force on everyone else, yet say those laws are for our own good (Proverbs 16:10). This is not equal justice, yet we allow it to occur. How did we get here?

Proverbs 23:10-11 says: "Do not move an ancient boundary stone, or encroach on the fields of the fatherless, for their Defender is strong; he will take up their case against them". Scripture isn't just talking about property rights, boundary stones are also a metaphor for the principles on which a nation are built. They're our societal rock. When different meanings are read into laws, the boundary stone is moved. Life becomes a matter of definition, marriage becomes whatever someone wants it to be, property ownership is only a source of revenue for the government, truth becomes hate speech, and on and on. How can we not have a passion to restore the plumb line that God intended for our use and the benefit of whatever nation in which we live?

The Book of Proverbs is rich in principles relating to personal accountability, bribery, punishment, indebtedness, honesty, hard work, lying, and even the poor. These sayings are practical tools to be applied with both care and

---

[80]     For instance: creating hate crime laws to elevate one class of victims over another; treating access to pornography in public libraries as a fundamental right; using eminent domain solely to gain more tax revenue at the expense of property ownership rights.

[81]     For instance: ignoring public obscenity ordinances, or refusing to deport foreigners that have illegally entered our nation or punishing employers that hire them,

persistence in all our relationships, and to the institutions of our nation. To ignore the relevance of God's truths to the governing of our nation is to bury His treasures to the detriment of everyone.

### *The Gospel of Matthew*

The New Testament is another rich environment to draw from, particularly the Gospel of Matthew. When Christ walked on the earth, Israel was under the authoritarian, iron-fisted Roman Empire. Given the tension between "church and state" that existed at the time, Jesus' teachings shed interesting light on our relationship to authority as citizens of the United States, or any nation for that matter.

Jesus taught that a house divided cannot stand (Matthew 12:25-30). As with the family of God, the same holds true for any nation, great or small. The more people stray from biblical truths and justice the closer the time comes that a nation will cease being a blessing in which to live. Without God's truths laying the foundation to judge right and wrong and energize our duty toward each other, people will drift toward anything serving their selfish interests and emotions. This selfishness, coupled with political expediency drove the people in Jerusalem to scream for the crucifixion of Christ as Pilot "counted the votes" and gave in to the mob instead of judging rightly (Matthew 27:21-26). If unchecked moral relativism judged Christ to be worthy of death, why would we ever expect our personal and religious freedoms to survive if we're not willing to actively protect and preserve them?

A similar teaching is found in Matthew 7:24-27 where the wise man builds his house on rock and not sand. God's Word is our unchangeable bedrock (Matthew 5:18) and He knows what's best for us all; Christian or not. Why wouldn't we want to apply it everywhere we can, while realizing that without our restraining influence our secular government will become more hostile to Christian influence every year?

For those who've lived a long life, interpreting the signs of the times as mentioned in Matthew 16:1-3 is instructive. Anyone living through the last generation has witnessed the transforming of our country from a relatively Christianized atmosphere, to a post-Christian era, to an ever increasingly anti-Christian era. Today the name of Christ is constantly being legally and forcibly removed from the public square. Granted, some wonderful victories are being won in the courts to restore many of our religious freedoms[82], but anyone with eyes to see has to acknowledge that evil has boldly come out of the closet to challenge everything we hold as pure and wholesome.

In Matthew 19:3-5 Jesus clearly teaches that marriage is the uniting of one man and one woman for life. Political correctness (radical feminist movement, no fault divorce), counterfeit marriages (domestic partnerships, civil unions), or unnatural same-sex marriages will not change what's best for us all. Jesus goes even further by condemning anyone trying to destroy a marriage (Matthew 19:6). As a gift from God, faithful, committed, monogamous marriage provides the societal foundation for our very existence – anything less is unfortunate at best, and profoundly detrimental to society at its worst. Since a stable family is so important, shouldn't we encourage government to do everything in its power to strengthen it, protect it, and incentivize it; while discouraging anything illegitimately trying to co-opt its role and worthiness?

It's no accident that when marriage is mentioned Jesus also talks about children (Matthew 18:5-6; 19:13-15). He warns against causing them to sin or hindering their coming to Him. In generations past, school children from

---

[82]   The creation of the Alliance Defending Freedom (ADF); Pacific Justice Institute (PJI); the National Center for Law and Policy (NCLP); and other likeminded, biblical worldview and Constitution-honoring legal firms fighting for faith, freedom and family issues has resulted in remarkable victories in preserving and protecting our freedoms. These, as well as other solid firms are listed in Chapter 18.

non-Christian homes were at least exposed to the existence of the divine and our deep Christian heritage as a nation. However, over the last generation anything specifically Christian has been methodically removed from schools and many times replaced with a dangerous; drug laden; coarse; disrespectful environment that encourages children to sin. Shouldn't Christians, as taxpayers if nothing else, demand better of government schools? Why should any support be given to an educational system that does exactly what Jesus warned against (Matthew 18:5-6)?[83]

What about our mandate toward the less fortunate? Loving our neighbor (Matthew 22:39) is easy when they can reciprocate, but what of those with nothing, or who are poor, sick or in prison because of their own sin or circumstances beyond their control? Jesus said we're to have compassion toward the hurting (Matthew 25:31-46) and serve them as if we're serving the Lord Himself. It's not government's responsibility to do this for us. When bureaucrats compete for our blessings, what happens? Our in-action is encouraged, the weak become dependent on government, and Christ is removed from the equation. Shouldn't government programs be the last option, if an option at all? Instead, government has been allowed to co-opt our mercy role to those in need without any moral foundation to guide it's efforts or ability to accurately diagnose and differentiate between physical and spiritual causes; much less treat them effectively (Matthew 6:3; 10:8; 19:16-24).

What of those aspiring to be leaders? Matthew gives us criteria to assess the worth of a candidate or public official. Have their decisions stood for righteousness, integrity, biblical morals, personal and governmental responsibility and accountability; or do they have a dismal record of self-interest and pandering (Matthew 7:15-20; 12:33-37)?

---

[83] Alternatives for Christian parents include private Christian schools, home schooling, charter schools, and even private schools that hold to moral values and principles consistent with a biblical worldview.

The same criteria applies to literally thousands government programs. Our concern over what government does is more than just worrying about the taxes we pay (Matthew 22:15-22), it includes asking what good fruit has come from every program and has it actually succeeded in correcting a problem or just created more life-destroying dependency?[84]

### *Prayer*

One of the clearest scriptural commands we have concerning our relationship to government leaders is to pray for them (1 Timothy 2:1-4). Not only is this an imperative but it's also a blessing. To come before Almighty God to intercede for the lives, decisions and well being of those that can so dramatically impact our lives is a labor too often overlooked or done in some cursory fashion. We diligently pray for our families, our friends, our church ministries, and any other relationship we have an affection or concern about. Is that same passion descriptive of our prayer for those that God has appointed over us for our good (Romans 13:1)?

For that matter, how much do we really know about those in elected office, or that serve on their staffs? Do we know which politicians claim to be Christians or what kind of church they attend? Do we have any real idea what they face each day in the political battles constantly being waged? Do we have a heartfelt concern for their spiritual health and plead with the Lord to grant them faith that's directed toward the only hope there is? Do we pray for them to recognize their accountability to a holy God for how they exercise the authority entrusted to their care? Have we sought out local elected officials to find out as much as we can about them personally so that our prayers for them can be tailored specifically?

---

[84] Chapter 16, Government Legislation Checklist provides a list of various questions that should be asked concerning any significant piece of legislation or public policy.

Or, if there are particular politicians that we don't like or that hold policy positions we find distressing do we find ourselves praying for their removal from office; or even worse?[85] When Paul wrote to Timothy to pray for kings and all who are in high positions, the purpose was for the people of God to have the freedom to live peaceful and quiet lives, godly and dignified in every way. The Roman Empire at the time was not known for its mercy and enlightened protection of everyone's individual freedoms, but for ruling with an iron fist. That Empire became particularly dangerous as persecution began to spread against Christians as a matter of state policy. Yet even that regime fulfilled God's will in this world as Christians continued to pray for those that had been placed in authority by a sovereign God (Romans 13:1).

Unfortunately, the spiritual weapon of prayer is oftentimes overlooked even though the Lord requires it from us. Since politics is just as much spiritual warfare as any other activity under the sun, our weapons need to be spiritual as well as physical. These include biblical reasoning, godly influence, and personal example, wise counsel, voting biblically, and yes, committed prayer for all those who serve us.

### Our Opportunity

It's been vogue in many Christian circles to submit to government authority as if it was a sin to not comply with everything we're told to do (Romans 13:2; 1 Peter 2:13-14), the exception being when God's clear commands are violated (Acts 5:29). In fact, Paul himself acknowledged his need to be submissive to

---

[85] On a personal note, I found myself re-telling jokes about President Clinton during his presidency. I eventually became convinced I was rather hypocritical in praying for the Lord's favor on the President both spiritually and physically, but then openly heaping ridicule upon him as a person and leader. Once I realized I didn't have a sincere concern for him, I changed my attitude and the content of my prayers, I came to respect the Lord's decision to place him over us as President, and I stopped publically denigrating a sinner in need of God's grace just as much as myself.

the law of the land should he be found guilty of doing anything that deserved death (Acts 25:10-11).

However, unlike biblical times, we have the opportunity to seek government positions of power, work to implement justice, and fight for life-mending not life-destroying compassion to those around us. We have the opportunity to provide godly counsel and warning to those in authority, and to work to restrain government to its proper role. Like the earlier examples, we truly have a noble calling to invest our lives for the common good through personal, church and political means.

Clearly, Christians have the biblical freedom to exercise their unique opportunity and responsibility to positively influence the culture and institutions around us. This should come as no surprise, since God knows what's best for mankind and His common grace is always present (Matthew 5:45; 7:9-10; Romans 13:6). Whether it's our "Salt-and-Light" responsibility (Matthew 5:13-14), or how we're to treat our neighbors (Matthew 22:39) and enemies (Matthew 5:43-44), God's Word is the standard. Whether we're to expose evil or not (Ephesians 5:11), submit to authority (Romans 13:1-4), pay taxes (Romans 13:6-7), implement environmentally sound policies (remember Genesis 1:28), or be good stewards of animals (Proverbs 12:10), each and every activity we undertake needs to be for God's glory (1 Corinthians 10:31).

Will this sit well with non-Christians, or even those Christians that don't see a need to get involved in politics? Obviously, opinions will differ, especially when the authority of God's Word is used. But our calling is clear, we're to be a blessing to the world (Galatians 6:10) and in doing so God's Word is our standard (2 Timothy 2:16-17). In fact, our personal credibility may be dependent on how diligent we are in laboring for the good of those around us, just as it is when we minister to each other (John 13:35).

Some believers argue that God worked through Old Testament saints in miraculous ways, but He doesn't work that way now. That reasoning may reflect more of an unwillingness to do what needs to be done than anything grounded in biblical teaching. Jesus Himself said that with the faith of a mustard seed incredible things could be done (Matthew 17:20-21), and even the gates of hell will be overcome for God's glory (Matthew 16:18).[86]

If we give up on defending the benefits of God's Word, and the destruction that inevitably follows unrestrained government and values-free justice, then what relevancy do we have to a decaying world, dying in its own filth? If we have no heart to work diligently and sincerely for someone else's (and society's) benefit through readily available political processes, why would we be looked to as a credible source when we share the gospel of eternal life (Matthew 28:18-20)?

The challenge for Christians is to be creative with the eternal Word entrusted to our care and apply it in new and relevant ways for the common good – in effect putting new wine in new wine skins (Matthew 9:16-17). An even bigger challenge is for the wider Christian community to do this in a united way. But always remember, God's Word is eternal and perfect, yet it's fresh and new to each generation with answers for every challenge they will face.[87]

Clearly the benefits of Christian political involvement could be immense, just as ignoring that slice of ministry have been devastating. But ultimately the greatest benefit will be the demonstration of the relevancy of God's Word to all of life, and the opportunity this gives to share the gospel.

---

[86]  Obviously, any verse must be evaluated in terms of whether it must be very narrowly applied because of obvious context, or whether we have artificially limited the application to a very narrow scope

[87]  God doesn't change; He's the same yesterday, today, tomorrow and into eternity. Likewise, His Word is eternal. The nature of man is the same also, until it's converted and a new heart is given. The challenge every generation faces is how to apply God's Word to the world in which we find ourselves. It requires wisdom and adaptation, but not compromise, in the basic truths of justice, righteousness, morality, and integrity.

# Chapter 4

# Separation of Church *from* State?

*"Do not be unequally yoked with unbelievers."*
**– 2 Corinthians 6:14**

*"Providence has given to our people the choice of their rulers and it is the duty, as well as the privilege and interest, of our Christian nation to select and prefer Christian's for their rulers"*
**– John Jay**

### A Confused Relationship

Few one-liners have been used and abused more than the iconic "Separation of Church and State". To the ungodly and the misinformed it's the final argument, the self-evident truth, the last defining word that trumps all Christian influence in the nation's political affairs at any level - whether local, national or international. However, not only is this contrary to our nation's history, but it also defies reason, logic and reality itself. Everyone has a personal belief system of some kind, and these beliefs directly impact a person's judgment, actions, how they vote, and even their understanding of the proper role of government.

Let's be candid, the real intent of arguing for a complete separation of church (or more accurately faith) from the political realm is to prevent Christian values from influencing public policy in any organized, methodical, or effective way.

Those who don't share our values have developed very sophisticated tools to eradicate what used to be a prominent and influential biblical worldview, or at least its values[88]. Lawsuits challenging everything from prayer in public schools and city council meetings, to the reciting of the Pledge of Allegiance, to the presence of a crèche on public property are routinely filed to remove any vestige of the spiritual within government-controlled environments. Not only that, but these actions fuel a broad public uncertainty concerning the role of faith in contemporary national life as well as giving a direct warning to all that would disagree. When anti-faith legal action is coupled with activist judges who reject and confuse what churches are allowed to legally do as 501(c)3 organizations, a palpable atmosphere of legal hostility (a chilling effect) is created, stifling our constitutionally protected freedoms and the historical role Christian faith has played throughout our nation's history[89].

If the battle with those who don't share our values isn't hard enough, sincere believers are also confused about the proper role of government and how the church should relate to it. In fact, any reasonable study of the history of western civilization since Augustine will quickly find a problematic track record of the abuse of power by both governmental and church authority, particularly when

---

[88]  Though lawsuits will be mentioned, other tools include a complicit news media that supports liberal causes and denigrates conservative positions through humor or dramatic portrayal of aberrant beliefs and behavior as normative; shouting down speakers at public forums, waging loud protests against any pending conservative legislation; implementing social and sexual policy requirements in schools and higher education that are offensive to our values; etc.

[89]  For excellent references on what a church can and cannot do under current 501(c)3 law governing church activities, refer to Chapter 18 Resources.

combined together.[90] Contrary to popular belief, the Bible doesn't appear to clearly justify or prefer any particular form of government over any other one.[91]

The two kingdom paradigm, the city of God and the city of man, the Lordship of Christ over all creation, differing eschatological views, the Reformation, monasticism, theonimism, the sinfulness of man and outright heresy have all contributed to a complex and contradictory understanding of the proper relationship of earthly governments and the Christian community. Add to this the egregious abuse of the term "Separation of Church and State" by the U.S. Supreme Court in numerous decisions[92] and any hope of a settled position on the subject quickly evaporates. For those interested in the historical context of this phrase and its misuse in recent years by our High Court there are a number of excellent books and resource materials the reader can consider in light of their understanding of our historical development as a nation.[93]

Another source of contention within the Christian community is when an overly optimistic view of government is promoted (e.g. thought of as equivalent to a para-church organization), or government is seen as just a nuisance to be tolerated. Both have serious consequences, with the latter particularly worrisome when the secular power of the state is thought to be benign towards religious freedom and ministry and only mentioned when used in sermon illustrations of sinful incompetence. Add a fuzzy understanding of

---

[90] One such treatment that reaches back even further than the New Testament era is: The Contested Public Square – The Crisis of Christianity and Politics" by Greg Forster (2008)

[91] Obviously, kings are mentioned very prominently throughout the Bible, and God raised up kings in Old Testament Israel. But the fact that the Lord very powerfully used kings doesn't necessarily prove that He prefers a monarchy to rule over man. In fact, when Paul says to submit to authority in Romans 13, the authority he was clearly pointing to was all earthly authority – with the pagan, violent, idolatrous Roman Empire the most obvious one.

[92] One of the most famous was in *Everson v. Board of Education* (1947). In this case Justice Hugo Black wrote: "In the words of Thomas Jefferson, the clause against establishment of religion by law was intended to erect a wall of separation between church and state".

[93] WallBuilders (www.wallbuilders.com) provides exceptional materials addressing the Christian roots of the nation, including: "Original Intent - The Courts, the Constitution, & Religion" by David Barton.

the dangerous nature of the world to the belief that government is either our friend, or just an annoyance, and naiveté clouds a person's appreciation for the possibility of widespread religious persecution – something we haven't yet experienced in our nation's history.[94] Can that change? It has in other countries, and as long as there's spiritual warfare it can happen anywhere.

That being said let me quickly state that I believe there is, and should be, a separation of church and state. I'm not referring to removal of every vestige of Christian influence from the public domain, or the disestablishing of the proper role of government in maintaining order. I'm talking about an obvious, intrinsic relationship that defines mutual responsibilities that are consistent with a biblical understanding. Fundamentally, faith and coercive government power must be separate realms, yet they cannot exist totally insulated from each other and remain faithful to Scripture.

It's important at this point to clarify what I mean when I use the term "church." By "church", what's meant is not just the community of individual Christians, the Body of Christ (1 Peter 2:9), but also the organized Christian church as it teaches and applies a biblical worldview to all of life. With that caveat, the following are some practical responsibilities the "church" has toward the state upon which most Christians can agree.

### *What Churches Are Not to Do Toward Government*

First, *the church does not have the authority to appoint public, government leaders.* Though practiced at various times in history, the church cannot claim a direct biblical imperative to select, approve and anoint those that rule over

---

[94]    This doesn't mean persecution hasn't occurred, particularly if the Church of Jesus Christ of Latter Day Saints (LDS) is included in the realm of Christendom. On the other hand, we haven't experienced anything close to a widespread Christian revival for over 150 years either. The last arguably being during the Civil War (see: *A Narrative of the Great Revival Which Prevailed in the Southern Armies during the Late Civil War* by William W. Bennett; published in 1877).

the affairs of this nation. To do so would quickly make government subservient to a particular religious belief system, eventually resulting in the state's physical power being wielded to enforce orthodoxy with little tolerance for any minority views, beliefs or matters of conscience. This type of abuse emerged in the Holy Roman Empire after Constantine and in lesser or greater measure in nations that embraced the Reformation (whether Lutheran or Calvinist). Even in early North American colonial days Puritan attempts to form a New World theocracy were tried with unsuccessful results. Once the power of the sword is granted to the church, the temptation to impose religious conformity becomes too tempting for the old sinful nature to withstand in any consistent manner, no matter how well meaning the original intent.

Secondly, *the church is not to wage war in this world.* By war I mean armed combat to further national interests. Biblically, the church has been engaged in spiritual warfare throughout its existence (Ephesians 6:12), but it's not commanded or encouraged to achieve kingdom advancement by the use of force. Instead, the Bible is very clear that the church is to use the weapons that are specifically granted to it (prayer, evangelism, truth, reason, etc.) and not the weapons the world uses (2 Corinthians 10:4-5). Although we know the gates of hell will not prevail over the church (Matthew 16:18), we can be assured this is referring to the spiritual battle that continues to rage around us and not to any literal, physical combat. In fact, nowhere do the apostles or Christ advocate violence or physical power to seize control of anything[95]. In the New Testament we find who is to wield physical power in this age, and it's government authorities that God has instituted for the common good to exercise justice (Romans 13:1-6).

---

[95] Some historical attempts to use scripture to justify the accomplishment of spiritual goals with the sword include Luke 22:36 and Matthew 10:34. But these obviously refer to the need for self defense and the effects that following Christ will elicit in the world's reaction to his disciples, respectively. We know this because Jesus explicitly taught us to turn the other cheek (Matthew 5:39), love our enemies (Matthew 5:44), do good to those that persecute us (Romans 12:14), etc.

Does this mean that as Christians we have no authority to defend ourselves against murderers or other direct threats to ourselves or our families well being? I believe we have that authority and freedom to do so (Exodus 22:2-3). Clearly this is a controversial matter among sincere believers, but biblically there's a difference between aggressive action to force obedience or submission of others and the practical matter of defending oneself or family against violence. However a sincere believer decides the matter toward his own personal safety, the fact remains that the church has no calling to independently conduct war to support the pursuit of national interests.

Third, *the church is not to establish national policy*. This involves those laws, rules, regulations and treaties that govern our national relationship with other nations. Government is specifically charged to maintain the peace and order in society, and to protect its citizens (Romans 13:1-6; 1Timothy 2:1-2). To fulfill these responsibilities it's critical to have the authority and the power to use the sword (Romans 13:4) if necessary to protect its very existence – as well as the well being of its citizens – from foreign dangers, invasions and even from self-destructive corrupting influences from within.

By contrast, the church (the Body of Christ) has no national borders that define or constrain its existence; it's a nation unto itself wherever it's found throughout the world (1 Peter 2:9). As a borderless family of God, under the kingship of King Jesus, it is to pursue spiritual matters relating to kingdom work no matter where it finds itself. It does this by representing Christ as his disciples and ambassadors whose citizenship is firmly and permanently held in heaven (Philippians 3:20). In fact, nowhere is there a mandate or imperative for Christians individually or as a church to negotiate separate alliances with national entities. The power to set national policy is vested in the authorities that God has instituted over us for our own good (Romans 13:4).

God raises up nations according to his plans and purposes, and deals with them according to his sovereign will (Acts 17:26-27). The church is not to act in competition with those authorities but to submit to them as they seek to deal with other nations. Does this mean Christians have no say in the laws of the land or national policy? Of course not.

Fourth, *the church is not to create or enforce civil laws for society*. Although authority within a church is to be exercised in a Christ honoring fashion toward its own members in order to maintain its purity (Matthew 18:15-17; 1 Corinthians 5:1-5), it does not have the authority to legislate civil and criminal laws applying to all of society. If it did, it would be acting in the place of government by exercising authority to punish evil and reward good over both the believing and the non-believing community. Interestingly, Paul acknowledges the existence of criminal courts to handle conflicts within the unbelieving community (1 Corinthians 6:1-7), and readily submits his very life to the authority of Caesar if he were to be found guilty of a capital offense (Acts 25:10-11).

In like manner, the church does not have the authority to force society's obedience to the state's laws through police actions or criminal punishment. The state wields this authority since it has been entrusted with the sword (physical power) for the common good. The sword also implies that judicial power over physical life and death in our land is held in the magistrate's hands in order to fulfill and support societal justice and to maintain proper order.

Fifth, *the church is not to levy taxes*. Although some Christians may see tithes and offerings as a form of spiritual taxation, biblically, we're to give to support kingdom work within the church from the heart, cheerfully, not coerced (2 Corinthians 9:6-7) and according to our means (2 Corinthians 8:3). The church doesn't have the authority to compel its members to give a certain amount to the Lord's work, and likewise it doesn't have any authority over the government or unbelievers in general to levy and collect taxes of any kind.

Tax revenue is intended for the common good to pay for the labor of those entrusted with governing the land (Romans 13:7). As in the famous words of

Jesus, we are to render unto Caesar (the state) that which belongs to the state (Matthew 22:15-22) for the worker is worthy of his wages (Luke 10:7).

The fact that the government must tax in order to support its functions is an obvious obligation and has been true throughout time and throughout the world no matter how much we may not like it or disagree with how government uses the tax it collects. As history and experience shows, in a very real sense the power to tax is the power to destroy. If the church had that authority over those outside the chapel walls it would quickly become coercive and punitive.

Are there other areas in which the church has no direct biblical mandate to exercise authority over in our society? There could very well be. But the above are some of the most important that have been entrusted to the state by the Lord for our own good. Realistically, most Christians would agree with the above limitations because they've grown up with, and experienced this separation and have had very little taught or preached to the contrary. That same situation many not be accurate in other countries or previously in history.

Given these limits on the influence of the church, the obvious next question is whether there are areas of government responsibility that the church is to influence for the common good, within our national context?

### *What Churches Are to Do Toward Government*

First, *the church is commanded to pray for those in authority over it (1 Timothy 2:1-2).* This covers a lot of territory if we consider all who have legislative and executive responsibilities at the local, state and national levels. Add those that are charged with exercising justice and maintaining order (e.g. judges, police officers, National Guard) and the imperative becomes overwhelming. In practical terms, we're to faithfully do what we can for those we know about, and entrust the results to God.

Individual and church-wide prayer for public servants, regardless of their spiritual status is our privilege and duty. By praying, we become sensitive to the responsibilities our leaders carry, and whether they fulfill those duties in a manner pleasing to God. It also prompts us to directly communicate both our concerns and thankfulness to them as decisions, actions and circumstances dictate.[96] Although all authority is ultimately accountable to God (Hebrews 4:12-13), we're accountable to encourage and correct as needed, as well as bring spiritual truths and blessings to those in leadership (Galatians 6:10). They may not understand or recognize it, but our representatives are involved in spiritual warfare, and the spiritual tools available to us (2 Corinthians 10:4-6) will have an impact on them as we seek the Lord's will, knowing that ultimately they are His servants (Romans 13:4).

One caution for all of us is to be careful how we pray. Scripture indicates that whether we're subjects to the state (1 Timothy 2:1-2) or captives of the state (Jeremiah 29:1-7), we're to pray for the nation's welfare and the common good, for in doing so we're also providing for our and our families welfare.[97]

Second, *the church can and must speak out on the moral issues around us.* If a friend came to you and asked for advice - wouldn't you want to help? In the same way governance in our country is designed to elicit our counsel on what constitutes good (acceptable) or bad (unacceptable) legislation and leadership (Proverbs 15:22). Even though everyone's endowed with a conscience (Romans 2:14-15), it would be unreasonable and unwise to expect government to always

---

[96] Another byproduct is that when we pray fervently for those in authority, when we diligently seek the best for them and God's blessings on them, it becomes very difficult to participate in demeaning personal jokes about them, or cast aspersions toward them since we would be demonstrating a real lack of true sincerity for their lives and actions.

[97] Admittedly, it's sometimes tempting to turn to the imprecatory portions of the Psalms for examples of prayer toward those in public service we're either disgusted with or know as callous toward anything holy (e.g. Psalm 69:22-28; 109:6-15; 139:7-9; etc.) . But Jesus commands us to love and pray for (not against) our enemies (Matthew 5:44). This should be our habit, until the clear demonstration of a hardened, obvious, hatred of a holy God and all things righteous (see also Proverb 24:17-18).

(or even often) know on their own what's just and to act accordingly. In fact, all levels of government reflect what we are as a people and a nation. If man's sinful nature and bankrupt worldviews become pervasive and dominant throughout society, then government will both reflect and powerfully project that nature.[98] If a moral atmosphere reflecting biblical values is commonly accepted throughout society, then the tool of government will be expected to be restrained and reflect that nature in its actions (Proverbs 14:34).

Because we've been entrusted with the very Word of God that applies to all of life (2 Timothy 3:16-17), why would we ignore opportunities to advise our government on what decisions would be closest to God's standard and best for the common good (Matthew 5:13-16; Proverbs 25:15). Not only is this true in matters of war and maintaining domestic order, but also in the exercise of justice. Since government is entrusted with the sword to govern everything within its realm why wouldn't we be committed and involved to ensure that that power is wielded properly against evil?

If we don't inform, restrain and direct government power we know who will; and it's almost guaranteed we won't like the answer. This isn't to say the work will be easy or that all Christians will automatically agree on everything. But that's one reason why the Lord has given to His people the gift of local congregations with all that they need to fulfill their purposes in this world (1 Corinthians 12:4-7).

Where better to grapple with the practical outworking of the Word of Truth towards the community around us than with the gifted teachers and preachers instructing and admonishing us in all other aspects of our lives? Where else can we turn to ensure proper accountability so that divisiveness

---

[98]   The aggregate power of government can be far greater than the sum of the power of individual citizens working independently or even as groups trying to make a difference since there are so many competing interests in our nation. Government has physical power that can be overwhelming, but even that can be overcome (albeit rarely) when an entire citizenry revolts against it.

doesn't corrode the Christian witness and engagement in political affairs (Titus 3:10)? Clearly, the church environment provides the best equipping ground for Christians to understand the times in which we live, the need to influence authority to fulfill their God-ordained responsibilities, and how to do this in a Christ-honoring way (1 Corinthians 10:31).

Third, *the church is to influence society for good.* Since God's pattern for living brings great blessings that are demonstrable, we can confidently use moral persuasion, logic, reason and facts to influence as many people as possible to do what's right for the benefit of society and our nation.[99] Instead of retreating from the world because of its bad influence, Christians have a legitimate right to publically and wisely expose evil for what it is (Ephesians 5:11) and challenge any legitimacy people want to give to it (James 4:7; 1 Peter 5:8-9). Exercising a salt-and-light influence helps create a broader moral consensus among those willing to be reasonable and teachable to pressure government to do what's right.

Even the example of our personal lives as we work and play in the world can influence others because of God's common grace[100].[101] This not only builds personal credibility with others, but also ultimately provides credibility when we have opportunity to evangelize. I realize only a changed, converted heart

---

[99] Before the inevitable argument is made that "true change must come from a heart change", let me state that I also believe that to be true. But, just as we train and equip our children to know right from wrong and that there are consequences to their actions whether they ever come to saving faith in Jesus Christ, so too we have the opportunity to influence those around us to see the consequences of sin, particularly since there's such a push to ignore and trivialize consequences by the major influence outlets of our day (major news media, entertainment industry, movies, etc.).

[100] At a secular company where I worked, when a difficult decision was faced, one or more would come to the point of saying: "What's the right thing to do?" Interestingly, everyone knew what was proper, and that would carry the day if there were any doubts as to the propriety of the action. This was in a non-Christian environment, but demonstrated the impact that proper values can have even among the non-churched.

[101] I've experienced the common grace of God many times in office situations at both a government research laboratory and a high technology company. By not swearing or using vulgar words and innuendo, and politely refusing to not listen to dirty jokes, there occurrence around me dramatically disappeared. In fact, apologies were given if a "bad" word slipped out by someone in a meeting.

will have eternal significance and value. However, our salt-and-light mandate (Matthew 5:13-17; Jeremiah 29:7) provides a powerful incentive to persuade others to reject corrupting decisions and chose ones that benefit themselves and others (Matthew 7:9-11). In effect, illuminating the consequences when wandering off the moral path God intended for the good of mankind, many can be persuaded of the benefits of proper values and choices (Proverbs 4:27; Deuteronomy 5:32-33). Ultimately, this provides greater pressure on our government leaders to act according to proper moral values.

Fourth, *the church should equip leaders for public office.* Where is a better place to grow the next generation of public leaders than within Christ-honoring churches that take seriously the discipleship of the next generation? How do we expect men and women[102] desiring to serve the public to gain the necessary knowledge and skills to govern and legislate in a godly way if the church doesn't equip them for the difficulties they'll face? What standard will they base their decisions on if they don't have God's standard constantly before them (Proverbs 22:6)?

Churches are a fertile ground to identify and mentor those who have an aptitude and desire to serve in public office.[103] Ask yourself if this is a priority in your church? If it's not, why isn't it? Second Timothy 3:16 declares God's Word is useful to equip for every good work; isn't godly governance in the public realm a good work? Isn't it also a testimony to the non-Christian world that moral standards, excellence, and accountability to God will yield rich blessings for

---

[102] The issue of women in political leadership is very controversial in some Christian circles. However, government is not a church, and even though God created men and women to complement each other, there are no Biblical injunctions against women seeking or obtaining high secular positions of authority. For a more detailed discussion of this issue see Chapter 10 Common Myths.

[103] Incidentally, even though elective office is the most visible and contentious, there are innumerable influential positions a person can be appointed to or hired to serve in a staff position. These become advisory in nature and can have significant influence on legislators and other policy decision makers.

all?[104] Do you invite Christians in elective office to speak at your church? These men and women can share directly what public service is like: its challenges, discouragements and its joys. We seek out missionaries to speak and share about their ministry efforts; do we seek out Christians who are performing kingdom work in just as spiritually hostile of an environment as examples for our youth of what it means to stand for Christ in the outside world?[105]

Better yet, if you have someone in your church who's been in elective office let them mentor those who have an interest in public service. Pastors often feel ill-equipped to do this because of a lack of direct political experience. However, they can surely seek it out from others and build an instructional program around them with timeless principles and truths from God's Word that apply to life no matter what the professional endeavor.

And finally, do we forget about Christian men and women after they're elected to office and just assume they'll continue to do the right thing? We should realize that once they're in positions of authority it's even more important to continue to mentor, advice and counsel them as well as faithfully pray for them as they struggle in the spiritual warfare that will rage around them.[106]

Fifth, *the church should equip its members to vote.* Besides working for the common welfare of our nation, Christians should responsibly exercise their duty

---

[104]　Many times while conducting lectures or seminars I've asked parents in attendance if they've ever encouraged their son or daughter to consider public service (elective office or even advisory staff) sometime during their lifetime or career. In over fifteen years I've had only one positive response that wasn't a blank deer in the headlights look, as if political service was somehow not a legitimate activity.

[105]　After meeting and talking with many different state legislators, the phrase "wickedness" was used more often in describing the California state legislative environment. Though each state will differ, some are more openly hostile to biblical values than others and those serving us need to be diligently encouraged, supported, and prayed.

[106]　I can't prove it, but I believe there was a significant drop off of prayer covering for President George W, Bush after he was elected for his second term. I rarely heard him mention prayer in public or private speeches like he did during his first term of office, and I didn't sense Christians were as engaged in praying for him the second four years. Yet, these are the times when spiritual warfare is the greatest: when the fight to finish well is the hardest. This is also the time we should be more diligent in our prayer ministry toward those who serve us.

to vote.[107] This means using biblical perspectives to study issues intrinsic to every ballot measure as well as voting for candidates that will do the greatest good if elected. In theory, supporting sincere Christians that are qualified to occupy elective office is the most desirable situation, but more often than not that option isn't available in many elections and we must settle for something less.

Obviously, a church has some legal restrictions on what it can do concerning candidates and how to treat them equally and fairly. However, there are few restrictions on what churches can do concerning pending legislation or ballot measures.[108] In addition, there are innumerable ways churches can equip their members on issues of the day; impacts of public policy and legislation on families and church ministries; and what activities can be done to influence legislation and even campaigns.

When these matters are openly discussed and addressed within a church environment – including from the pulpit – the opportunity for divisiveness and resentment is going to be dramatically reduced since the pastoral shepherding role is readily available to ensure differences are handled in a Christ-honoring way.

Final thought: *The government isn't a church.* The responsibility of the church and its members toward government is quite significant for the benefit of the nation, community and everyone affected by government. Where many difficulties and conflicts originate is when Christians either assume government is some benign entity they can ignore, or they treat government as if it were some type of organization operating like a church where everyone's best interests are taken to heart.

Government is not, and never should be thought of as a church or some benign entity. It's a tool that will be used for good or evil, depending on who

---

[107]  Though data is not exact, virtually all polling shows Christian voting turnout to be as poor as that of the general population.

[108]  For a more thorough treatment of what a church can and cannot do legally, see Chapter 15: Practical Steps.

leads it or strongly influences it. Our duty and responsibility is to do all we can to ensure government is a blessing as it exercises justice on evildoers and ensures a healthy environment for kingdom work to prosper and flourish. Since it won't do that on its own, it needs to be actively engaged in a Christ-honoring, biblical manner to keep it within its rightful sphere of power; no more, no less.

So, what is the government's proper role relative to the church? That subject is explored in-depth in the next chapter.

# Chapter 5

# Separation of State *from* Church?

*"Righteousness exalts a nation, but sin is a reproach to any people"*
**– Proverbs 14:34**

*"Render to Caesar the things that are Caesar's, and to God the things that are God's'"* **– Mark 12:17**

*"That the power to tax involves the power to destroy. . . [is] not to be denied"*
**– Chief Justice John Marshall**

### The Impact of Worldviews

A classic battle of political worldviews has been growing more passionate and open in the past several decades. In fact, the increasing hostility between "right" and "left" seems to make every election the most important one we've ever had.[109] Presidential elections in particular focus our interest

---

[109]   In actuality, if a bankrupt, destructive worldview (and ideology) continues to have increasing influence over our nation, then every succeeding election does in fact become more important to try to reverse, or at least stop this slide.

since they provide opportunity to decide which of two competing views of the world will drive the national decisions we'll either suffer under, or be blessed by for years to come.[110]

At a basic level, one worldview sees mankind as fundamentally good, with government an obvious tool to extend and apply that nature with unlimited potential and incredible power for the benefit to all. The second worldview, based on God's revealed truth, sees mankind's intrinsic nature as fundamentally evil (Jeremiah 17:9; Romans 3:9-18) with unbridled government inevitably becoming an abusive and powerful reflection and expansion of that nature.

The concept of limited government implemented by our nation's founders clearly assumed the biblical view was the correct one. But over time, particularly during the last generation, the worldview permeating much of politics seems to believe in mankind's basic "goodness", if not perfectibility. As a result, inordinate amounts of trust have been placed in the hands of an insatiable bureaucracy to control virtually every aspect of life. It's not too much of a stretch to realize that a government that's big enough, powerful enough, and ideologically driven enough will see biblical values as a threat to keeping its power. As that happens, freedom to openly speak, teach and preach God's Word will come under increasing pressure to bow to "political correctness" and relegated to the realm of private thought only.[111]

Before addressing what a proper government role would be toward the church, it's instructive to remember a few national questions that are in

---

[110]    By saying this I don't want to imply there's always a clear and consistent distinction between two major presidential candidates facing off every four years. Most people are neither consistent over time nor at any given time across all policy issues. This is due to complexities involved in most public policy matters which pit many principles against each other, or a lack of a coherent worldview underlying decisions.

[111]    In my lifetime I've noticed that what used to be in the closet (man's depravity) has openly come out and been celebrated, while biblical values and morals have experienced unrelenting pressure to be forced into the closet. Consider the mainstreaming of gay "pride" parades as family events, while mentioning the name of Christ in prayers prior to the opening of city council meetings is considered divisive and intolerant.

desperate need of the wisdom of a biblical perspective. Should government: be limited or unrestrained in power; run the economy or incentivize free markets; incentivize individual dependence or responsibility; provide disincentives or incentives to wealth creation; increase or reduce its own indebtedness; increase or decrease individual tax burdens; abolish or strengthen traditional marriage; ration health care or allow competitive growth; increase or decrease dependence on foreign energy; unilaterally disarm or strengthen defense; treat life as utilitarian or made in God's image; grant citizenship to illegal aliens or incentivize their departure; ignore or respect state's rights; promote immoral lifestyles or incentivize sexual purity; invent hate crimes or ensure equal justice; encourage faith in the public domain or eradicate it.

What should be obvious is that the worldview that prevails in elections will determine policy decisions for years to come on these and many other moral judgments. But most people I've met, including many Christians, believe that man's nature is fundamentally good. This conviction not only trivializes biblical truth, but accepts a relativistic post-modernism that basically denies the very need for the gospel.[112] Is it any wonder that many Christians are befuddled about how our government has become so pervasive in controlling our lives and becoming anti-Christian? After all, if everyone is basically good, then government is only a greater and more powerful expression of that good.

When people misunderstand the battle, they become unwitting accomplices in growing the very government that will reflect man's sinful nature.[113] In reality, politics is a shadow of the ongoing spiritual warfare struggling for the soul of our nation (Ephesians 6:12). With that context, the following summarizes some practical relationships government should respect concerning the church

---

[112]   The obvious consequence of this thinking is that the necessity for a Savior (Romans 6:23) and personal repentance (1 Peter 3:9) becomes trivialized since sin is not really as bad as the Bible clearly proclaims it to be (Jeremiah 17:9).

[113]   In fact, when government loses its fundamental acknowledgment of accountability to a holy, righteous God (as is clearly stated in the Declaration of Independence) it will do everything in its power to become the focus of man's attention; in effect a "god" to replace "The" God.

that are natural extensions of the purpose for government as summarized in Romans 13:1-6, 1 Peter 2:13-17 and elsewhere.

### What Government's Should Not Do Toward the Church

First, *the government must not establish a religion.* This is a well-known restriction in the United States, and is clearly embodied in the First Amendment to the Constitution: "Congress shall make no law respecting an establishment of religion, or prohibiting the free exercise thereof." The founder's original intent is well documented; prevent the formal recognition or establishment of any national Christian denomination. States on the other hand were free to acknowledge or even promote religious activities as they saw fit. Contrary to what anti-faith organizations believe, allowing or even encouraging the presence of varied manifestations of Christian faith in public service is not the same as establishing a state-sponsored and state-run religion.[114] This is a far cry from today's judicial activism that often shows open hostility toward any vestige of Christianity in the public, policy realm.

Just as government is not to force religion on its citizens, it must not impose the religion of secular humanism or atheism as the *de facto* national belief system.[115] If it does, this is in itself a discriminatory action against the prevailing, self-proclaimed faith of most of the population. To the other extreme, when government embraces cultural and religious pluralism by treating anything from animism to Islam, or witchcraft to orthodox Christianity as equally valid

---

[114] This is implicit in the 10th Amendment to the Constitution, which states: "The powers not delegated to the United States by the Constitution, nor prohibited by it to the States, are reserved to the States respectively, or to the people." With decisions of this nature residing closer to the voting public, changes and corrections were able to be made easier than at a national level.

[115] Scripture provides some very intriguing examples of this idea in Genesis 47:20-22 where Joseph respects the priests of Pharaoh and in Daniel 2:24 where Daniel saved the lives of magicians and astrologers. In both cases the religion of the Jew could have been mandated for the entire country but it wasn't done. Likewise, when Nebuchadnezzar tried to force false worship, God miraculously intervened to prevent it (Daniel 3 and 6).

(or invalid) expressions of truth, it naturally leads to embracing a morally relativistic (secular) standard with no room for biblical truth and accountability to the God of the Bible.

Unfortunately, government has elevated all sorts of non-Christian faiths to moral equivalency while removing Christianity from its historically prominent role. The net result is an unofficial denial of any transcendent reality and rejection of any claim on spiritual truth. By trying to appear "tolerant", government is in fact forcibly discriminating against the most widespread, indigenous form of faith that has formed and guided most of our national life and been the basis for our many freedoms being fixed in law.

Second, *the government must not define church government*. The existence of incredible varieties of church governments (ecclesiology) illustrates the freedom we enjoy to organize according to biblical convictions on how church authority is to be exercised. Large hierarchical denominations as well as independent churches; conventions; senates; fellowships; synods; affiliations; and associations all exist today. Inside churches we find pastors, elders, deacons, priests, lay pastors, ministers, bishops, vicars as well as examples of no recognized leadership at all. The leadership may operate as a plurality, a hierarchy, a staff position reporting to a board, or any number of other combinations.

But in all of this, government should not impose its will on how the wider church or an individual fellowship organizes itself. Church governance must be allowed to follow the dictates of conscience in light of scriptural convictions; something government is incapable of understanding or implementing. To do otherwise would result in the church quickly becoming only an extension of a soulless bureaucracy.

Although subtle, government encroachment does occur when a church applies for a 501(c)3 designation in order to obtain a tax-exempt status.[116]

---

[116]  Whether a church should become a 501(c)3 organization or not for tax purposes is controversial, and beyond the scope of this book. However, it's something that should be thoroughly

Similarly, church hiring actions that are not directly pastoral in nature can potentially be subject to anti-discrimination laws.[117] These types of government interference try to distinguish between "spiritual" and "non-spiritual" activity in order to force conformance to secular beliefs, contrary to our historically protected legal freedoms of religion and conscience.

Third, *the government must not establish church doctrine.* Government has no right to define spiritual truth or what constitutes valid, fundamental beliefs of a person or a church. Not only is it incapable of doing so, but it's also incompetent to do so. The dictates of one's own conscience under the authority of Scripture form the foundation of individual beliefs and a church's statement of faith. When government assumes this role, inevitably persecution will follow toward those not adhering to the dictates of the state.

Similarly, government is not to establish a *de facto* "faith-less" state religion by showing hostility toward expressions of faith in the public domain. Though not directly forcing religion on anyone, by restricting its free expression government creates a "chilling effect" on the legitimacy of Christian biblical imperatives having any role in the handling of national affairs (Matthew 10:32-33).[118]

Clearly this has been an unconstitutional activity by hostile judges toward Christianity for years.[119] However, in spite of constitutional protections, activist groups continue to exert immense pressure to purge the very mention of the name of Jesus Christ from public invocations or benedictions, city council

---

researched and decided in the light of scriptural understanding and legal ramifications (Ephesians 3:8-11; 4:11-16).

[117] This has been legally challenged in many ways, such as whether a janitor or choir director can be refused an employment position solely because they're openly homosexual even though the church views homosexual behavior as sin.

[118] One possible exception is when the exercise of religious convictions violates necessary civil law concerning obvious health and safety issues. But even here, in my opinion, government cannot rule on the validity of the belief, but only on its impact upon life and health.

[119] This fact was re-affirmed by the United States Supreme Court in May 2014 when it ruled in favor of the Town of Greece, and that the town's practice of beginning legislative sessions with prayers does not violate the Establishment Clause of the First Amendment

meetings, school graduations, or even book reports in public schools. While intimidated city councils may allow "divinity devoid" moments of reflection these self-imposed conditions actually compel conformance to a non-Christian, non-biblical viewpoint completely contrary to the purpose and pattern in seeking God's blessing in the first place (John 14:13-14; 1 John 5:14-15).[120]

Fourth, *the government must not rule on spiritual matters.* What constitutes sin and what's biblically required to reconcile a person to God and to others is not a government responsibility to define, interpret or enforce. This responsibility lies within the church (Galatians 6:1), a believer's convictions (Romans 7:7-25), and the bounds of biblical truth (1 Corinthians 4:6). Church discipline, specifically, is not an activity that the state is capable or qualified to adjudicate.[121]

Association with the Body of Christ demands acknowledgement of, and adherence to standards of morality, unity and action consistent with the Lordship of Christ in the person's life (Titus 3:10-11). Mature spiritual leadership is in the best position to determine if someone has violated clear biblical warnings against gross sinfulness and brought dishonor on the name of Christ. For the government to insert itself and attempt to protect a person's public reputation (e.g. accusations of libel), or ensure secular norms of evidence collection, jurisprudence and that rights of appeal are followed is inconsistent

---

[120]  This also occurs when terms like "father of mankind", "god of the universe", "holy one", are tolerated but praying directly in the name of Jesus Christ is strictly prohibited. The fact that Jesus' name and His name alone are being targeted as offensive or non-inclusive shows that the issue is truly spiritual warfare and not just some administrative accommodation made in the name of tolerance.

[121]  Though it will vary among churches, common causes for exercising church discipline include public immorality (1 Corinthians 5:9-11; 6:9-10; Exodus 20:12-17); divisiveness (Titus 3:9-11; Romans 16:17-18; Hebrews 13:17); and denying the faith (1 Timothy 1:19-20; 6:3-5; 2 John 9-11); none of which will typically violate existing civil or criminal law. Obviously, discipline can take many forms, including the barring from the Lord's Table (excommunication), removing from membership and/or treating as a non-believer in social or personal interactions (Matthew 18:15-17).

with the God given authority that pastors and church members have to wisely judge the wicked and praise the righteous within their fellowship.

As a matter of fact, the Constitution ensures that freedom to assemble is self-regulated. This important freedom not only legally guarantees the rights to form a church but also to determine the qualifications needed to be met in order to be part of that fellowship. Conversely, membership privileges can be denied to those who violate the known tenets of the church and should not be subject to secular legal recourse.[122]

One important caveat, however, is when criminal behavior has occurred and the offender is subject to the civil authorities (Romans 13:4). There are consequences for violation of civil law (such as child abuse, theft, mayhem, etc.) independent of church actions; but the government is not to determine what is or is not a violation of God's commands. Its duty is to enforce civil law as established for the good of the community and not spiritual law that governs the hearts, minds and activities of the faith community.

Fifth, *the government must not appoint church leaders.* Those who occupy positions of authority within a church are to demonstrate qualifications consistent with biblical requirements for leadership (1 Timothy 3:1-13; Titus 1:5-9; Hebrews 13:17), not some government litmus test that changes with the prevailing political climate. For government to appoint church leadership in any capacity would be devastating to the nature of the Christian church, its spiritual health, and it's calling to be the voice of moral conscience to government itself.[123]

It's also not up to government to judge the competency of pastors by examining their education background, giftedness, aptitude, racial status,

---

[122] The Constitution of the United States; Second Amendment: "Congress shall make no law respecting an establishment of religion, or prohibiting the free exercise thereof; or abridging the freedom of speech, or of the press; or the right of the people peaceably to assemble, and to petition the Government for a redress of grievances".

[123] A review of the history of government and church melding together is far beyond the scope of this book.

physical attributes, or policy positions on political matters. How could a secular bureaucracy ever be competent to assign, much less accurately assess the quality or validity of spiritual leadership within an area it's inept to even understand?

Our Constitutional freedoms are built on Western political thought, natural law and a biblical worldview. Though this foundation protects our religious liberties, we can never take it for granted or stop being vigilant to defend them whenever and wherever necessary. Though the above list may overlook some inherent limitations on government, it's important to continually assess the government's attitude and actions toward the Christian community. It can never be assumed government has our spiritual health and freedoms at heart, or that it's doing all it can to provide an environment conducive to the "free exercise thereof", much less be capable of rightly discerning spiritual matters.

Government has assumed far ranging authority over our lives and every existing institution we hold dear, including the church. Given its ubiquitous nature, are there any clear roles the government should have toward the church and spiritual matters? The next section covers a few of the most important ones.

### What Government's Should Do Toward the Church

First, *government must recognize its accountability to God*. Government is a natural consequence of the fall of mankind, and though it can be abusive, it's ultimately intended for our good (Rom 13:1-5). The United States is rather unique in its Declaration of Independence by declaring independence from England and at the same time dependence on an almighty God as the Creator of the universe.[124] It's not just a coincidence that every one of the 50 states of

---

[124]  It's very instructive to read the Declaration of Independence and note the four references to the divine. Specifically: ". . .and to assume among the powers of the earth, the separate and equal station to which the Laws of Nature *and of Nature's God* entitle them. . ."; "We hold these truths to be self-evident, that *all men are created* equal, that they are *endowed by their Creator* with certain unalienable Rights. . ."; ". . .with a firm reliance on the *protection of divine Providence*. . ." (Emphasis added).

the United States also acknowledges a divine God in some manner it their state constitutions.

Our national Christian roots clearly show the use of God's biblical standard as the foundation on which all government responsibilities, and civil justice itself, should be judged. It's not a matter of might making right, but of government doing what's right before the Judge of the universe. Those in authority over us are put there by God and are accountable to God, whether we can clearly understand the specific reasons or God's purposes or not. Ultimately, our prosperity, our security, and our freedoms are completely dependent upon the grace and mercy of God. Though this was openly and routinely recognized publicly by our national and local leaders for much of our nation's history, the increasing trend to ignore this dependence as the source of our blessings will eventually result in God's withdrawal of his mercies.

Second, *government must commend what's good.* To commend is to uphold, highlight, and even encourage or incentivize. Government shouldn't be creating stumbling blocks to our promotion and cultivation of moral purity and virtue, justice, strong families, life, compassion, or the proclamation of the gospel. In fact, government should do what it can to complement the righteousness the Christian community strives to example and inculcate in our culture. This is not only reasonable; but it's also consistent with life experience, conscience, and innumerable studies that show the devastating consequences of sinful behaviors and the blessings that come from living moral lives of character.

God has revealed for mankind both through his perfect Word (Psalm 18:30; Proverbs 30:5; 2 Timothy 3:16-17) and natural law (Romans 1:20; 2:14-15)[125] that there's a way that may seem right to a sinful heart, but in the end lives lived in disobedience to God will only lead to destruction (Proverbs 14:34). Thankfully, the virtues our nation has valued since even before our

---

[125]   These two sources of truth are commonly referred to as God's Special and General Revelation.

founding have reflected God's truths and empowered the greatest outreach with compassion and the gospel the world has ever seen.

Government can provide a fertile environment for the church to fulfill its biblical imperatives without establishing a formal religion or trying to force its citizens to believe certain articles of faith.

For our part, Christians are responsible to ensure government fulfills these duties consistent with the biblical standard for what's good for our society and the moral conscience that God has granted to humanity (Romans 2:14-15). Obviously, God's eternal moral standard (Exodus 20:1-17) doesn't change over time, although wisdom is needed in each generation to apply it effectively and without compromise given the demands of the time. This wisdom approach was exampled by Paul, when he confessed that he was all things to all men for the sake of the gospel, but never outside the law of Christ (1 Corinthians 9:19-23).

A final point on this topic. If Christian influence is removed from direct involvement with government and politics, then like any other legitimate human pursuit it will rot and eventually be used as a weapon against us.

Third, *government must punish evil*. Our topsy-turvy world is no different than the experience of mankind throughout the ages. When given an opportunity the fallen nature will define evil as good and what's good as evil to their own shame (Proverbs 17:15; Isa 5:20)[126]. Euthanizing a person is thought of as death with dignity; killing unborn babies for any (or no) reason is merely a simple choice and a cherished legal right; and sexual impurity of all types is seen as personal freedom independent of the inevitable destructive consequences. Government is not to mirror the worst of society, it's to embrace a high standard of virtue, integrity and morality consistent with God's proven standard.

Who is going to define what evil needs to be punished (or discouraged) if we don't? Since we of all people understand the destructive power of unrestrained

---

[126] A powerful way to re-state this is that the world around us will use as many tools as possible to make that which is ugly appear to be beautiful and inviting (Proverbs 5:1-6).

human nature, shouldn't we do all we can to persuade, influence, guide and at times force government to not fall into the trap of moral relativism; or being manipulated by evil influences; or eventually promoting what's wicked (Proverbs 29:2)?

Criminal and civil laws reflecting a righteous standard of justice allows government to discourage the unrighteous deeds of darkness (Romans 13:5), as well as enforce peace and order for the good of everyone (1 Timothy 2:1-2). Even in ancient Roman with all the pagan idolatry and violence it still maintained strict order on society and granted rights to citizens that were carefully defended (Acts 25:10-12).

Fourth, *government is to protect free expression of religion*. Basic Christian teaching shows us we cannot impose faith on someone else; they must respond to the dictates of their own conscience and conviction (Acts 2:36-38). This belief is integrated into our national thinking through the First Amendment to the Constitution: "Congress shall make no law respecting an establishment of religion, or prohibiting the free exercise thereof."[127] This principle was intended to ensure the national government wouldn't establish a religion (or denomination) to the exclusion of all others, and that any one of the varieties of Christian and other belief systems would not be officially discriminated against or favorably treated.[128] It's understood, however, that this amendment doesn't give license for religious activities that clearly violate common moral standards and comprise criminal actions.

---

[127] There's a reason why this is the First Amendment to the Constitution. Without freedom of religion and religious conscience, no other liberty or right defined and protected by the law of the land is safe from being taken away.

[128] It's also instructive to note that Article VI, paragraph 3 of the Constitution states that for members of Congress, members of the state legislatures, and for all executive and judicial officers at the national and state levels: ". . .no religious test shall ever be required as a qualification to any office or public trust under the United States". By rejecting a religious litmus test, a variety of expressions of faith were encouraged to participate in governance.

Why is freedom of religion so important? The government's power to tax can be very capricious and vengeful. As a consequence, government should have no right to regulate churches through taxation since this would unnecessarily constrain the good works churches are called to do.[129] These freedoms allow Christians to exercise their beliefs in a full, open and public manner such that God's truths will be shown through any objective investigation to be far superior to any other worldly belief system.

The second protection the government must give is the free expression of our faith.[130] As a nation we grant Muslims, Eastern religions, and even atheists the same freedoms. But when government goes out of its way to selectively discourage just the mentioning of the name of Jesus in any government setting, it's selectively censoring the free expression of our faith. This discriminatory means by which government shows its revulsion for Christianity is another mark of the spiritual warfare underway around us, and the need for Christians to hold the government to task to respect our fundamental freedoms and the biblical principles upon which they're based.

Lastly, the imposition of government authority into the exercise of our faith doesn't end with issues of safety, taxes or mentioning Jesus' name; it includes approving tax exemptions, zoning restrictions, and limitations on a church's freedom of speech and finances to accomplish moral (political) objectives (Galatians 5:9). The merit of any particular exercise of government authority in these areas can and should be debated (facility use permits for example), but the bottom line is the same: is the government action restricting religious expression or not? If it is, on what basis can it be clearly justified and shown

---

[129]   Rightfully so, it has been said that the power to tax is the power to destroy. Although kingdom work will not be extinguished if the government chose to tax churches like any other entity, its labors would be a little more difficult.

[130]   Even Joseph in Egypt honored the existence of pagan religious entities by not using his power to persecute or eliminate those that served Pharaoh (Genesis 47:20-22)

to eventually be instrumental to the furtherance of the protection of the free expression of religion?

Final thought: *Government and the church are not inseparable* Clearly the current administration[131] embraces an ideology that believes government is benevolent and knows what's best for us all, independent of evidence to the contrary. History shows quite plainly that unrestrained power rapidly becomes corrupt and the enemies of all that biblical Christians hold dear. But when government is restrained to its proper role of punishing evil and commending good (Rom 13:1-5; 1 Peter 2:14), the result can be incredible freedom for churches to openly exercise religious liberties, pursue our mercy mandate without government co-opting our role, and openly proclaiming the gospel and biblical truth to all of society. This is clearly a battle worth fighting for.

Can government's massive intrusion on our freedoms, lives and businesses be restrained? If the 2010 Congressional House of Representatives election, and the 2014 Congressional House of Representatives and Senate elections demonstrated anything, it showed the general public was finally willing to push back against an out of control government that sees little if any restraints on itself.

So, what group is clamoring for government to be restrained to its proper and limited roles? Libertarians eschew government control of our lives; and individuals severely harmed by government overreach may selectively hate government power; also survivalists and loners may try to evade notice by government as long as possible. But realistically, the Body of Christ is undoubtedly the greatest threat to the government assuming authority over every detail of our lives or the promotion of values anathema to the common good.

There are two giant influences in our nation, the government and the church. Though they fulfill different purposes, we that comprise the church

---

[131]  Specifically, the current administration is that of President Barack Obama. However, vestiges can be found in greater and lesser amounts in many modern presidential administrations.

are also the government. Christians are a big determiner of what values and standards government will implement and enforce. This same government is to encourage and protect what's good, and enforce law, order, and especially justice. Our challenge is to continually refine the government's role to ensure acknowledgement and fulfillment of its biblical purpose toward everyone it serves throughout this nation. The trick is to do this while at the same time not looking to wield government power as an end in and of itself.

This battle must be recognized for what it is, and the fight engaged to restore to the public debate an understanding of the nature and rotting fruit of sin, as well as the dangers of a government unbridled by biblical restraint. We know that earthy government will eventually pass like the rest of creation (Revelation 21:21), but in the meantime it's a valuable tool that can be used for good if it's used in a manner consistent with biblical insights and truth.

# Chapter 6

# What About Zealots?

*"True friends stab you in the front"*
– *Oscar Wilde*

*"If the iron is blunt, and one does not sharpen the edge, he must use more strength, but wisdom helps one to succeed"* – ***Ecclesiastes 10:10***

## *A Personal Experience*

Let's face it, when we talk about such a volatile subject as secular politics and the role of the Body of Christ, few things give pastors more concern than a true zealot in the midst of their membership. By zealot, I'm not talking about someone with a love for our nation, or the one with a passion for a particular ministry such as pro-life. I'm also not talking about the mental cases in front of Wal-Mart screaming at customers that the end of the world is at hand. Here I'm talking about someone, either a man or a woman, who has a single-minded life focus on an issue that becomes, in effect, the energizing principle and passion of their daily lives, and who are constantly trying to win converts to their team.

Zealots have very unique characteristics immediately recognizable by anyone in leadership. My own experience has brought me several times in close fellowship and ministry with what I'd consider zealots. I can honestly say that each time has been personally challenging and discouraging. One instance in particular illustrates many of the weaknesses this book is addressing, and revolves around what would normally be considered a minor issue by most people. Let me start by describing how I was confronted by two different individuals:

*"His wife supports destroying embryos to harvest stem cells, how can you as a Christian even think about supporting a man like him as a candidate for office?"*

*"You call yourself pro-life, but you're just as bad as everyone else that's pro-death if you support this guy"*

Wow – these are quite some accusations, ones that shouldn't be taken lightly. How could I ever be so naive and taken in by what I thought was a staunch, pro-life legislator who was a stealth supporter of the bio-medical industry's lust to methodically destroy human life? Even if this candidate did support solid pro-life legislative initiatives in the past, would he really be willing to compromise his outspoken, conservative, evangelicalism in order to gain higher office?

These were serious charges against both the candidate and myself if they're true. Obviously, this needed to be given serious thought, and if I was wrong I had to know about it as soon as possible. If it was just a misunderstanding, I felt compelled to clear up any confusion in the Christian community so godly candidate voting decisions could be made.

As more and more information came to light over the next four months, it became obvious that the "guilt by association" factor had taken a toll on any reasonable assessment of the situation. The candidate's wife worked as a representative of a very large bio-medical firm, but never in the areas of embryonic stem cell research. In actuality, her personnel testimony of faith, and selection of work she was willing to represent, demonstrated her commitment to Christ and the sanctity of life to corporation executives that wouldn't otherwise have had such an example. The legislator really did have a stellar record as a pro-life representative, and was recognized as such by many pro-life organizations.

In effect, the condemnation of the legislator was equivalent to rejecting all of Disneyland because both good and evil people go there. I realize an argument can be made to boycott Disneyland because one of the Disney's many corporate divisions produces both good and offensive films, but as Paul reminds us that principle can't be applied consistently in a fallen world (1 Corinthians 5:9-10).

The same rationale would preclude any sincere Christian from running for public office since the legislature may pass vile legislation. Illustrated another way, the fact that a person is a member of the legislature would be *prima facie* evidence that he's guilty of being associated with every evil decision made – in other words, a classic quilt-by-association scenario.

Even after a fuller understanding of the situation became known, the followers of the two zealots making the accusations against the legislator wouldn't listen to facts or reasoning that contradicted their leader's rants. This Pied Piper situation served to energize and focus a segment of the Christian community against what they were convinced was the typical, vile hypocrisy of a two-faced politician who needed to have their cover blown. This single-mindedness, and unrelenting tenacity illustrated quite clearly how zeal for the things of the Lord can sometimes be misapplied at the expense of extending grace and understanding to someone committed to representing Christ in a hostile, thankless environment.

If the example ended here, it'd be instructive enough, but it didn't. Since I couldn't resolve the issue, and I was being publically condemned for "compromising with evil", I approached each zealot's church leadership in an attempt to follow Matthew 18:15-17. If nothing else, these pastors would have the opportunity to apply Galatians 6:1 to each of us so we could confess whatever sin was found and be reconciled. In both cases the zealot's pastors refused to engage to resolve the issues, even when I made it clear I was willing to submit to their judgment on whether I was in error (or sin). Finally, I offered to bring the issue before my own Elder Board to weigh the two sides, judge the situation and determine whether correction was needed. This offer was also turned down by both zealots and their church leadership.

### Not Just an Individual's Problem

I belabor the above example because it highlights some incredible weaknesses in the Christian community. Zealots wield an inordinate amount of power if they fill a leadership vacuum within the church. Their single-mindedness, apparent purity of devotion to God's truths, and their hatred of evil fashions them into a type of modern day prophet sounding the alarm that no one else is willing to sound. Typically hard to shepherd, many times unwilling to listen to counter arguments, more often than not reluctant to extend grace and understanding to others, and you have a recipe for disaster. The net result: zealots become virtually non-accountable and also shamelessly intimidating, even to pastors. If they did recognize and submit to pastoral authority, it may only last until the first time the pastor disagrees with them. Is it any wonder that the application of Matthew 18:15-17, or even Galatians 6:1 in these situations is so rare?

If you've actively and publically engaged the major moral issues affecting the Christian community, you've either heard about or encountered the classic zealot. They don't have to wear a badge for identification, just listen and you'll immediately recognize them. As a matter of fact, they'll know pretty fast where you stand on their pet concerns since you're going to be sized up quickly as a disciple, a possible convert to the cause, or an enemy.

Even non-believers are well aware of them since the news media loves the opportunity they give for both shock value and Christian stereotyping. In all fairness, the zealot phenomenon is not new, and an objective assessment shows there are actually good, as well as bad and ugly qualities. The real question to ask ourselves is whether zealots are our enemy or friend. Although generalities have their limitations, my experience is that most zealots will exhibit some or most of the following traits, but never every one of them[132].

### On the Positive Side

The most remarkable characteristic is energy and fire for a cause, and a level of personal commitment that can inspire many others to do what's right. The enthusiasm to attack evil and any perceived compromise is not only invigorating; it can be infectious. This zeal isn't necessarily wrong, since we're commanded to "...not be slothful in zeal" but to be fervent in spirit (Romans 12:11). As a matter of fact, many times those who are timid by nature find themselves emboldened to take action and defend things that they otherwise never would have done on their own. This new-found enthusiasm breeds a strong loyalty toward the zealot by those who need an example for their own lives. The disciple now has access to an authoritative source of information and specific actions to take that they didn't have before. As you can imagine, this situation could become a source of frustration for any pastor who may have seen little ministry involvement by the same person after sitting for years under their faithful preaching.

---

[132] In characterizing a zealot, it's instructive to identify the variety of traits that may exist, but it needs to be obvious that no one person will exhibit each and every one. In talking with pastors, when zealotry is mentioned, there's an immediate recognition of the type of person being referred to. This stereotyping has some merit, but won't be true in every case.

Sometimes it happens that there's been compromise in the Christian community, whether overlooking a sinful life of a prominent member of the congregation, or buying into homosexuality being a God-given gift that should be celebrated, or even denying clearly orthodox beliefs. By taking God's Word as the authoritative standard, zealots don't easily buy into incipient incrementalism that can easily entrap so many without even being aware of what's happening.

Zealots hate hypocrisy, and can sometimes clearly see when compromise has occurred, either through clever wording, manipulative argumentation and reasoning, or downright rejection of clearly established biblical truths. When they focus on who or what the enemy is, they can be like a laser beam in accuracy and a bulldog in tenacity, oftentimes throwing the opposition into confusion and retreat.

Admirably, zealots typically are jealous for the things of God, and want to do kingdom work on God's behalf. They see themselves as a modern-day Jeremiah fighting the good fight against evil in the land (Jeremiah 6:27), or as an Ezekiel pointing out sin and warning the faithful (Ezekiel 3:16-19). Because they believe this is their calling, they usually grow a thick hide that's not easily penetrated.

Thus, having little regard for their own safety, zealots may go places and talk to folks we would never think of going to or doing ourselves. Their nature is to change the paradigm of engagement and confront evil directly, and not live a life that's satisfied with the status quo. By thinking out of the box, they can sometimes create significant public exposure to wrongs that would otherwise never have been known to a broad audience. This happens during city council meetings when photos of sexually explicit gay pride participants are shown as the council considers a supportive public proclamation. It happens when adult bookstores are picketed with signs of small children to illustrate the impact the repulsive material inside can have on innocent lives. It can also happen when embarrassing questions are asked at public forums following lengthy and arduous Internet searches of the past dealings of a public figure or bringing to light some questionable activities conveniently overlooked by a complicit media.

The more apathy and weakness that emerges in the Christian community, the more we need those who will stand up and correctly identify and condemn it, particularly if pastoral leadership is in short supply or compromised in doing so. Also, with so much Christian energy focused internally "within a chapel's walls" the major outside threats trying to do us harm may be completely overlooked if it wasn't for the vigilant zealot looking out for us and giving warning, akin to the Old Testament watchman on the wall (Ezekiel 3:16-21).

Those who fall into the category of being a zealot can lead a lonely life because of their intense passion for the cause of righteousness. We need their example of what it means to be committed to kingdom work and not just biding our time until the Lord returns. In that sense, they're a needed reminder of the weakness of our own affections toward compromise and evil.[133]

### On the Negative Side

Zealots tend to be unique, rare individuals that display leadership qualities that energize those starved for direction. But consistent with the ancient Greek *hubris*, their greatest strength is sometimes their greatest weakness. In providing leadership, they'll tend to isolate themselves from any accountability and become their own judge and jury. This can quickly extend to private interpretations of Scripture to bolster their particular view of something.

The problem is that what may sound like a reasonable application of biblical truth may not stand the test of orthodox understanding after a little more diligent research. This can be particularly troublesome when isolated quotes of

---

[133] Just having one zealot in a church can be an extremely challenging experience. Having more than one at a time can be overwhelming to any pastoral leadership. If these types of shepherding challenges are ignored, they generally won't improve over time but will only get worse.

Old Testament prophets are directly applied to obscure legislation. Obviously, if one is not teachable the time will come when open conflict will flare up and correction becomes unavoidable. Even if correction is acknowledged, it may only be on the zealot's terms so that their motivation and righteous indignation can be sustained without challenge.

Probably the most difficult zealot characteristic to deal with, however, is a sense of indignation when a fellow Christian doesn't agree with their "agenda". Zealots tend to be outspoken advocates for moral purity and the need to confront wickedness. If someone appears to fault their tactics or question the strength of the biblical justification, it'll often be seen as a personal attack on them as well as truth itself. This often leads to more conflict than would normally occur if complex issues were just accepted for what they are, and disagreements addressed gently and deferentially. I'm not implying zealots have no humility, but only that a tender heart is more likely to show itself in other areas than the focus of their passion: engaging spiritual darkness, or exposing shortfalls in the Body of Christ or with pastors.

This stridency or "take-no-prisoners" approach can create tremendous collateral damage, particularly with those of tender conscience. Many times they will tend to lack sensitivity to the frailties' of others or any patience for indecision or time-consuming introspection by those not quickly onboard with the rightness of their cause. Rightfully so, this sinful divisiveness is consistently condemned in Scripture and must be directly confronted (1 Corinthians 12:25; Romans 16:17-18; Titus 3:10-11) for what it is; a lack of gentleness and grace (Galatians 5:23; 6:1). Not surprisingly, these same characteristics can make it difficult for zealots to mentor or disciple others, except to try to mold them into their own image.

Since patience tends to be a rare commodity with zealots, many sympathetic Christians can become discouraged, burned-out and, after a time, completely walk away from any involvement. When this happens, or there's a significant difference of opinion, a zealot may write-off a former comrade in arms because "retreat" and "compromise" are not words in the their vocabulary. In more extreme situations that I've both witnessed and been on the receiving end of, one's personal salvation is questioned because of a sincere stance on a controversial issue over which believers may legitimately disagree. To be fair, more often than not when agreement is lacking the zealot may only question the person's level of commitment to the cause of Christ – which is itself damaging enough.

Besides an attitude that can chaff many people, zealots can also have a low opinion of any spiritual leadership that doesn't fully agree with and promote them. By believing their calling is a gift from God, they can think they're above correction because of their unique insights and understanding, thus correction or mentoring isn't needed. When this happens, submission to authority tends to become optional, and at times only expedient. When this happens, a zealot's zeal will end up contributing to the disunity and contention that can so easily weaken a church or cause division throughout the Christian community. I've seen this firsthand a number of times, and I believe it's ungodly pride at best and destructively sinful at worst.

A particularly bothersome result of a zealot's total commitment to confronting evil is how often they can become the darlings of the news media. Reporters can be assured of some great quotes to spin as representing the broader Christian community. This feeds media sensationalism and can fuel a pejorative stereotyping of Christians as intense, far right, narrow, intolerant, simplistic people deserving contempt and not understanding. This situation can also make the evangelical community cringe when their concerns and faithful work is misrepresented by a hostile media that cherry-picked some extreme statements out of context. As zealots become more widely known, the swath of their influence can become greater and more problematic. Unfortunately, media not only feeds a zealot's desire to influence as many people as possible, but they can also be a trap to fuel a self-righteous attitude. As pastors know, when someone becomes a widely known public spokesman with little personal accountability it's just a matter of time before catastrophe strikes for both the person and the Christian community they claim to represent.

In reality, the numbers of believers who fall into the true zealot category are few. But even a small number can create large amounts of discord within a church, or among Christians across the larger community. Though the good that's done may be beneficial for the ultimate cause of Christ, the investment in spiritual energy to prevent discord, bitterness, and resentment can be more than most pastor's are willing to invest. So, the proper question to ask is what should be done when these zealots are in our midst?

### *What Should We Do?*

Scripture doesn't say zeal by itself is wrong, but it does warn that if not balanced with knowledge, it can be counterproductive and even sinfully divisive (Romans 10:2; Galatians 4:18).The Proverbs especially are replete with warnings about the tongue and a foolish heart that speaks or takes action before carefully considering the consequences of what is said, how it is said, and the need for charity and grace in order to truly honor the Lord.[134]

Concerning the zealot's view of their biblical role, I don't believe that today we have the equivalent of the Old Testament prophet speaking the revelatory words of God. I do believe, however, that we're to proclaim God's truths as accurately as possible, be salt and light in every legitimate endeavor, and to influence as many as possible to do what's right for the common good and the glory of God (1 Corinthians 10:31). Some may call this "forth-telling", using a "prophetic voice", or some other descriptive term, but however described there needs to be great care in wielding God's Word as accurately as possible

---

[134]  Though there are many Proverbs that would apply, a few samples include: Proverbs 10:11-19; 11:12; 12:18; 13:3; 15:1,4,23,28a; 16:13,21,2324; 17:27,28; 18:13,21; 20:25; 21:23; 25:11,15; 29:20. Obviously, the book of James also gives strong warnings about the tongue.

(Hebrews 4:12)[135]. In using the authority of Scripture, the question to ask is whether the zealot is building up the Body of Christ to mature it unto good works (Ephesians 4:11-16), or pursuing their own self-righteousness while wrapping themselves in a holy purpose (2 Timothy 3:5).

Sadly, there's much that's lacking today in the visible church. Although there are many remarkably strong congregations faithfully preaching and teaching God's Word and equipping the saints for woks of service to each other and to the outside world, there are many more that are spiritually weak, comfortable and compromised. For spiritually weak churches, the zealot is going to be a very real threat. For generally strong churches, he may provide a much-needed wakeup call in weak areas that are being overlooked (Proverbs 27:6a). If that were the total extent of the zealot's impact, they'd be serving a valuable role for the sanctification of the Body of Christ.

However, given the prickly nature of dealing with zealots, and the intrinsically volatile nature of politics, they need to be approached very carefully.

First, listen carefully and with discernment to what they're saying and why. Our impulse is to reject correction and dismiss those for which we may not highly regard. But, even though the messenger may be incredibly flawed, the message may still have some validity (James 1:19). We're always to examine ourselves to determine where the Lord may be bringing needed correction in order to be more fruitful in kingdom work. Unfortunately, a confrontational attitude can be difficult to overcome to see clearly what has merit. We personally may be more subtle in our manner of speaking and ministering to others, but that doesn't mean we're any less susceptible to pride and blind spots[136]. In fact, some who are attracted to zealots for leadership may see in them what

---

[135] When Scripture is clear on what constitutes sin or a spiritual imperative, then our response is much more straightforward. When general principles from scripture are mined for application, then wisdom, charity and graciousness must undergird our heart and our actions toward each other.

[136] Smooth talkers can be just as sinful as those that are in our face. As Jeremiah 17:9 reminds us, the heart is deceitful above all things. . .who can understand it?

they think is lacking in their own pastor, i.e. strong exhortation to pursue the practical outworking of our faith in a community and toward a government growing ever more hostile to our faith.

Secondly, the zealot needs to be shepherded. Whether this is a disciplining relationship, an accountability program of some kind, or just a close friendship it's needed to help the person grow in grace and sensitivity toward God's sheep. The zealot needs to know that he's to deal as gently with us as God has dealt with us (1 John 4:19-21). He needs to realize that even though his issues are important, there are many other life, family, church and outreach demands on our lives that are just as important in submitting to the Lordship of Christ. He needs to realize that God jealously guards His people and hates divisiveness (1 Corinthians 1:10). Even harder, he needs to learn how to cultivate a large measure of grace toward those who may not completely agree with his strongly held views in order to help foster unity within a fallible church.

Third, the zealot may need to be called out and publically exhorted if destructive patterns can't be corrected or at least curtailed.

Ephesians 4:29-32 captures the heart that all of us, including the zealot, are to have.[137] Sowing divisiveness under the cloak of proclaiming truth is both vile and destructive. And anyone who is unwilling to submit to spiritual authority is setting themselves up as the final arbiter of what God's will is. That's a very dangerous place to be, and one that won't produce the type and quality of fruit the Lord demands from us (Matthew 7:17-20). Sowing discord and division doesn't fulfill the Lord's design or intent for His flock (Romans 16:17-18). As a matter of fact, if someone is stirring up problems among the sheep, biblically they're to be warned several times, then we're to have nothing to do with them

---

[137]    These verses deserve to be spelled out: "Let no corrupting talk come out of your mouths, but only such as is good for building up, as fits the occasion, that it may give grace to those who hear. And do not grieve the Holy Spirit of God, by whom you were sealed for the day of redemption. Let all bitterness and wrath and anger and clamor and slander be put away from you, along with all malice. Be kind to one another, tenderhearted, forgiving one another, as God in Christ forgave you." (Ephesians 4:29-32)

(Titus 3:10-11). A severe example of where this could lead is described in 3 John 9-10 where Diotrephes places himself above any other authority, has his own loyal disciples, and is puffed up with pride.

Finally, the zealot needs our earnest prayers. They hold themselves up publically as representing God's will, and as such become a lightening rod attracting a lot of attention. As Christians, we tend to be naive in the ways of the world and a bit timid when it comes to public exposure. The zealot, however, has been honed by attacks and backlashes that we may never face ourselves, but that we need to be equipped to handle. Many times they come from incredibly difficult and challenging life experiences that we only read about. But through it all a zealot's personal example in withstanding the world's evil can become an encouragement for us to do likewise when called upon (1 Peter 5:8-10).

Given the zealot's unique role, can we really be a help to them?

It's difficult, but by remembering God's example of patience toward us, there's always hope that a zealot will mature and become an even more effective advocate for what's right when we minister to, and with them. Though a bit counter intuitive, what I've found is that the role of zealots will tend to decrease when godly leadership rises up within the Christian community to fill the vacuum the zealot occupied. Remember, cleansing must always begin in our own home first in order for the Lord to powerfully use us. Sometimes that's why zealots are needed: to wake us up; and to challenge the status quo when there's an absence of solid biblical preaching and the Body of Christ is weak or apathetic.

The bottom line is that every generation will have, and also needs zealots. Even King David learned humility when Shimei condemned him (2 Samuel 16:5-14); Nineveh repented when faced with the spectacle of Jonah preaching hellfire and brimstone to them (Jonah 2:1-10). Even in their own sin they were fulfilling God's purposes. Take and learn what you can, don't become discouraged, and realize that a zealot's life could be part of the chastening that the Lord provides to His church for its good and His glory (Hebrews 12:7-11).

# Part 2

# Fratricide Amongst Believers

# Chapter 7

# How to Approach Your Pastor

*Obey your leaders and submit to them, for they are keeping watch over your souls, as those who will have to give an account." – Hebrews 13:17*

*"Never criticize a man until you've walked a mile in his moccasins"*
*– Native American Proverb*

### Have We Walked in Our Pastor's Shoes?

It's pretty easy to tell someone else how to do their job. I mentally do it all the time when government decides to raise taxes or make it more difficult to buy a simple thing like a light bulb. More often than not our judgment is limited since we've never actually performed the other person's work. If we had we may be a lot more merciful to the struggles and complexities involved.

Now consider the church. Do we ever have a critical spirit when our favorite hymn hasn't been sung for three months or the hospitality coffee is too weak? Let's face it; we probably have a judgmental nature more often than we care to admit. This is no less true when we take aim at those who shepherd us. Since pastors are immersed in the ministry needs of their flocks, it's not surprising that Congress' crazy schemes are not at the forefront of their thinking. What does occupy his attention are things like someone struggling with pornography, or the teenager threatening suicide, or researching a difficult verse of Scripture for his next sermon.

Though we want our pastors to be passionate about fighting a hostile government, we need to do a reality check on priorities and balance.

Pastors can't be equally involved and competent in everything. Those immediate spiritual matters with eternal consequences in individual lives will always be of greater concern than secular, political issues, or the creation of a new citizenship ministry.

### What Should be a Pastor's Focus?

Ultimately, pastors will give an account to God for their diligence in caring for the spiritual health of those entrusted to their care (Hebrews 13:17). They're to equip us to live godly lives in obedience to Christ through:

- Faithfully preaching and teaching the Bible (Acts 2:42; Ephesians 4:11-12; 1 Timothy 3:2; 5:17; 2 Timothy 4:2; Titus 1:9) while exercising their authority in all areas of doctrine and practice
- Shepherding the flock through counseling, exhortation, encouragement, and prayer (1 Peter 5:2-3; Acts 6:4; 20:28; 1 Thessalonians 5:12; Titus 3:9-11)

Whether Christian activists like it or not, the Pastor's primary biblical calling is not political activism or aggressively transforming the culture, but equipping believers for "every good work" (2 Timothy 3:16-17) while laboring for the unity of the Body of Christ for the glory of God (Ephesians 4:11-13).

Where friction so often occurs is when "every good work" excludes, or overlooks, or trivializes our duty to be salt and light to the world (Matthew 5:13-16).

Although the average pastor is just as concerned about the world's evil encroaching upon our lives and ministry, he physically doesn't have the time or inclination to engage it as passionately as you. Does this mean he can ignore government hostility toward kingdom work, or his duty to fully prepare us to influence elections, laws and government actions; or the simmering political conflicts just below the surface within the church? Of course not!

Given this common mismatch between a pastor's primary duty and so many church members' expectations, how can a citizenship or salt and light ministry ever be established? First, by understanding the pastor's unease; and secondly, by approaching him in a Christ-honoring manner.

### *The Concerns Many Pastors Share:*

Divisiveness is a destructive force. Even when a pastor pours his heart and soul into the Lord's sheep, churches have split over anything from obscure doctrinal issues to the color of chapel carpeting. Because a pastor desires the flock to have spiritual oneness and maturity, controversial matters like flawed political candidates, climate change (global warming), energy independence, federal bankruptcy, or even red light traffic cameras may be relegated as sermon illustrations instead of opportunities to apply a biblical worldview and encourage influencing for the common good and the gospel.

Clearly, with thousands of contemporary issues the further a problem is from a clear command of Scripture, the more "opinion" grows. And with that the opportunity for contention – the very thing a pastor tries so hard to prevent.

Enter the zealot, a particularly problematic situation for a pastor. When a zealot is politically focused they present almost a worst case scenario: they're embedded in a biblical environment; claim the Lordship of Christ; are probably knowledgeable about a volatile issue; and usually have a number of "disciples" looking for leadership. Though zealots serve a purpose, they can consume a pastor's attention and create the potential for open controversy at any time, on any subject[138]. When faced with this situation, is it any wonder a pastor may become apolitical.

Another concern is whether a clear biblical mandate exists for pastors, or Christians in general, to engage in politics. Many seminaries are loath to treat the Christian's role in political activity, much less to view it in a positive light. And Scripture doesn't unambiguously proclaim it on every page. Yet the Bible is full of personal examples and principles that imply a citizenship duty that's consistent with our obedience to the Lord and a passion to transform the nation for the common good and God's glory.[139]

Believe it or not, a pastor can even suffer a touch of "Jerk-a-phobia".[140] Pastors are looked up to as spiritual leaders, counselors and experts in handling the Word of God. They of all people recognize the care needed with every word they speak (Matthew 12:36; James 3:1) Not surprisingly, it can be threatening for a pastor to publically show a superficial understanding of some egregious legislative action. Add to this the possibility of having a local news reporter stick a microphone in their face and ask why they're homophobic and what's the incentive to be outspoken?

---

[138] This is such a difficult and important issue that Chapter 6 (What About Zealots?) is dedicated solely to its implications.

[139] This claim is developed in much more detail in Chapter 3 (Do We Have a Political Mandate?) as well as Chapters 4 and 5 where the issue of church and state is addressed from biblical, wisdom and reasoning standpoints.

[140] I don't know where I first heard this term, but it describes the biggest fear many in public leadership harbor. It's one thing to miss-speak, or get our facts messed up, or to be completely wrong about something; but in our modern electronic age of You-Tube, Facebook, and the like, our gaffs become public fodder to be used by anyone in any context they like in an effort to create as much embarrassment as possible. This is not a new phenomenon (Romans 1:29-30), but it should cause us to consider whether we fear men more than God.

Whether admitted or not, many pastors are also concerned about their 501(c) 3 tax exempt status.[141] The average church may have tight budgets, so anything that may jeopardize ministry resources (including missionary support) could be seen as too risky. Add the widespread misinformation about legal requirements resulting from the "separation of church and state" myth and the comfortable decision to ignore politics becomes the path of least resistance. Needless to say, uninvited public scrutiny, threatened litigation, and tax implications are powerful disincentives to engage in public spiritual warfare.

Finally, pastors that take a stand on political issues or try to treat them in a balanced way can appear to be favoring a particular political party instead of just standing on biblical truth. Once the perception of political bias develops, the tendency is to think that person accepts every policy position the political party espouses, even though that may be far from the truth. Accurate or not, it's a concern many pastors would rather not have to deal with.

### Classic Mistakes in Approaching a Pastor

"You're a coward!" Isn't that a great way to win your pastor over to becoming more politically astute and informed? "He's rejected his calling and prophetic voice"; "He's. . . ." – You fill in the blank and I can guarantee I've heard it from a frustrated church member disgusted with what they perceive as a lack of spiritual leadership in political matters. Given the pastor's primary duty and concerns, you'd better take heed of the following common mistakes in approaching spiritual leadership if you ever want to have a citizenship (or salt-and-light) ministry established and properly shepherded.

1. ***Don't*** tell your Pastor "You should be doing. . ."

---

[141]   There are many excellent resources available that clarify the legal freedoms churches and pastors have to influence the political realm. Chapter 10 Common Myths summarizes the Do's and Don'ts of which every church should be made aware.

Whenever we tell someone else what their job is, we're basically saying we know it better than they do and we're here to make sure they realize that. This may be true in rare circumstances, but even then we're to approach to someone humbly, gently and with great care (Galatians 6:1). It's presumptuous and arrogant to tell a pastor he's not doing something when we don't know or appreciate the burdens he's bearing or how we can come alongside to help him in those difficulties.

2. ***Don't*** blame your Pastor for the lack of church political involvement

Accusing your pastor of dereliction of duty, when they may not see the importance of a citizenship ministry impugns their motives. Are you sure you're right, or are you just frustrated? Unless there's clear evidence that no salt-and-light ministry of any kind will be tolerated, than the assumption should be that they haven't yet seen the need to create one within the balance of church ministry demands.

3. ***Don't*** forget your Pastor is probably already overwhelmed with ministry demands

Never underestimate the overwhelming amount of spiritual energy and time that a pastor puts into the flock. Creating and nurturing a citizenship ministry, though important, will be ineffective if the Body of Christ isn't healthy. Because the wellbeing of the church is the pastor's focus, it will consume everything he has if he's faithful to that calling. Our duty is not to add to that burden, but to creatively work within existing constraints and priorities to provide balance with existing ministry labors.

4. ***Don't*** underestimate a natural resistance to "outside" influences on ministry

There's a plethora of Christian books, sermons, and resource materials to assist in scriptural exegesis, counseling, and maturing the Body of Christ. The nature of a citizenship ministry, however, is that activist passions can be influenced by dubious facts, slanted information, urban legends and hypothetical implications that sound plausible, but with closer scrutiny may be bogus[142]. Like it or not, it's easy to be manipulated by others who appear sincere but are pursuing an agenda that's ultimately not consistent with our values when challenged by solid biblical research. If wolves can masquerade as sheep (Matthew 7:15), how much more will those outside our fellowship try to use us for their purposes?

5. ***Don't*** try to convince your Pastor to lead this new ministry.

In any organization, if something has to get done we tend to look for the person that's already overworked. We do this because we know they're the ones that'll get the job done! That may work for smaller tasks, but for complex and high risk ones, unless the pastor has a personal passion for salt and light then someone else needs to lead the ministry. This mistake is closely related to trying to tell your pastor what his job is. He needs to shepherd the ministry not necessarily lead it.

6. ***Don't*** expect your Pastor to read long papers on issues of concern to you.

---

[142]  I've learned a hard lesson over the years. I try to never forward anecdotal information, supposed historical facts or events; statistics, outrageous quotes, or "smoking gun" revelations that have no source information that can be used to independently verify the information. If it seems like a blockbuster "gotcha" e-mail, it may just be too good to be true (Proverbs 18:17).

When we have a passion for something we develop an amazing ability to absorb lots of information relating to it. But when we have serious responsibilities relating to people's personal lives that can require incredible time commitments, giving time to read and understand a tome written on an obscure policy issue is not going to be welcome. The clearer, concise and well sourced the message, the closer it is to biblical truths, the more receptive he'll be to becoming acquainted with it (Ecclesiastes 12:12).

7. ***Don't*** contend with, threaten or demean your Pastor, directly or indirectly

You'd think this warning would be obvious. Unfortunately, many who've lived in and been hardened by the political arena can forget how combative or impatient we've become. Remember, we'll all stand before the Lord and account for our lives. And how we deal with the spiritual authority God placed over us is no trivial matter (Hebrews 13:17; James 3:5-12). The Lord demands we be humble, winsome, and also long-suffering with each other. This is true in our families, jobs, communities; but especially when trying to convince our pastor to make a major change in church ministry.

8. ***Don't*** try to counter everything your Pastor says – be quick to listen

Often we can get caught up with our own arguments and talk over someone else, trying to beat them into verbal submission. I can assure you this doesn't work with people in general, and it definitely won't work with pastors. If we have the iron clad answer to every objection, we sound like a classic telemarketer from whom we can't stand to get calls. They're trained to give a plausible response to every excuse for not buying what they're selling. Doing the same with your pastor will only frustrate him.

Not only that, you'll probably miss hearing what his real concerns are since you're formulating your next rejoinder instead of actively trying to understand his apprehensions. Scripture is clear, we're to be slow to speak and quick to listen (James 1:19). This applies across the board, but it's especially true with those that watch over our souls.

9. ***Don't*** think your ideas are clearly the best and he just doesn't understand

If we think we have all the answers, we better take a closer look at what we're trying to do. You're passion is for one ministry, while your pastor has many. What you want to do may sound easy and low risk to you, but to him it may seem overwhelming and with the high risk of unnecessarily offending church members who see no church role in politics.

A pastor has many more things to consider in fulfilling his leadership calling and protecting the health and well being of the church than you do. If he's willing to take time to consider how to equip the flock for effective political engagement, we need to respect that, assume the best, and to work with and not against him.

10. ***Don't*** throw simple Bible verses out and expect him to be convinced

Think about it. Between the two of you, who has the most extensive theological training? Are you trying to correct him with some new understanding that you alone possess? This approach can seriously backfire by appearing to speak down to your pastor instead of grappling together with how to apply general scriptural principles to our contemporary times (Proverbs 27:17). The other impression you risk giving is that you understand these verses and you're shocked he doesn't. To win a person over takes time, patience, and some good references from respected sources to open a dialogue and a greater appreciation for a wider application of scriptural truth.

### 11. *Don't* let your ego get in the way of submitting to your Pastor

Remember, he's a shepherd over you for your welfare and spiritual health. Be willing to submit to his authority and work with him over the long haul. This will take humility and patience on your side and a willingness to clearly show that you respect and honor him. When we've self-identified with a ministry we're passionate about, our ego can easily get in the way if we sense what we're promoting is being rejected

Our purpose should be to wrestle together with what would be an appropriate and fruitful ministry given the limitations and strengths of the church.

### 12. *Don't* become impatient while striving for unity

Remember your goal: to establish a mature, long-lasting church-based citizenship ministry that has probably never before existed. For most churches this will be a major change from "kingdom work as usual" and requires a long-term perspective to prevent frustration with slow progress[143]. If the immediate objective is a quick, knee-jerk reaction to some pending legislative action, and there's no solid ministry foundation already established you'll only create conflict, tension, and probably strong resistance.

### 13. *Don't* sow seeds of divisiveness within the church toward your Pastor

---

[143]   It was over six years before I was able to establish a Christian Citizenship Ministry at our church that was properly shepherded and thought through. A mega-church down the street took over three years to formalize a citizen's ministry to begin to equip its members.

Unfortunately, it's quite tempting to talk with other church members about frustrations with a pastor. The question to ask yourself is whether you're seeking wise counsel on steps to take, or just trying to build yourself up while tearing down your pastor, Be very careful you're not sowing seeds of discontent among the flock at the expense of the unity the Lord wants us to have (Ephesians 4:1-3). Sowing divisiveness – like gossip – are terrible sins we should constantly be on guard against (Romans 16:17).[144] It's much better to speak highly of your pastor and stress the things you can agree on as you work through this ministry formation process.

14. **Don't** blind-side a Pastor by taking action without their approval beforehand[145]

A quick way to destroy credibility or trust with your pastor is to take unilateral action with members within your church who are sympathetic to your cause. It's one thing to engage likeminded friends in political and policy battles outside the church. It's quite another to use fellowship time before or after church services to recruit willing activists, hand out literature or pass petitions not vetted or approved through your leadership. It may seem like a small thing to you, but it shows disrespect to leadership and opens up the opportunity for unnecessary offense that they'll have to deal with.[146] I gave a presentation once

---

[144]  The entire thrust of this book is how to biblically and practically maintain our unity as brothers and sisters while dealing with political issues within the Body of Christ. Divisiveness has destroyed more churches and our witness to the world than probably any other factor that I've seen.

[145]  Otherwise known as "acting first, then seeking forgiveness later"

[146]  Examples I've seen include petition signing, political pamphlets being handed out, candidate brochures being distributed, flyers for political meetings being placed on car windshields during worship times, etc. Not only is this irresponsible, but it will also probably create some major "blowback" from members who think this is not supposed to be done on church property and then blame the leadership. These types of activities must be approved ahead of time so church leadership can properly prepare the membership for whatever is finally agreed to be distributed or talked about.

during a Christian Salt and Light development seminar where I strongly made the point that pre-approval was critical. The organizer, however, was convinced that mobilizing the church to respond to some particularly vile time-critical legislation was worth the risk of having to seek forgiveness later.[147] I think this attitude, maybe commendable in other venues, is shortsighted and potentially disruptive within the Body of Christ. Building trust is critical to successfully establishing any kind of citizenship ministry, and violating that trust may cause irreparable damage.

15. ***Don't*** develop a "My way or I'm going down the highway" mentality

Finally, don't pull the "I'll leave otherwise" blackmail card. It won't work, it makes you look immature, and it sends a message that your staying in membership requires full support into the future. To a pastor, this means it's just a matter of time before you'll find some reason to leave – so why should he invest time and effort trying to work with you now to form a fruitful ministry?[148]

## Top Things to Keep in Mind

If you've mastered the above list and taken it to heart you're ready to work with, come beside, and help your pastor figure out what, if any, Christian activism, citizenship or salt-and-light ministry can be done in your church. There could still be a long way to go, but the following reminders should make it easier.

---

147 Not surprisingly, I wasn't invited back to be a speaker at the next development seminars.

148 Really test yourself in this. Have you bounced around from church to church because they "didn't get it" (i.e. those things obviously very important to you)? It could mean the state of pastoral leadership concerning political issues is abysmal, but it could also mean you have a more fundamental problem – how you relate to authority and what the priorities are in your life (Hebrews 13:17; 2 Timothy 2:23-26).

1.  Every church, pastor and ministry leader has their own strengths and priorities

Be sure to remind yourself of the strengths and blessings that are distinctive of your church. They're probably the reason you're there, and why you've a burden to build upon what the Lord is already doing. In any attempt to create a new ministry it's always important to stress the good that's already being done. This not only helps to ensure a proper balance of priorities, but it also builds long-term confidence and trust. In addition, since politics isn't your pastor's strong suit (otherwise a ministry would already be in existence), the practical result will be a gradual maturing of a political engagement ministry that doesn't detract from or overwhelm other fruitful ministries.

2.  Pastors have the same concerns about the government that you do

Pastors are just as concerned for their own families as you are for yours. Don't underestimate their anxiety about the environment in which they're raising their children, or their disgust with the culture or how our government leaders are imposing immoral values on us all. The issue with them will more than likely be what the role of the church and its leadership should be, not whether great evil exists and is trying to destroy the kingdom of God. Whatever reticence they may have, at least acknowledge to some degree they're aware of the dangers around us, even though they may not know where the trends are heading or what to specifically do about it.[149]

---

[149] A practical example of this was the controversy in California in 2008 with Proposition 8, where the voters were to decide whether the state Constitution should officially declare marriage as between "a man and a woman". Although most evangelical pastors agreed with the proposition, they saw little need to address it with their congregations - until the full implications of it not passing were clearly explained. That type of information came from legal experts, historical research, and investigation into other states and countries that legalized same-sex marriages.

3. Compared to the Pastor's full range of responsibilities this ministry is small

It's always best to assume that your pastor is close to being overwhelmed with the extent and burden of ministry. His calling is not a 9-to-5 job that's left "at work" at the end of the day. It's also not just preparing an hour sermon on Sunday morning. Think back about the hardest, more stressful time of your own life and recall how difficult it would have been to take on a new, unknown, potentially large endeavor that could alienate many of your closest friends and consume any energy you had left. Talk with him from that perspective so that an immediate defensive wall isn't put up. This will take wisdom and empathy on your part, and a realization that compared to the potential life-death issues he may be facing in some families, that politics may be an unnecessary distraction at this point. Balance, a longer time perspective, and a willingness to provide the necessary talents and labor for him to use could be the key to making progress.[150]

4. Find a church leader that's sympathetic to your ministry concerns

Most people want to go straight to the senior pastor to get things done since they carry the greatest weight. Although probably true, often it is better to find a person that's part of the church leadership that's sympathetic to your concerns and work with them. You understand the significance and importance of citizenship ministries, but they'll understand the inner leadership process, how decisions are made, and what concerns will need to be thought through. His insights are critical to ensure major road blocks to new ministry are dealt

---

[150] Because every situation is different, it's important to understand the primary responsibilities of your pastor. If he's the sole pastor or elder, then his responsibilities will be multi-faceted and literally touch everything. As churches grow there's a necessary division of labor and ministry emphasis consistent with primary giftedness, though core biblical duties will remain to one degree or another.

with ahead of time to prevent unnecessary difficulty or confusion later on. Work with and listen to them. It may take longer, but the investment is worth the effort and will dramatically increase the probability of success.[151]

5.   Test your own heart

You may think you're as pure as the driven snow, but it's very important to assess your own heart before the Lord while pursuing politically oriented ministries within your church. Are you disgruntled about how slow or non-responsive church leadership is to your ideas? If so, maybe you need this delay to mature your understanding of what has weightier eternal value. It could also show a need to develop humility and a submissive attitude, while recognizing a pastor's primary role is shepherding the flock (Hebrews 13:17). Next, do you really have the honor of Christ and the sake of the gospel as the central focus of your heart and passion for politics, or is it a need to correct your pastor, draw attention to yourself, or to get you own way?[152] These are tough questions, but ones that need to be sincerely considered.

6.   Be patient, humble, and respectful at all times

Remember who you're talking to – a man that's concerned about the spiritual condition of your soul. He's called of God to be an under-shepherd to you. You need to recognize that fact, and submit to his authority. Ways to fulfill that include not being argumentative, being humble, patient, and respectful at all times. Just as you would reason gently with someone that's very precious to

---

[151]   For a detailed treatment on how to create a Christian citizenship ministry, read Chapter 15 Practical Steps.

[152]   In the secular world it's called "requirements traceability." Is there a direct path from what you want to do and how it brings honor and glory to our Lord and Savior? In effect, everything should be traceable to fulfill 1 Corinthians 10:31: "So, whether you eat or drink, or whatever you do, do all to the glory of God."

you, so you're to be with those God has placed in your life to mature you, care for you and love you. Not only is this proper, but it will also help build a long lasting respect and trust between you when issues arise in implementing and pursuing such a controversial ministry.

7.   Be aware of what other churches and Pastors are doing

Some pastors can acclimate to a new challenge even if it hasn't been done before. Most, however, need a little more assurance that this less-traveled ministry path has actually been done fruitfully by other churches they respect. It's helpful to have examples of on-going church-based salt-and-light or Christian citizenship ministries in your general area that your pastor will recognize.[153] The best case would be churches that have the same or very similar doctrinal positions as well as philosophy of ministry. Lacking that, find out about the mechanics of how other churches have implemented their ministries and how they're shepherded. If there are none in your local area, then Internet searches will help find ones anywhere in the nation.

8.   Be aware of readily available legal advice

Like it or not, in the back of every pastor's mind lurks a nagging suspicion that doing "politics" in the church environment is against the law. Activities by the ACLU, the mainstream media, and other organizations hostile to Christianity are continually promoting this misunderstanding to shut the Christian community down from having any impact on public policy or who will represent us in elective office. Unfortunately, they have been persistent and successful in perpetrating unfounded fear and uncertainty. There's a reasonable

---

[153]   Chapter 15, Practical Steps has a lengthy listing of types of ministries that churches have implemented. A single church can't do every one of them, but there are at least several that could immediately be added to your church's ministry tool kit, depending upon interest and giftedness.

balance in what churches have a legal right (as a 501(c)3) to do concerning political issues, and there are exceptionally good resources available that not only set the legal record straight but also defend churches if there's a legal challenge.[154] Being fortified with this information will go a long way to alleviate any concerns your pastor may have[155].

9.   Connect a spokesmen for salt-and-light with your pastor

Helping to arrange for an experienced, knowledgeable person who understands pastoral ministry to talk with your pastor about Christian citizenship duties can be beneficial. The advantage of this invited "hired gun" is two-fold. First, it's not just you who is concerned about the state of affairs in our nation and what role the church could be playing. This can provide some much-needed credibility to what you've been talking about. Second, it may provide an independent view of what would make sense for your particular church. Like it or not, your relationship with your pastor has history behind it, so having a person without that background talking with him may make the discussion more profitable. The reality is that an "expert" is held in higher regard just because of their acceptance in a broader community, credentials which you may not personally enjoy. Also, an "expert" will probably have numerous illustrations of what other churches are doing and the insights gained from their efforts. In the best of

---

[154]   Many legal groups exist to defend churches and individuals in the exercise of their religious rights. Each has good materials available that clearly delineate what a church can and cannot do. Some of these organizations are: Alliance Defending Freedom (ADF); Liberty Council; Pacific Justice Institute (PJI); Advocates for Faith & Freedom (AFF); and the National Center for Law & Policy (NCLP). In addition, a summary of church do's and don'ts is given in Chapter 10 with a resource list provided in Chapter 18.

[155]   The major contention point is whether churches can legally endorse a candidate for public office or not. Current interpretations of law say this is illegal. However, there are initiatives underway with hundreds of congregations across the United States to force the IRS to officially determine whether that is an illegal act or not under existing law. While there is debate on this point, pastors can legally discuss political issues from the pulpit.

all worlds, a peer pastor that is passionate about engaging Christians would probably have even greater influence if available (see point No. 16 below).

### 10. Try to find common goals, then identify how to incrementally get there

A common mistake is to try to create an entire full-service, wide-ranging salt-and-light ministry all at one time. This may be the last thing your pastor wants to do if there's any initial hesitation on its merits. It may be more fruitful to first identify general goals you have in common, and work toward achieving one or two before attempting more aggressive ones. Simple but important actions include registering Christians to vote, then encouraging them to vote biblically. It may be inviting guest speakers who are experts in financial matters to address the current government financial meltdown and its impact on our families and the future. Or it could be current public school policies and parental rights. Activities can be expanded once an approach is worked out and its merits assessed. Starting with simple goals fosters success and allows the building of trust and procedures that will make leadership comfortable.

### 11. Remember that Pastors may change, but it typically needs to be on their terms

We've all had the experience of convincing someone to reluctantly do something, but they never truly buy into the decision. The same is true with church leadership. You may be able to start a citizenship ministry, but the support may be half-hearted or even counterproductive if it hasn't been agreed to on terms the pastor owns.[156] Eliciting and then accommodating his ideas and not going

---

[156] My personal experience is that most pastors want to see things done their way. I call this, doing it on their "own terms". Basically, they have to come to a comfortable position in their own way so it's personalized to them; based on their own reasoning and not someone else's. In doing so it creates personal ownership not attributable to others. This may be driven by caution, or a

beyond his comfort zone will increase the likelihood of pastoral ownership, ministry support and encouragement for you. If the pastor has strong buy-in, it can also provide a layer of protection should you come under fire by others within the congregation.

### 12. Be willing to do whatever's necessary to support this ministry

If you think your pastor is going to personally lead a new political activism ministry, you'll probably be disappointed. Church ministries are fruitful because they honor the Lord and have a champion (leader) with a passion for it that's willing to invest the time, talents, and yes – even treasures if necessary. There'll be many hours of preparatory work, research, meetings, approvals, purchasing of materials, coordination, recruiting and working out glitches. To help win your pastor over, you need to be the primary resource that invests in whatever it takes to be successful. If you're not willing to invest yourself heavily, then you've only identified a problem with no real solution.[157]

### 13. A Pastor may define a "zealot" differently than you

This may be a very touchy area, but many Christian activists would never think of themselves as zealots.[158] However, keep in mind that from your pastor's perspective, your passion and zeal for political issues may already brand you

---

desire to be able to defend what's being done; or it may even involve a bit of pride interfering with objectivity.

[157]    I know of a classic example of this: a group of members wanted to strengthen their church's evangelistic emphasis. They faithfully met for several months, generated a detailed paper identifying the scriptural mandate, the current church shortcomings, and many wonderful recommendations on what needed to be done. This report was given to the church leadership, with the expectation that the pastors would do what was necessary to implement the committee's plans. The committee subsequently disbanded and provided no follow-up involvement. Guess how much was actually implemented?

[158]    The reader is encouraged to find more detail on the zealot situation in Chapter 6.

as one to carefully watch.[159] As hard as it may be to accept, it could be that for a ministry of this type to be started and to flourish within your church, you may not be the one to actually lead it. It could take someone that the pastor believes is more mature, has better interpersonal skills, is older, broader in understanding, has more refined biblical understanding, or even more open to different activities and approaches. If that's where you find yourself, are you willing to support someone else leading this type of ministry?

14. Even if you need to start small, do everything with excellence

Sometimes we become discouraged when we have to start small. When this happens, our attention can become less focused and the result may not be good. Always remember you're doing this unto the Lord for His glory not yours, big or small, so do it with excellence. Remember also that the church leadership will be watching and evaluating. If small things are handled well, then greater things can be entrusted to your care later (Matt 25:14-30).

15. Always keep your pastor aware of what you're doing

No one likes to be blindsided. This is just as true in the spiritual community as it is in the secular world. Why would we ever think that taking unilateral action of a political nature in our church, one that could very well cause embarrassment and consternation for the leadership, is something that would endear us with pastors to create a more robust ministry in the future? Gaining leadership confidence in you can take time, so keeping them informed of your every move before you do it will build that confidence quickly. Using e-mail, face to face reports, or even written reports on progress and planned activities

---

[159] Interesting side-note, every time I've mentioned to a pastor the importance of not placing a "zealot" in charge of a salt-and-light, Christian citizenship, or citizen's type of ministry they immediately show their agreement.

before they happen will go a long ways to allowing more freedom to act in the future. Don't ever take this freedom for granted, however, since one major gaff can result in loosing much if not all the gains you've made. [160]

16. Pastor's will probably be more influenced by peers they respect than by you

It's the nature of any "profession" or position of authority that one tends to be more responsive to peers than to those that are not as skilled in their calling. You may be right on the issues, have the best ideas, and even understand the implications of inaction better than your pastor. You may even know the scriptural foundation better in some area. But you may not have the credentials that will speak as forcibly to him as a fellow pastor. This could mean you have to do your research to identify pastors that have salt-and-light ministries, or that have well known understandings of their advantages and disadvantages. These contacts could go a long ways to influencing your leadership to allow a ministry of this type to form and develop.

17. Always prepare yourself through diligent prayer

Sometimes we overlook the obvious: diligent prayer will help us to maintain the proper focus on our activities and why we're doing what we're doing (1 John 5:13-15). It's not to create a mythical Christian nation in our time, but to honor Christ and fulfill our mandate to be salt-and-light to the world for the sake of the gospel. Its spiritual warfare and we must be spiritually strong for the battle. Our pastors are critical in helping us on this path, just as we're to be a blessing to them in helping to equip Christians to apply a biblical worldview

---

[160] Remember that just passively keeping leadership informed isn't enough. If they have a different idea on how to proceed you need to be able to adapt your plans as necessary.

to all of life. Be patient, be respectful, be flexible, and above all be available to do what will be needed to help maintain the unity God desires for His flock, and to be an effective witness to the world of God's truths for His glory and the common good.

# Chapter 8

# The Lesser of
# Two Evils Conundrum

*"One of the penalties for refusing to participate in politics is that you end up being governed by your inferiors."* – **Plato**, 429-347 BC

### The Classic Head Scratcher

"How could you possibly vote for Schwarzenegger?" With this invective, a personal friendship and a significant ministry collaboration effort came to an abrupt end.

In early 2003 California faced its worst economic and financial climate to date. The incoming re-elected Governor Grey Davis was a career politician elected in 2002 over a committed Roman Catholic conservative. But Governor Davis was so feckless in his leadership and the handling of state fiscal and energy crises that almost immediately a petition drive was started to recall him from office.

Eleven months later, for the first time in California history the citizens recalled a sitting Governor in a lopsided vote.[161]

What was particularly difficult about this election, however, was the ballot also contained the names of 135 candidates wishing to replace him if he was removed[162]. Literally, in one election the citizens had to vote to remove or retain Davis, and then vote for a replacement if he's successfully recalled. There was no primary, there was no selective process to winnow down the competitive field beforehand, and there were minimal qualification requirements to be on the ballot. In effect, the office was up for grabs for anyone with money and name recognition.[163]

It was painfully obvious during the campaign leading up to the recall vote that there were only three real contenders to replace Davis: Actor Arnold Schwarzenegger, Lt Governor Cruz Bustamante, and state Senator Tom McClintock. Here-in lays the problem: McClintock was a strong fiscal and social conservative; Bustamante was a radical fiscal and social liberal, and Schwarzenegger was considered a fiscal conservative but social liberal. Polling consistently showed Schwarzenegger and Bustamante as the front runners and with a significant lead over McClintock.

As the election drew closer it was obvious that Schwarzenegger or Bustamante was going to be the next governor.[164] Yet this political certainty became a major source of contention amongst the state's Christians. Realists saw the possibility that Bustamante could win election if enough of the conservative voting base split between Schwarzenegger and McClintock, thus they held their nose and voted for Schwarzenegger. Those who couldn't

---

[161]  Percentage approving recall: 55.4%; total against: 44.6%..

[162]  http://en.wikipedia.org/wiki/California_gubernatorial_recall_election,_2003;

[163]  Candidates included a pornography "actress"; a sumo wrestler and Hustler magazine Publisher Larry Flynt.

[164]  The final vote was: Schwarzenegger 48.5%; Bustamante 31.5%; and McClintock 13.4%.

stomach Schwarzenegger saw those focusing on stopping Bustamante as sell outs rejecting conservative principles and maybe even denying the faith. Those who supported McClintock felt justified in standing by their "biblical" principles and saw exercising any other option as not just compromise but maybe even sinful.

It's also instructive to know that many Christians made very passionate, heartfelt claims that "if all Christians had voted, McClintock would win", or that God "was going to bring about a miracle".[165] Not surprisingly, many of these same individuals took no active part in the election campaign itself and stood on the sidelines. I even had friends who watched the exit polls before they voted to ensure Schwarzenegger would win (i.e. Bustamante would lose), then safely voted for McClintock to be able to say they voted on principle. Finally, it was very clear that if McClintock had not been on the ballot many Christians would not have voted at all.

What the Christian community faced was the classic decision of voting for the lesser of two evils. Granted, there was another option on the ballot representing conservative values but the general population of California would not support that outcome. The bottom-line reality was that the most qualified candidate (McClintock) did not have enough name recognition, grassroots support, financial backing or media gravitas to carry the day. His campaign impact was primarily in articulating conservative values in an otherwise muted values race and potentially being a spoiler for the Schwarzenegger campaign.

---

[165] I would never say the Lord is incapable or unwilling to bring about astounding outcomes in elections (Ecclesiastes 9:11); only that depending upon such divine action may be an excuse to do nothing on our own (James 2:26). Also, this is a good reminder of the importance of prayer in all that we do, particularly in political matters.

### *A Reality Check*

In the rough-and-tumble world of political campaigns many practical truths can put the Christian community at a distinct disadvantage. Obviously the Lord is sovereign in every election outcome, and He's not caught by surprise by anything that happens. But for us, history and experience says if we make decisions relying on a miracle for a strategy instead of hard work then more often than not the results will be discouraging.

The governor's race in California in 2003 was not driven by classic social or moral issues but by high visibility name recognition (Schwarzenegger), tremendous amounts of money (Schwarzenegger and the Republican Party), revulsion for the outgoing governor (Davis and his Democrat party base), and the extremely poor fiscal climate (which favored a well-known businessman, Schwarzenegger).

Given this environment, at least three things would have been needed for McClintock to carry the day: the entire Christian community would have had to vote solidly for him; large amounts of financial resources and volunteer time sacrificially given to his campaign from its inception; and a massive advertising and promotion onslaught to convince a large percentage of the general voting public to support a staunch social conservative.

Unfortunately, none of these three necessities were present for McClintock. What was present, however, was divisiveness among brothers and sisters in Christ, a split community of believers, and another illustration of the political naiveté that surrounds Christian activism. Over the years, I've encountered innumerable Christians that have no appreciation for what it takes to win an election; but are quick to condemn fellow Christians if they don't vote solely on principle independent of the election realities. The result is the growth of animosity amongst those that should be more gracious and understanding of each other. Sad to say, the harm experienced in that one gubernatorial election has continued to affect some ministry relationships to this day.[166]

So, why do we run into these situations so often? In practical terms, voting is the very end game of a long, complex, and demanding process. Campaigns begin many years in advance of any balloting, and candidates that invest the time, treasure and talent to gain an upper hand early on have a much better opportunity of success. The need to: network; build alliances and strong financial commitments; generate name recognition; build trust; learn how to be articulate with a hostile media; and be able to counter unprincipled opponents requires time and maturity to develop and master.[167]

But even having a perfect candidate may not be enough. Too many times believers think they're fulfilling their citizenship duty simply by voting. But just as the candidate must be intentionally prepared, they also need a large support base that is willing to commit campaign time and energy to move the electorate to their side. This too takes planning and effort that begins long before an election. Understandably, most Christians are working hard to provide for their family and are church ministry focused. Adding the burden of campaign support can be a hardship, but it's absolutely necessary to help godly candidates achieve elective office to serve us all.

---

[166]  This isn't an antidotal statement. I've personally experienced the long-term resentment of others based on this one decision, even though there's been agreement on the vast majority of other voting and political decisions since then.

[167]  Christians are often enamored with the "White Knight" syndrome. The attitude that the right person can be recruited at the last minute to run for elective office and that the faith community will rise up and sweep them to victory. This may happen, but in most races the outcome is decided by the "mushy middle" of the voting public and not by a large, informed, and motivated Christian community.

## *Preventing the Greater Evil*

A stumbling block for many sensitive Christians is making a choice when there's no desirable candidate. The phrase summarizing this situation is "voting for the lesser of two evils". Unfortunately, saying it this way only creates a conscience issue that's hard to overcome since evil isn't something we want to support. The predictable consequence is that many won't vote at all. This can be devastating when the top of the ticket[168] is a turn-off and the voter ends up staying home entirely. That one decision literally affects every other elective office on the ballot by removing one vote other good candidates need. Multiply this by thousands feeling the same way and election outcomes at all levels can be compromised, particularly those that are razor close. This can also prematurely end an aspiring candidate's career from ever maturing since lower level elective offices are often the precursor and necessary training ground for higher offices.

A simple way to soften the conscience concern is to rephrase the decision as "voting to prevent the greater evil (or damage)". It is more than semantics; when said that way there's a clear moral imperative to minimize the damage that truly offensive candidates will cause if elected. In effect, given undesirable options we still have a responsibility to protect our families as best we can, which may mean making a distasteful, but necessary, voting decision. Clearly this was how many assessed the California gubernatorial race mentioned earlier.

What about write-in candidates? While writing in a candidate's name may allow us to make a protest statement against the listed candidates, it only serves to remove oneself from the election outcome.[169] The same situation applies

---

[168] The top of the ticket refers to the highest office voted for in any election. Every four years the Presidential race is the top of the General Election ballot, in off years it will be a Congressional seat. In local elections it may be the office of Mayor. The key point, however, is that more often than not there are other "down ticket" offices being voted for that also need to be filled.

[169] Three Congressional seats have been won by write-ins: Senator Strom Thurmond (South Carolina, 1954); U.S. Representative Joe Skeen (New Mexico, 1980); U.S. Representative Ron Packard (California, 1982), but in general they're exceptionally rare and require massive effort.

when an acceptable but unelectable candidate is voted for when there are more than two candidates from which to choose. This may make a voter feel better about themselves, but in a small way they're contributing to a potentially more disastrous outcome. I'll be quick to add, however, that in those extreme cases where all candidates are vile and a person's conscience before the Lord sincerely prevents them from voting; the better option is to skip that race and move on to the rest of the ballot decisions.[170]

### *Which Candidate is the Greater Evil?*

Another voting complication is figuring out which candidate really is the most damaging if elected. If nothing's known about a candidate except their political party affiliation, then choosing the one whose party platform is closest to your values may be the best choice, though it's not assured.[171] This type of situation is more common when "non-partisan" local offices are on the ballot, whether city council or mayor, sheriff, city attorney, water board, or even Superior Court judge.[172]

One of the most difficult decisions is when a liberal candidate is facing off with a candidate that's fiscally conservative but soft or compromised on important social values. For Christians with a "non-negotiable" list preventing them from

---

[170]    Conscience issues are not trivial since they involve questions of whether a person's decision is sinful or not. In church parlance telling a person they must vote no matter what is "binding their conscience". Demands like this better have solid and unambiguous biblical justification since Scripture is clear we're to be sensitive to one another's conscience before the Lord (Romans 14:1-23).

[171]    Where I live in California, I can go to the County Registrar of Voters and access an on-line database that provides the party affiliation (if any) of every registered voter.

[172]    In reality there's no such thing as a non-partisan office. Every candidate brings their own worldview and political affiliation or affinity to office. In fact, lower level offices are the training ground for reaching higher elective offices in the more openly and combative "partisan" campaigns.

voting for anyone that doesn't meet all their criteria; they'll probably remove themselves from voting entirely and in a small way make matters worse.[173]

Particularly egregious choices occur when a candidate associates with a conservative party but is either pro-choice or supportive of homosexual activist goals. These candidates have the potential (and desire) to change the fundamental party platform in such a way that abortion and same-sex-marriage eventually become non-issues and are no longer fought against. As these morally compromised politicians become more numerous the inevitable time will come when biblical values based on the dignity of human life (made in God's image) and God's gift of traditional marriage are no longer defended by a major political organization. These types of candidates are far more destructive to Christian political goals than those belonging to a liberal party since they're destroying from within (Matthew 7:15-20). Once this happens, biblical values will no longer have a broad-based political home to help Christians fulfill their role as the moral conscience of the nation on life, family and sexual morality issues.[174]

### Deal Breaker or Deal Maker?

Where Christian values are generally held in high regard, Christians, or those strongly sympathetic to biblical values have a much easier time of being elected.[175]

---

[173] Many "non-negotiable" lists include things like requiring a candidate to be pro-life and for traditional marriage. There are many other important moral issues such as fiscal responsibility, size of government; gun control; immigration reform; school choice; etc. Clearly, the longer the list of uncompromising factors the harder it'll be to find a viable candidate that'll meet every criterion.

[174] This exact situation existed in Southern California in the Congressional General Election of 2014. A liberal candidate (Democrat) faced a fiscally conservative, articulate, openly gay opponent (Republican) that didn't represent the existing national party platform. The long-term impact if the Republican was elected could be the normalizing of behaviors traditionally rejected by conservatives and preventing any future home for Christian conservatives to promote godly moral values relating to sexual morality and traditional family structure.

[175] Clearly this is the case in "fly-over" country, otherwise known as the Bible Belt in the central and southern parts of the United States. There are also such pockets in liberal states, though

In these situations Christian influence can be a strong "deal maker" and in effect be a vetting mechanism for candidates who are worthy of support by the Christian community.

However, far too often throughout many states[176] there's only a small concentration of conservative voters who are insufficient to carry the day in major elections. Although discouraging, the primary role they may play is to stop unworthy candidates from leveraging the Christian base of a conservative party for their own self-serving or party-transforming goals. By organizing and openly withholding support for a completely unacceptable candidate, motivated Christians can stop a political career early instead of allowing them momentum to create devastating long-term party compromises.[177] When organized and willing to exert this type of "deal breaking" influence there's also greater potential to impact which candidates will eventually rise through the ranks.

### Bottom Lines

Politics can be a messy business, and every campaign has its own opportunities for believers to become frustrated or even sinfully divisive with each other.

But the Lord hasn't left us alone (Ephesians 1:13-14). Christians, who are called to accomplish good works for His glory (Ephesians 2:8-10), are to use the spiritual weapons and tools God provides (prayer, truth, reason, discernment,

---

their influence on state politics will tend to be limited.

[176]    The West coast isn't called the "Left Coast" for no reason. Also, the New England and central Eastern States tend to be very Liberal.

[177]    This exact circumstance occurred in a recent mayoral race in the city of San Diego California. One particularly ambitious candidate cultivated the persona of being a conservative with Christian roots. In reality this candidate supported liberal agendas that were completely contrary to clear biblical teachings. The Christian community effectively intervened in this election and became a "deal breaker" to ensure this career didn't proceed any further.

etc.) and not the weapons of the world (2 Corinthians 10:36).[178] One of those spiritual weapons is to realize each election is a battle in a never-ending spiritual war.[179] Whether an election outcome is favorable to our values or not, there'll be many more political skirmishes in the future requiring Christ-honoring collaboration. In all of these fights we're called to be faithful co-laborers and not required by God to guarantee results. Those are ultimately in the capable hands of the Lord, where they belong (Romans 8:28).

In facing political differences among Christians, it's instructive to keep several principles in mind. First; sincere believers have much more in common through Christ than they'll ever have in politics. Eternal life, heavenly rewards, God's daily mercy and grace; as well as knowing we're brothers and sisters in the same kingdom of God should cause us to work for unity in our decisions and labors and not just try to get our own way.

Second, when differences can't be resolved, do everything possible to remain on good terms with each other (Romans 12:18), knowing there'll be many more opportunities to collaborate in the future. In fact, the goal should be to continue to speak well of each other no matter what the stance eventually taken. If Christ has loved us so much even in our own sinfulness, how much more should we demonstrate that same affection and support for others for whom Christ has died (1 John 4:11)?

Third, in this world there's no perfect candidate for office. Each one will have strengths and weaknesses just like the rest of us. Accepting only the ideal or perfect candidate and nothing less will only lead to frustration at some point and eventually an excuse to not become involved. Ultimately, everyone falls

---

[178] Many of the political weapons the world uses can be summarized by five "D's": Delay; Deny; Distract; Deceive and Destroy. For a very insightful understanding of how these tactics can be effectively used for ungodly purposes, see the classic "Rules for Radicals" by Saul Alinsky.

[179] Never ending in the sense that they continue throughout our lifetime; but ultimately these spiritual battles will cease when the Lord returns in glory to claim His own (1 Thessalonians 4:13-18)

short, so our full trust is to be centered in the Lord and not a candidate or some political party (Proverbs 3:5-6).

Fourth, more often than not, it's important to remember the general public needs to be convinced of the superior qualifications of the candidate we support. Many times the Christian community is insufficiently organized or united to carry the day in an election. Either through limited voter turnout, a poor appreciation for a consistent biblical worldview, or even personal compromise on God's moral standards can all result in a poor showing on Election Day. To overcome these realities a broad public base of support is usually needed in order to win an election. This doesn't mean conservative Christian values must be compromised. It does mean, however, that articulating scriptural principles in the general language of the day instead of using uniquely Christian terminology and biblical references may be critical to winning the public over.[180]

Finally, as we seek to prevent greater evil from winning at the ballot box by choosing electable candidates closest to our core Christian values, we must be balanced and grounded with openness to the realities of the political world. If we stand on principle to the exclusion of all else in the political realm we may end up standing alone. That may be required some day, and when that comes may the Lord grant us the wisdom we need to stand tall and fight the good fight (1 Corinthians 16:13).

---

[180] The political term for this is to "know your audience".

# Chapter 9

# A Common Grace Basis for Political Engagement

*"For when the Gentiles, who do not have the law, by nature do what the law requires, they are a law to themselves, even though they do not have the law"*
**– Romans 2:14**

### The Tactical Advantage of Using Common Grace

For Christians, the Bible is God's only revealed, inerrant, infallible truth. From its pages we know a truly changed heart only comes about by the redemptive work of the gospel (Romans 10:17). However, because we rightfully place such a high priority on the condition of a person's soul, sometimes it's easy to overlook the opportunities God's common grace provides to influence other people's decisions and even the nature of government for the glory of God (1 Corinthians 10:31).

Clearly, the Lord has given a conscience and reasoning abilities to everyone (Romans 2:14-16). Knowing this, conservative lobbying groups with Christian values eventually realize that to influence legislation or political decisions they must appeal to more than biblical truths to sway the public and gain its support. Using reason, information, research, and examples of consequences from similar situations in different states, or even countries, they can influence political leaders in terms in which they can not only understand but also relate.

It's one thing to study the Bible in a church environment and apply it to our lives; it's a different challenge to apply godly principles in a rough-and-tumble political environment. It's in this tactical application that unnecessary confusion and disagreement divides many Christians and prevents our influence from being as powerful as it could be.

It's not uncommon to find conflict between those using only the Bible to convince others to do what's right and those that use other means. Some believe that reasoning with non-Christians will never carry the day and that God's Word can speak for itself without resorting to facts and figures. Others withdraw completely from political battles since they see no hope in trying to "fix" a fundamentally flawed, worldly system. And still others reject any compromise that smacks of using the weapons of the world with the weapons of the Spirit (2 Corinthians 10:3-6).

Political reality, however, is that much of the nation is unconvinced of the authority of Scripture and immediately rejects it as an argument.[181] In fact, this is even true within liberal parts of the broader Christen community. To overcome this difficulty, election campaigns, political lobbying efforts, and new legislative initiatives find they have to persuade the broader public by using tools consistent with God's Word, but not overtly identified with it.

Is this a violation of Jesus' warning about denying him before men (Matthew 32-33)? If this approach is out of fear of repercussions then our commitment can rightfully be challenged. If it's because we're unconvinced of the applicability of God's Word, or are ashamed of our faith, then our very reasons for being in

---

[181] By saying this I'm not rejecting the power of God's Word to bring conviction to the soul; but what I am saying is that in political discourse in our post-Christian era there's a widespread predisposition to turn off when overtly biblical phrases are used in an argument. Much of this is due to a hostile media community that routinely portrays Christians as ignorant, intolerant and shallow.

the political battle are probably misguided. But if our purpose is to enlist the support of the widest number of people by using easily recognizable common grace blessings that result from conformance to his will (Joshua 1:7; Proverbs 4:27), and we are willing to point to the scriptural basis (and the gospel) as opportunities allow, then we're probably on good ground.

Take the example of well-reasoned arguments that are fully compatible with Scripture (Isaiah 1:18). Quantifying the consequences of sin on societal health is a valid form of persuasion (1 Timothy 5:24); while using life examples to illustrate what happens when a person, a marriage, a family, a community or a government stray from God's ordained order (Joshua 1:6-7; Proverbs 4:27) can be very powerful. In fact, even the moral conscience of someone hostile to any faith can be moved to consider what's right when approached in the proper way (Luke 18:1-8; 1 Corinthians 9:19-23).

These "tactics" aren't intended to compromise God's Word, but to leverage God's common grace gifts of conscience, reason and even self-evident blessings to mankind (Matthew 5:45). Obviously, fruitful results aren't dependent on these tools alone since politics involves spiritual warfare, and in that type of warfare we're ultimately dependent on the Holy Spirit to move people's hearts and minds.

To develop this concept a little further a series of questions and answers follow below. The purpose isn't to justify any rejection of the power of God's Word, or to somehow make a better pagan, or to ensure our nation has merit with God. It's to ease the conscience of those who have a hard time justifying involvement in politics because of an unnecessarily narrow view of the means God has given us to use for His glory and ultimately the furtherance of the gospel (Jeremiah 29:5-7; 1 Corinthians 10:31).

### Is Redemptive Change the Only Real Change?

I've heard the following said many times in different ways: "Real change will <u>only</u> come about when the heart changes."[182]

Like most authoritative sounding statements, it's true if context and application are well understood. Hopefully, all evangelicals agree that coming to saving faith in Jesus Christ is the most significant event in a person's life (Romans 12:2; 1 Corinthians 6:9-11; Colossians 3:5-11). While some will mature faster than others, the Holy Spirit gives us new eyes to see the world differently (Romans 12: 2-3). When "real change" refers to this transformation the above quote is clearly true. But what if the heart isn't regenerated? Can any "real" change occur in a person or in our nation?

Obviously, in emphasizing heart change as the only opportunity for true change there's an imperative for evangelism to the exclusion of any political "ministry", no matter how important politics may be in helping to ensure our freedom to evangelize. On the surface this may sound noble, maybe even biblical. In reality, though, it only dampens enthusiasm for any broader range of Kingdom work. In fact, we work for change all the time if we're good citizens and try to fulfill Jeremiah's admonition to the exiles to work hard for the land we dwell in so that it will go well for everyone (Jeremiah 29:7).

Does trying to influence our nation by convincing as many people as possible to accept our values trivialize the need for the gospel – absolutely not!

Political labors, even if noble or beneficial will never earn merit with God. The issue is whether there's benefit to our families and our ministries by using godly means to influence the political realm, or whether these means are biblically

---

[182] This statement is often used as a self-evident truth that's often given to prevent any further discussion on the merits of political involvement. The underlying logical conclusion is that no change of any kind can ever occur unless a person comes to faith. This is obviously not true in most life experiences.

limited to sharing the gospel. Like so many of life's pursuits[183], I believe we're free to work for the good of everyone (Galatians 6:10), and in so doing improve the opportunities to minister the gospel to our nation.

### Can We Change a Non-Believers Thinking and Behavior?

On a basic level, this is a silly question. If we own a business we probably advertise in order to gain more business by influencing peoples buying decisions.[184] Why set a godly example at work[185], or in a babysitting co-op, or while buying cabbage at the local grocery? Besides bringing credit on our Lord, it influences others to do the same. As a matter of fact, we raise our children to know good from evil even if they never make a credible profession of faith or show evidence of a redeemed heart.

When we set an example or call attention to a common moral value, most people will recognize and even appreciate it even though they may be too weak to conform to it.[186] The question isn't whether we can influence others; it's whether we can influence them to accept the values, principles and truths in God's Word for the benefit of all.

---

[183] This shouldn't be surprising. We use moral persuasion in work environments since we know it's best for a company's business. We use logical reasoning, facts and data to derive solutions to complex social, technological, financial or business problems. Jesus, in fact, used moral persuasion when using His parables. But for some reason many may ignore these means when spiritual matters are involved.

[184] Consider the return on investment businesses expect by changed buying habits as a result of a simple, multi-million dollar, 30-second commercial during the Super Bowl.

[185] Countless times in my professional career others have quickly apologized to me when an "expletive" was blurted out during a meeting, whether I was in charge of the meeting or not. This is just a small example of God's common grace of salt and light influencing the presence of evil.

[186] In the technology company I worked in for over twelve years, many times a question would come up on how to best approach a customer. Someone would eventually ask; "what's the right thing to do?" Almost invariably, the majority immediately acknowledge what that option was.

If people can't be influenced, why are our values so methodically removed from public schools? Is it to invade a student's heart with relativism, post-modernism, and hedonistic influences instead of godly light (Romans 2:14-16)? By omission or through outright hostility our values are being ignored and the next generation is being conditioned to accept a destructive worldview at odds with a biblical worldview that ultimately points to true hope.

Why are facts about the destructiveness of the homosexual lifestyle so hidden? Activists know shortened life spans, debilitating diseases, broken relationships, emotional damage, and a high incidence of pedophilia would turn public sentiment against this immoral and in-your-face lifestyle (Romans 1:18-32). By diminishing the public's awareness of sin's consequences and redefining what's normal, the general public is conditioned to accept what's clearly destructive by any objective measure. Obviously facts, information and even terminology are powerful tools in swaying a person's views one way or another[187].

Other weapons at our disposal are reason, logical arguments, and well-known stories that illustrate truths. These help others understand the nature and consequences of bad decisions and the blessings of good ones. Is this a sure thing every time, obviously not! But as someone's destructive life decisions may not convince every friend to live the straight and narrow life, in general they'll know better and, many times, act accordingly.

Our arsenal also includes personal experience, a big factor in ones decisions and outlook on life.[188] The book of Proverbs, replete with common, pithy statements of life truths, resonates with people because they're consistent with

---

[187]   As mentioned earlier, Scripture is clear that the Lord has a righteous path, and any that walk to the right or the left of what He intends for our good will suffer the consequences (Joshua 1:6-7; Proverbs 4:27)

[188]   A proverbial saying consistent with this notion is that a young person who is not liberal is one without a heart, an older person who is not a conservative is one without a brain.

everyday experiences. Teach these truths, like Solomon did with his sons, and one will probably do well in life (Proverbs 22:6)

What about laws themselves, do they have any merit in teaching what's right or wrong? Even the apostle Paul said he wouldn't have known what sin was except for the law (Romans 7:7). Although he was talking about spiritual truths, laws of the land that reflect moral truths have a similar effect. Knowing there are consequences when a public standard is violated shows that our society values certain behaviors and condemns others. If public sex wasn't prohibited and also repulsive to most people, the behavior would become more commonplace as more and more citizens learn to ignore their own conscience.

Historically, one purpose of biblical law is to show a person's inability to meet God's standards (1 Timothy 1:8-11). When Christians have a united voice in what's morally acceptable and not acceptable, and are winsome in convincing others, the civil laws change accordingly. This in turn influences people's behaviors. In effect, God's common grace, man's conscience and biblical truths mutually support the recognition of natural law for the broader good.

### Do Most People Try to Be Morally Good?

It's inflammatory in some Christian circles to imply a non-believer can do something morally good. Clearly only God is absolutely good, and the only intrinsic goodness we have as believers is the righteousness of Christ imputed to us (Philippians 3:7-9). But keeping the biblical view only at this level does a disservice to the role of God's common grace and mercy in the world.

Even Jesus himself taught that the ungodly do good things for their own families (Matthew 7:10-11), and that an unrighteous judge can still give a just ruling (Luke 18:1-5). This shouldn't be surprising, since God made mankind in his own image (Genesis 1:26), and from that image good works emerge from a heart softened by conscience, experience and the influence of others.[189] The fact that anarchy doesn't reign supreme throughout the world is a testimony to God's mercy and also to a universal moral code that's generally understood by people and governments (Romans 2:14-15). When this reality is appealed to in an articulate and united way by Christians the moral drift by our government will become that much more difficult.

### Are God's Moral Standards Known to the World?

It's easy to think that since we hold God's Word in our hands, His truths aren't available in any other way in the world. This is far from the truth. Not only does mankind have a conscience that undergirds natural law principles, but any number of non-Christian moral codes reflect (albeit imperfectly) values sometimes remarkably similar to ours.[190] This really shouldn't be surprising since mankind has a common ancestor – Adam. .

From the time of Adam a moral code has been inherited throughout the world. The preciousness of human life was clear from the very beginning since God created man in his own image (Genesis 1:27). God instituted and sanctified marriage between one man and one woman as a universal command for the benefit of all nations (Genesis 2:24). And God gave man a responsibility to care for and nurture the created order, not to abuse it (Genesis 1:28; 2:15); including a high respect for the animal kingdom (Genesis 8:1619).

Even after man's nature was corrupted by the Fall, God's divine pattern for man's good continued on. God reaffirmed the importance of life by putting safeguards around it (Genesis 4:15; 9:5-6) and re-established the Kingdom

---

[189] During the 1995 Kobe, Japan earthquake, thousands of non-Christians gave sacrificially to dig out those trapped in the rubble. I wondered at the time how it could be that those who haven't heard the gospel exhibited the compassion towards others that we as Christians are to freely show towards the less fortunate around us.

[190] For example, the Golden Rule (Matthew 22:39) can be shown to be a universal concept well documented throughout history and in many different civilizations and religions.

mandate by charging Noah to be fruitful and fill the earth (Genesis 9:1; 7). Later, during the Exodus we find one of the purposes for the laws given to the people of Israel was to be a witness to the world of God's righteous standards and demands (Deuteronomy 4:5-8). If there was no capacity to recognize the rightness of these moral standards, what purpose would they serve to instruct other nations? In fact, the existence of Israel was known by much of the world, and God's decrees resonate with many other nations down to this very day (Psalm 96:1-13; Psalm 98:2-3; 1 Kings 10:23).

### *Who Should Provide the Moral Compass for Society?*

We know that secular laws are at best a mere shadow of God's perfect standard. But even in their imperfection they point to the true standard behind them. In establishing just laws, policies, or community rules the question is who should define and defend them for the common good? If Christians don't fulfill that role, somebody else will definitely seize the opportunity to do so.

In the Old Testament the watchman on the wall exhorted men of courage to sound the alarm when danger was imminent (Ezekiel 3:16-21; 33:7-9). Of all people, Christians should be that moral watchman on the wall since we recognize the consequences of man's sinful nature and the blessings that come from behaviors consistent with God's will for humanity.

Obviously living a good, moral life alone will not merit eternal life (Ephesians 2:8-9). But defending the standard that speaks to the ultimate standard-Giver demonstrates there's more to life than just random chance and survival of the fittest. There's a profound transcendence of truth that recognizes man's basic selfish nature and disregard for ultimate accountability. Man's conscience and exposure to natural law serve to bring awareness of personal failings, and the inability to perfect oneself. This is the first step to recognizing the inability of anyone to merit for themselves any assurance of eternal life or ability to stand without guilt before the Judge of the universe (Romans 2:1-6).

Pastors provide the primary watchman role in the church gathered (Ephesians 4:11-16); while all Christians comprising the church scattered can fulfill the watchman duty to the nation (Ephesians 5:11). As stated earlier, the imperfect reflection of the law of God in our nation's moral codes serve to show what's evil and what's good (1 Timothy 1:8-11; Galatians 3:24). If this standard is withheld, or watered down, or allowed to be challenged without response by a divided and inconsistent Christian community, then we've squandered a powerful means to uphold God's moral standard for the benefit of everyone. Without opposition, evil will continue to metastasize and use political weapons to remove what last vestige of Christian light remains.

Clearly, Christians are the only salt-and-light to the world. If we're concerned about the well being of our families and those we love, why wouldn't we diligently work to influence the powers around us to do what's right, instead of just expecting the best to happen on its own?

Jeremiah's letter to the exiles is very telling in this regard (Jeremiah 29:7). He told them to diligently work for the prosperity of the city (and by extension the nation) they were exiled to, as well as pray for that city's well being. We have a similar cultural mandate in our nation as well as freedoms to engage the entire political process for God's glory. Why would we ignore that freedom and duty?

### Can We Judge the Ungodly?

I've met sincere Christians who believe they have no biblical right to judge anyone. More often than not this is due to a misunderstanding of Matt 7:1-5, where Jesus is teaching his disciples about hypocritical judgment, not judgment itself. In fact, Paul specifically calls for believers to judge those inside the fellowship of believers, and not those in the world outside (1 Corinthians

5:12-13). If no judging of any kind was allowed, then church discipline could never occur (Matthew 18:15-17), and no one would be confronted to bring about spiritual restoration like that commanded in Galatians 6:1.

Does this extend to the world around us? In many ways it obviously has to. We make decisions every day on what we watch on TV, who we listen to, or what we read or indulge in on the Internet. Our lives are to honor the Lord, and in doing so we train ourselves to reject evil and pattern our lives in honorable pursuits. Not surprisingly our society and our government are not passive bystanders while this is going on. Left to their own devices, they'll do everything in their power to remove any godly influence that openly or passively calls into question ungodly behavior (Ephesians 6:12). Since our representative government implements laws reflecting the values of the society they represent, why would we ever want to ignore the opportunity to implement proper values: in dispensing justice; in defining what standards of behavior should be encouraged and discouraged; and in what our public schools should or should not teach? If we don't do so, who will?[191] All of these decisions and thousands of others involve making judgments on what's right or wrong, good or evil, and what should be encouraged and discouraged.

A classic example of an out-of-control government legislating injustice is hate crimes; where one class of individual or group is literally valued higher than others when a crime is committed against them. This ignores the reality that we are all created bearing the image of God (Genesis 1:27) and that all crimes are hate crimes in one form or another. It doesn't take a lot of imagination to realize the ultimate goal of such politically correct thinking will be to criminalize hate speech as the pre-cursor to hate crimes. Once this step is taken it's only a matter of time before preaching the full council of God on such

---

[191]   This is obviously a rhetorical question. Someone will define the values that will govern our nation. If we don't, or can't defend our values, then the evil one will willingly fill the vacuum.

egregious evils as abortion or sexual perversion will be legally attacked, with evangelism not far behind.[192]

Fundamentally, standards that society uses to govern itself reflect the very soul of the nation. When a righteous standard is no longer respected, then sin is not condemned for what it is: an offense against an almighty God. We should not be judging a person's heart or where they are spiritually since that's the prerogative of God; but we can judge actions, behaviors and the destructive consequences that result from them.

### Remove the Right Standard, and What Happens?

If my wife and I raised our children without teaching them do's and don'ts, or to understand what's right and wrong, or the good to do and the evil to shun what would happen to them? They'd become like the classic unsure person tossed by the wind (James 1:5-6). Obviously, Christian parents want to teach their children God's righteous standard whether they ultimately become regenerate or not. And even if a child rebels later in life, Proverbs teaches us that the morality taught to them while young will still be a guide for them later in life (Proverbs 22:6).

Is promotion of godly, moral standards important? Let's test ourselves by asking a few questions.

What would happen if biblical morals and principles were removed from the government-run public school system? Who would benefit if government decided who's worthy to receive "entitlement" support? What would happen

---

[192] If this seems farfetched, consider the legal restrictions in Europe and Canada against speaking out publically against homosexuality. In California, SB48 was signed into law in July 2011, prohibiting any school material or instruction that reflects adversely on homosexuality, bisexuality or transgenderism, while prohibiting parents from being able to remove their children from classes containing offensive material. In fact, Christianity is sometimes already publically equated to militant fundamentalist religions (Jihadist Islamists) or openly called brainwashing or a form of child abuse. It's not a huge step for this type of attitude to seek legal restrictions on our freedom of conscience and religious practice.

if government determined what a fit parent should be like; or whether a child molester is cured and no longer a threat to society? What difference would it make if personal character; unfaithfulness to a spouse; or blatantly deceptive campaign promises are considered irrelevant in judging one's qualifications for public office? What would happen if an artificially created, fundamental right to chose took absolute precedence over the life of an unborn baby? What higher good would be promoted if libraries refused to filter pornography, bestiality, homosexuality and every other type of deviant behavior from access around children? What's the harm if every vestige of Christianity is removed from government schools and held up to derision by educators; while mother earth, spiritualism, Islam, Yoga and witchcraft can be studied at will?

We know the answers to the above questions, and the consequences aren't pretty. As a matter of fact, when righteous standards are openly denigrated (or willfully ignored) doesn't this play into the hands of the Devil (1 Peter 5:8)? When a moral compass consistent with God's revealed will for mankind is no longer championed, it's a matter of time before a nation arrives at the same place the ancient Israelites did when they followed their own standard instead of God's (Judges 21:25). Spiritual darkness is all around us; and its greatest enemy is the light of truth (Matthew 5:13-16).

It's pretty clear what happens with any legitimate profession or pursuit that doesn't have a godly moral standard infused into it: spiritual forces of darkness will take over (Ephesians 6:12). Though we know this, many times we fail to realize the devastating effects non-engagement will have on the lives of those we love (Proverbs 29:2), our religious freedoms, and even our opportunity to share the gospel.[193] The alternative is also clear. When we live out our salt-and-light mandate evil will flee (James 4:7b).

---

[193] Clearly, spiritual darkness has no desire to allow any light to shine forth. Given opportunity, mankind's sinful nature will corrupt anything (Jeremiah 17:9), and then use those corrupted means to restrain or eliminate the gospel as much as possible.

### How Does Government Determine What's Evil or Good?

Throughout history, wise kings gather counselors around themselves they can trust for good advice (Proverbs 12:15; 15:22) and strive to fulfill the proper role of governing (Romans 13:4-5; 1 Peter 2:4-5). A foolish ruler ignores these valuable resources to his own detriment (1 Kings 12:1-20; Proverbs 12:34; 28:12).

There are many examples In the Old Testament of God's people influencing rulers to do what was right:. Consider Joseph with Pharaoh; Daniel with Nebuchadnezzar; Jonah and the king of Nineveh; and even Esther with King Ahasuerus. Although access to rulers in the past had to be provided providentially by the Lord, in our day we're blessed with an incomparable degree of access to those wielding power over us.

Our election system not only allows us to participate in selecting who will represent us in the councils of government, but also to influence them after they're elected. This includes writing, questioning at town hall meetings, lobbying, petitioning, and meeting directly with representatives or their staffs. We can also influence by peacefully demonstrating, advertising, and through legal challenges if necessary. Just as gentleness and wisdom has accomplished great good for entire cities and nations (Ecclesiastes 9:13-15; Jeremiah 29:7), we can use the same approach to influence today's leaders by speaking truth to power whether the hearers are believers or not (Proverbs 25:15).

Our influence doesn't stop there. We can also confront our representatives during re-election campaigns by supporting candidates who are more representative of our values. In many states the initiative process allows egregious legislation to be overturned by bringing the issue to a vote of the people. The laws of our land at the federal and state levels, as well as public policy, are all subject to change and interpretation over time. If we don't ensure just laws aren't ignored or used to violate our fundamental freedoms, we know who will.

We must never forget that government is just a tool, albeit a very powerful one. By itself government is neither intrinsically good nor evil[194], but as a tool it's used for good or evil by whoever can gain the upper hand in its use. Unfortunately, once control is lost to those who don't agree with our understanding of justice, morality, dignity, and character it's extremely difficult to rein it back in.[195]

### Is There a Rationale Basis for Political Activism?

Our daily lives, our experience, and wisdom itself demonstrates very clearly that we can exercise incredible influence on those not just in our own family and community, but also in the halls of power in our government.

When we're prosperous, ignorant or apathetic, it's only a matter of time until evil finds a way to attack us and eventually our message of hope. We're in a war that will continue until the Lord returns to establish his righteous Kingdom. Until then, every election, every law, every public policy decision is an opportunity to implement a value system that's consistent with the desires of God for the good of the community and for His glory. Not only that, but these are also opportunities to speak to the conscience of those in public office who are ultimately accountable to an almighty God to give an account for their lives and decisions.

Our task isn't an easy one, but it's an important one. We're to be godly, educated citizens exercising our freedoms and duty as Christ's salt and light to influence those elected to rule for our good (Romans 13:4a). Scripture clearly

---

[194] There's and argument that an intrinsic, institutional evil can exist in government that becomes virtually independent of those that wield governmental power. However, those characteristics are still only a result of decisions made beforehand to allow that type of abuse to exist.

[195] A good example of this in California was the failure of the "stopsb48" referendum to overturn the repugnant SB 48, a statute by the California legislature signed into law by Governor Jerry Brown that forces the treatment of LBGT influences in social science classes for grades kindergarten through twelfth, without any opportunity for a parent to opt out children out.

shows we're to contribute to the common peace and prosperity of our land (2 Timothy 3:16-17; Jeremiah 29:7), as well as set an example of living quiet lives in godliness and holiness as a reminder to the world of what it means to live under the Lordship of Jesus Christ (1 Timothy 2:2).

Although we're able to appeal to man's conscience, it's not the changed attitude or behavior that's important, or the creation a law that is the perfect civil reflection of God's moral code, but the recognition of the moral foundation that brings conviction that a holy, just God is behind it all. Obviously, God must bring about any change, whether in our nation or in an individual's heart. But in this process God uses His people to display and defend His perfect wisdom and standards to the world (Num 14:13-19; Matt 5:16; Col 3:17; 1 Cor 10:31). For us to do otherwise would be missing an opportunity to bring glory to God and would border on irresponsibility (James 4:17).

# Chapter 10

# Common Myths

*"Have nothing to do with foolish, ignorant controversies;*
*you know that they breed quarrel"*
*– 2 Timothy 3:23-26*

*"The trouble with our liberal friends is not that they're ignorant;*
*it's just that they know so much that isn't so"* – **Ronald Reagan**

### The Power of Myths

Myths are tenacious little creatures. They generally have a bit of reality embedded in them and ring true with someone already thinking along those lines. For others, they become truth itself if there's no further investigation into their validity. Although most myths are probably not that consequential, when they deal with faith and politics it can become emotional very quickly.

The following issues are just a few that have helped stoke the hostile environment we currently have in our national political debate. Some our adversary's use against us, while others percolate within our own Christian ranks. But each of these canards are unnecessary sources of contention, confusion, and even divisiveness if not handled appropriately within the Christian community, creating an uncertain sound when engaging a secular world that has a hard time understanding us to begin with (1 Corinthians 14:8).

### Christians Want America to be a Theocracy

There's definitely a portion of the Christian community that believes the Lord is Lord over all the earth (Joshua 3:13; Psalm 22:28; 103:19) and that He will rule directly on the earth <u>after</u> His people win the spiritual battle currently raging in the world.[196] Even though these believers (Theonomists) are a distinct minority within Christendom, their views feed the fears of unbelievers who think Christians want to impose an iron-fisted, autocratic, moralistic theocracy akin to radical Islamists. To unbelievers, the major difference between the two groups is only whether Old Testament law or Sharia is implemented.

For the record, there's not been a true biblical theocracy since the Lord directly ruled in the Israel of the Old Testament. The Holy Roman Empire attempted to combine church and state; and Puritans tried to re-create a new Israel on America's shores when colonies were first formed. But biblically, a Christian's most important citizenship is in heaven, and the Body of Christ has no national borders or mandate to create a unique Christian nation (1 Peter 2:9).

The vast majority of Christians in the United States have no desire to form a theocracy and find no biblical warrant for one. The real issue is whose values will prevail in the public sphere, not whether a religious belief system becomes the law of the land. Unfortunately, the enemies of Christ continue to portray concerns over societal values and the use of government for destructive

---

[196]   This is aligned with a Post-Millennial view of the end times; i.e. Christians come to dominate the world and usher in Kingdom rule, followed by the bodily return of Jesus Christ.

purposes as equivalent to the heavy-handed theocracies associated with Islam. The intended result is to instill fear in those who don't understand or appreciate Christianity's love and belief in freedom of conscience.

### Christians Don't Care About the Mother, They Only Want to Criminalize Abortions

On the face of it, this is a bold-faced lie. Christians have consistently been on the forefront of adopting "unwanted" babies[197], providing counseling services and material support to women experiencing crisis pregnancies, and disciplining young women in how to live sexually moral lifestyles that yield blessings and not regrets for the rest of their lives.

Abortion, however, is one of the most shameful consequences of a nation that's lost its soul. Like a disease, abortion has infected the moral conscience of society so deeply that any pushback is viciously attacked with every ungodly tool available to agents of darkness: name calling, denigration, intimidation, misrepresentation, lies, legal challenges, and as much financial support as it takes to crush any threat to any restrictions, no matter how small.

Once a mother's natural instincts to love and protect their unborn child are replaced with a belief that the young "fetus" is nothing more than flesh (or property) the stage is set to attack other phases of life that bear God's image from conception to natural death (Genesis 1:27). It's no wonder then, that after the Roe *v.* Wade decision infanticide, euthanasia, physician-assisted suicide, embryonic stem-cell harvesting, cloning, and other life-ending decisions are becoming more pragmatic.

Whether abortion should be criminalized or not is a needed national debate once the true humanity of the unborn and the emotional, physical and spiritual impact on the mother (and father) becomes widely understood.

---

[197]    This is true even in cases where the child has severe physical or mental challenges from birth.

Reaching this point would be the equivalent of the long national cleansing that took place once slavery was recognized for what it was – a devaluing of life for the benefit or convenience of others. Until this happens, Christians must continue to protect and nurture innocent life, and defend the worth almighty God gives it.

This is where the debate must lead: to recognizing the sanctity of life as far more important than an artificially created mother's "right to choose". Only then will significant strides be made in encouraging mothers to carry their unborn children to term. Only then will godly means to openly address the moral implications of fornication be widely acceptable. Only then will the number of abortions drop significantly and the questions concerning criminality have a just basis on which to proceed.

Ultimately, making abortion and participation in it punishable or dis-incentivized in some fashion for deterrence purposes will be consistent with the moral revulsion that will naturally follow a broader understanding of the value of the life the mother carries, no matter how or under what conditions it was conceived.

### *Christians Are Irrational Homophobes*

In the battle over homosexuality, the small numbers of people who have succumbed to this type of sexual impurity are an incredibly potent political force. Homosexual activists and their willing supporters have successfully stifled any open opposition or even objective discussion of their lifestyle through every legal, economic, and outright deceptive means conceivable. This has occurred in spite of the fact that homosexuality is still considered repugnant to many and has a blatant in-your-face activist component. Part of that activism involves publically denigrating and marginalizing any resistance to granting special protective legal status to homosexuals, the redefining of marriage to include same-sex partners, and allowing adoption of children by same-sex couples. A common tool used by gay activists is to maliciously label anyone with an opinion different from theirs a homophobe.

In California this battle is extremely hot, with the public school policy being used as a weapon to normalize and promote same-sex practices to children as young as kindergarten age.[198] This not only neuters freedom of religion, but it tears away at parental authority, destroys freedom of speech, denies the use of scientific and sociological facts as well as rational thought to consider the consequences of alternative lifestyles. Make no mistake, this assault isn't just to normalize immoral values, it's to force acceptance of a sexual lifestyle that's abhorrent to Scripture and anathema to God's intended sexual design.

For prostitution and pornography the degradation of men and women for base purposes corrupts and degrades what God has designed for mankind's good. However, with homosexuality, lesbianism, transgenderism, and bisexuality the natural order of God-created gender relationships have been rejected at an incredible cost.[199] At the least, government shouldn't be promoting these demonstrably destructive behaviors, particularly when they're objectionable to most people with an understanding of the inherent practices involved.

Promoting these behaviors creates societal confusion and results in undesirable social consequences that are well documented. Whether there's a compelling public interest to criminalize homosexual (and other) behaviors in an attempt to change a person's private life predilections is arguable at best (1

---

[198]   Current California state law mandates instruction in social sciences for all school ages to include the role and contributions of lesbians, gays, bisexuals and transgender to the economic, political and social development of California and the United States, with a particular emphasis on portraying the role of these groups in contemporary society. Of particular note is the lack of a parental opt-out option, or anything that may "promote a discriminatory bias" towards these groups; i.e. anything perceived as negative.

[199]   These costs include the social consequences that result from high-risk sexual practices; transmission of STD's; lifelong emotional and psychological distress; as well as the irrational destruction of businesses that cannot in good faith service activities such as same-sex marriages or the creating of gender-neutral bathrooms and showers in public schools.

Timothy 1:8-11). But for the government to force acceptance by every man, woman, child and business of objectionable sexual behaviors performed in private is clearly unjustifiable coercion by authority and not homophobia by those that would oppose these measures on biblical grounds.

### *I'm an American, so I'm a Christian*

Unfortunately, not everyone calling themselves Christian are truly "born again" as a new creature in Christ (Romans 12:1-2; 2 Corinthians 5:17). Our long national Christian legacy has made it common practice to be considered a Christian just because one lives in the United States and respects God to some level.[200] In fact, much of the world categorizes the United States as a Christian nation and *de facto* thinks of everyone from here as being a Christian.

Time and time again national polls show the number of people that self-identify as Christians can be as high as 80%. However, when degree of adherence to specific orthodox beliefs becomes the criteria the percentage drops dramatically.[201] In effect, Christianity as practiced in our country is a designer religion where one picks and chooses what they're willing to believe (Acts 17:21). This shows itself when one considers Jesus Christ as their Savior ("He died for me"), but be very selective about the Lordship of Jesus Christ in their lives.

Though there are many reasons why this is the situation, it's not surprising that the practical consequence among Christians will be disagreements over:

---

[200] This situation has been commonly characterized by the term "cultural Christian", one that identifies them self as a Christian solely because they're in the United States, independent of an understanding or belief in the fundamental orthodox tenets of Christian faith.

[201] Analysis conducted by the American Culture and Faith Institute and the Barna Group use distinct questions to determine born-again status, such as: is their faith important to their life; do they have a personal responsibility to share their religious beliefs about Christ; do they believe Satan exists; do they believe eternal salvation is possible only through grace and not works; do they believe Jesus Christ lived a sinless life on earth; do they believe the Bible is accurate in all the principles it teaches; etc.

public policy; who's a good candidate for elective office; whether gays should be granted marriage; whether a woman should have the right to choose; or whether government should be giving handouts to the habitually dependent to curry their favor and grow more government.

No, not everyone who calls themselves a Christian is really a member of the family of God (Ephesians 2:13-22). This is a sad commentary on the health of the "visible" Body of Christ, but we need to remember, it was true in Jesus' time also (Matthew 7:21).

### You Can't Legislate Morality

There's primarily one reason why the world challenges a Christian's involvement in the public battle over morals, values and laws – and that reason is sexual immorality. Obviously there are countless ways the biblical worldview can influence policy and legal decisions concerning everything from the environment, to business, finance, safety standards, to international relations. But fundamentally, the greatest motivator of the unbelieving world's venom toward conservative Christians is that we represent God's standard concerning sex and its proper, beneficial role. Why else would homosexual activists be so vehemently anti-Christian; marriage so disparaged by society; sexual purity laughed at; so many movies glorify adultery, sexual perversion and fornication; or Christians be called intolerant, uneducated, prudish, even Neanderthal?

It's obvious that Christians are the one segment of society that holds to a different standard. Christians understand the unique perspective of the marriage union reflecting the marriage of Christ with His body, the church (Ephesians 5:22-33). They also understand God's promises concerning sexual fulfillment within marriage according to His perfect design for all of mankind (Genesis 2:24; Matthew 19:4-6). But the world can't stand this truth so it'll do everything in its power to destroy it.

Legislating morality, therefore, is code-speak for anything that may detract someone from plunging into sexual dissipation and encouraging others to do the same (1 Peter 4:3-4; Romans 1:32). Using this obvious conflict, anything that Christians stand for is then lumped in with the sexual immorality issue as religious intolerance and backwardness independent of any objective merit.

The truth of the matter, however, is that every piece of legislation, law and policy is an expression of someone's moral values. When something is regulated, there's a value decision as to whether there should be more or less of the activity, or if there are right or wrong ways to conduct the activity. The same is true with the application of taxes, criminal statutes, family legal code, and on and on. All law (legislation) is a direct implementation of a moral value. The only question that's really germane is whose morality will be pre-eminent in our society?

### It's Illegal For a Church to be Involved in Politics

This is one of the greatest myths perpetrated on churches in our lifetime – thanks to the never-ending efforts by the ACLU (and others) to remove anything relating to Christ from the public. Is it any wonder the ACLU also warns churches across the nation that anything they do that even hints of being political is illegal and could result in federal action against them? No wonder Christians are overly concerned about offending anyone or speaking out about political issues – even though our very existence is an offense to the unbelieving world if we're living our faith at all (2 Corinthians 2:15-16).

For anyone willing to do a little research, they'll find that churches and pastors have a lot of freedom to be actively involved in "political" matters. By remembering a few rules of thumb there's no reason why a church can't preach and teach on moral issues that have profound political implications. Church leaders can talk with elected officials to express support or concern about pending legislation of any kind. They can even have candidates come and give their testimony, a sermon, or teach a class, as long as they're not using it as a campaign appearance. In fact, as long as all candidates are afforded the same opportunity a church can host question-and-answer forums and even allow each candidate to tell why they're the best candidate for an elective office.

For detailed lists of what can and cannot be done by either the pastor or the church, there are many resources available. The Alliance Defending Freedom (ADF) and Liberty Council have excellent guidelines for church use, and recently the National Center for Law and Policy produced a helpful booklet providing great advice on do's and don'ts. Besides clarifying the political freedoms and rights of the Christian community, the other recent development has been the availability of legal representation should the government ever challenge churches or pastors for exercising their religious freedoms while equipping their flocks to be godly citizens. A short list of these organizations is contained in Chapter 18 Resources.

### Churches Should Address Only Moral Issues Not Political Issues

If it's conceded that the church has a biblical duty to address moral issues, then it'll address political issues. Trying to differentiate between a moral and political issue is useless. In fact, try to find any significant moral issue of concern to Christians that's not also a political issue. Moral issues aren't just relegated to the privacy of an individual's life between themselves and God. Sure, it's possible for a person to only harbor sinful thinking with no actions, but even those sinful thoughts have been influenced by the long arm of government policy in one way or another. Most people, in fact think that if something is legal then it's OK. Likewise, if it's illegal, then there's something wrong with it. Paul himself implied this when he admitted he wouldn't have known what sin was unless the law pointed it out to him (Romans 7:7).

On the flip side, every significant political issue is a moral issue.

Values are applied every time a law is passed. A judgment is being made whether something needs to be corrected, protected, encouraged, or punished. These are moral decisions to influence behavior whether the intended result occurs or not. Since government's duty is to punish evil and commend what's good, it goes without saying that it must make a value (moral) decision on what evil to punish, and what good to encourage. And clearly a legislator's worldview will influence their understanding of what's good or bad, beneficial or detrimental.

To claim there's no relationship between politics and biblical morals is patently false. This artificial distinction only serves as cover by some to ignore any responsibility toward the actions of government even though we have the opportunity to influence it to act rightly.

### *America Is Not Exceptional*

With the conflicting dynamics of the American experience over the last generation, and the battles raging over the future direction for our nation, the term American Exceptionalism seems to have made a comeback of sorts, particularly with Christians. President Ronald Reagan, President John Kennedy and even de Tocqueville in his "Democracy in America" referred to America as the "shining city on the hill". This phrase captures the unmistakable belief that God's hand has been directly involved in the entire life of the United States. Of course, biblically we know God raises up nations and marks out their seasons (Acts 17:26) and their eventual accountability (Psalm 110:6). The question is whether we're exceptional in a unique spiritual way or only narrowly as President Barack Obama sated: "I believe in American exceptionalism, just as I suspect that the Brits believe in British exceptionalism and the Greeks believe in Greek exceptionalism."[202]

---

[202] As reported in James Kirchick in the Los Angeles Times, "Squanderer in chief" on 28 April 2009.

Truth be told, the United States is both exceptionally good and exceptionally wicked. Our personal freedoms and opportunities are in sharp contrast with the rest of the world. Our right to worship, evangelize, support missionaries "to the uttermost parts" is unparalleled in history. Our compassion for the less fortunate in our own nation and around the world (Matthew 22:39; 5:43-44) demonstrates a unique understanding of the sanctity of life created in the image of God (Genesis 1:27), and the privilege to give sacrificially out of our abundance to those in need due to warfare, genocide, famine, sickness, or natural disasters. U.S. Army General Patrick Brady captured it well by pointing out we're a courageous people, a competitive people, and a compassionate people.[203] Our blood and treasure, our technological and engineering creativity, our ability to create wealth, our system of justice, our generosity, and our acceptance of immigrants who want to legally start a new life are a uniquely powerful example of a nation built upon biblical principles and western political thought grounded in natural law.[204]

However, we have the proverbial evil twin to our national nature. There's incredible arrogance and condescension toward other, less developed nations. We're by far the world's greatest mass producer of pornography. The United States has legally protected and financially supported the slaughter of over 55 million unborn children; and subsidized millions more such deaths around the world. Our criminal incarceration rate is one of the highest in the world, as is our abuse of drugs, resulting in destroyed lives and families. The majority of states sanction legalized gambling, ignoring the social destructiveness to countless lives, and marriage is relentlessly under attack to be re-defined or no longer treated as a gift to be protected and encouraged.

---

[203]   General Patrick Brady, World Net Dailey Commentary on 2 July 2011; "Why we should all believe in American Exceptionalism"

[204]   Many conservative commentators have used the following question to evaluate the significance of the American experiment: "If the borders were removed completely, would people rush into our country or run out of our country?"

What's one to make of this? The open moral vileness and government's growing irresponsibility makes one wonder why God's wrath hasn't destroyed this nation. But that's the nature of the spiritual warfare around us (Ephesians 6:12). Whatever's good should be enjoyed and continue to leverage for the greater good and the glory of God. The exceptionally evil, we should expose for what it is (Ephesians 5:11), and counter its devastating effects on our witness to the world (James 4:7).

If the term American Exceptionalism is used, it should be used advisedly to prevent unnecessary confusion. It's not worth creating division over, but it's important to understand how the American people use it and how it can lead to deeper conversations.[205] Bottom line: is America exceptional? Yes and no.

### *America Is a Christian Nation*

This is a very emotional credo for many people. It also causes a lot of confusion about our Christian role in living in this unique nation. Was this country founded on biblical principles by committed, talented and gifted men: Yes! Has Christianity's moral virtues and principles undergirded much of our society, laws and politics throughout most of our shared national experience: Yes! Have some founders, Supreme Court justices and even presidents made statements about our being a Christian nation: Yes! Do these statements determine whether this is a Christian nation or not: No!

If someone claims to be a Christian, yet their actions were a mixture of good works, a caring heart, but also vile passions and idolatrous pursuits should they be considered a Christian? You'd be right to have doubts, but the key determiner would be their personal relationship to Jesus Christ even though still a sinner (Romans 7:7-25). There's an analogous situation with our nation.

---

[205]  Any general phrase like this can be used to segue to spiritual conversations. With our rich Christian national roots and legacy it can be a lead in to highlight God's truths

The salt-and-light in our country isn't organizations doing good works, or a benevolent government creating economic safety nets, or even just laws, the people of God are the only true salt-and-light (Matthew 5:13-16). Institutions, organizations and laws may be tools for salt-and-light purposes, but they're not salt and light in and of themselves.

Also, there's no biblical warrant for a Christian nation to exist, but there is one for the universal Body of Christ (1 Peter 2:9). In one sense the United States may be thought of as a Christian nation just like Israel is a Jewish nation. But the governing documents of our country don't specify Jesus as our nation's Lord or King; they don't call out the Bible as the law book to base all other laws on; and they don't declare Christianity as the official belief system of our land. Clearly our nation is blessed with large numbers of Christians, as well as a legacy of Christian values, morals and understanding of justice. But these do not make us a formal Christian nation. If we were, church and state would be one and the same just like Islamic countries are when under Sharia law.

The bottom line is that this shouldn't be a divisive issue among Christians, but if the phrase is going to be used it needs to be explained clearly what's meant so wrong conclusions aren't drawn or inferred.

### God Will Bring About an Election Miracle

It's unwise to question what God can or will do to fulfill His purposes. He holds the heart of kings (and presidents) in his hands; He also raises nations up and brings them down for His own glory (Proverbs 21:1). However, it's always amazing how many sincere Christians believe the Lord will bring about a great miracle at election time and sweep their candidate into office. The problem is when their favorite candidate doesn't win the excuse becomes: either a lack of faith or not enough Christians voted.

There's a saying at work: "Expect the best and plan for the worst". This phrase relates a positive attitude with the necessity of good, old-fashioned hard work (Nehemiah 4:15-17). Obviously the Lord can bring about a miracle anytime He pleases. It can be in circumstances, events, changed hearts, medical healings, and any number of ways – including elections. But what's not found in the Bible is a mandate to rely upon a miracle to occur without any effort on the part of His people.[206] This is testing God, requiring Him to do something that may or may not be what He desires to happen. In a backwards way, it acknowledges God is in charge, but says only this answer is the right one, hence He'll make sure it happens.

In contrast to this thinking, Christians have a great and high calling to be faithful and diligent laborers in Kingdom work. As the athlete vigorously trains to compete for the prize (2 Timothy 2:5; 1 Corinthians 9:24-25), or the farmer works hard to bring forth a crop to provide for his family (2 Timothy 2:6), so we are to work hard for results that'll please the Lord. In the parable of the talents (Matthew 25:14-30) the ones who invested and worked hard received their reward as well as affirmation by the Master. The one who hid the talent in the ground, equivalent to saying the Lord will do whatever He wants, was scolded for being slothful. Everywhere in Scripture we're told to be diligent, work hard, discipline ourselves, and labor for others, the gospel, and righteousness (Matthew 6:33). Nowhere are we told to relax, sit back and just let God do all the work. It may give the appearance of being holy and trusting only in the Lord we serve, but more often than not it's an excuse to do nothing.

Winning elections is hard work. Grass-roots campaigns take time, financial resources to pay for costly campaign materials, and initiative to talk to people

---

[206] A cartoon many years ago illustrated this by showing a bunch of scientists staring at a white board full of complicated equations leading into an empty box, with an arrow exiting the box and pointing to the result they all wanted. With no known way to get from their sophisticated analysis to the desired result, one of the scientists pointed at the box and said "this is where the miracle occurs".

and create new venues to get the word out. Likewise, influencing decision makers is difficult when they don't share our values. Many people won't take the time to confront evil or are intimidated into inaction. But scriptural examples are quite the opposite. The gospel doesn't go out unless someone brings it to the unbelieving world (Romans 10:15); a tower isn't built unless someone diligently plans for and builds it (Luke 14:28-30); a nation doesn't go to war without doing everything it can to ensure success (Luke 14:31). Even the Israelites had to fight hard and long to conquer and occupy the Promised Land (Exodus 23:29-30); it wasn't just given to them.

Reason and wisdom would dictate that in any race, battle or election we're to plan well, work hard, and entrust the results to the Lord. To do the latter, and ignore the former is only an excuse to do nothing while giving the appearance of great faith. The Book of James addresses this very situation and draws the conclusion that faith by itself, if it travels alone without works, is for all intents and purposes dead (James 2:14-17).

### If All Christians Voted, We'd Turn This Country Around

Though this seems right in theory, it's just not true. For reasons discussed in other chapters, much of Christendom in our nation is politically fragmented and divided. There's a wide spectrum of views concerning the authority of Scripture, how it's to be interpreted and whether it's even applicable to our day. Add to this the artificial complexity of the problems our nation is facing and the lack of pastoral leadership to equip the flock and the magnitude of the task to provide a consistent Christian voice is staggering.[207]

---

[207] For example: Anglicans have recognized and normalized homosexual behavior, as has the Evangelical Lutheran Church of America; while the liberal wings of the Presbyterian Church have supported secular government-based social programs, globalization of our country, and anti-Israel positions.

If all who called themselves Christian suddenly voted, the outcome would probably be no different than the common public in today's world. In fact it may be preferable that a biblically ignorant Christian, one uninformed on the major issues of the day not vote at all since they'll be more influenced by emotion, TV commercials, and personal opinion than a scriptural worldview. Given this state of affairs, it's surprising how many election outcomes are still determined by a small percentage of votes. As discouraging as this can be for values voters, it's also encouraging to see what happens when clear moral arguments are presented to the electorate. A case in point is the 2008 California vote on Proposition 8, the defense of marriage initiative.

In 2008, Obama carried California with 61% of the vote; homosexual activism was at a feverish pitch; $40-plus million was spent to defeat Proposition 8; the California Supreme Court authorized same-sex "marriages" for months prior to the November election after overturning Proposition 22 earlier in the year[208]; and virtually every major news and newspaper outlet came out against Proposition 8. Yet it passed with 52%.

The broader self-identified Christian community saw the moral imperative to protect marriage at all costs and as a result the evangelical community, Roman Catholics, Mormons and even minority groups worked together to pass Proposition 8.

Christian values can triumph over political correctness, but for Kingdom work to continue to influence politics in a Christ-honoring way it must become a routine part of what the church understands its salt-and-light mandate to be, and a biblical worldview must inform that mandate.

---

[208] Proposition 22 was passed in California in 2000 by over 61% of the vote. It used the same language as Proposition 8 to define marriage as only between a man and a woman.

# Chapter 11

# Assessing Your Own Church

*"You are the salt of the earth, but if salt has lost its taste, how shall its saltiness be restored?"* – **Matthew 5:13**

*"I know your works; you are neither cold nor hot. Would that you were either cold or hot! So, because you are lukewarm, and neither hot nor cold, I will spit you out of my mouth"* – **Revelation 3:15-16**

*"And I tell you, you are Peter, and on this rock I will build my church, and the gates of hell shall not prevail against it"* – **Matthew 16:18**

### Do You Know Your Own Church?

"Is the moral climate in this country improving, growing worse, or staying about the same?" Every hand in the class[209] went up for the "growing worse" option. What most struck me was who made up the class: 20-something's (with several seminary students) and older saints nearing retirement. I

---

[209] For inquiring minds, the name of the class was: Cultural and Political Engagement Discussion Group, and it was conducted on a Saturday morning.

expected the older audience to think things are worse since they've had a long life of reflection. But when the younger crowd responded the same way it told me the rate of public moral decay was rapid enough even they could see the difference[210]. We spent the rest of the class evaluating whether our church was adequately equipping its members to confront the growing evil around us, or if that was even a proper biblical purpose of the church.

This chapter enters dangerous ground. Everyone with a passion for ministry will eventually begin to see everything through the lens of that ministry. If it's worship, you want it to honor Christ in every way, and you'll continue learning, refining and applying everything you know to ensure it brings glory of God (1 Corinthians 10:31). If you're a pastor, you're concerned with the spiritual health of the flock. You'll seek after stray sheep, bind up the sick and injured, and do everything you can to point those under your care to the glories and promises they have in Christ Jesus (Hebrews 13:17). Similarly, if you have a passion for Christian activism (Matthew 5:13-16), to encourage believers to engage political darkness for the sake of the gospel, you'll want that ministry supported and encouraged by your church's leadership as much as possible.

### Inward or Outward Focused?

Realistically, the opportunity to develop a church-based ministry to influence the political realm is highly dependent on the pastoral understanding of the church's biblical role toward the world.[211] Understandably, pastors are the major driver of what types of ministries should be encouraged, resourced, and promoted through sermons, small groups, formal teaching and the like.

---

[210] Clearly this isn't a scientific poll; but the results are consistent with many whom I've talked to over the years. The open hostility toward anything Christian is becoming more blatant in the major liberal news media, the Hollywood entertainment industry, and in religious freedom challenges in court.

[211] For a fuller examination of the implications of this fact and the reasons why politics are so overlooked, see the first three chapters of this book.

Unfortunately, some churches with strong biblical preaching and teaching can become isolationist in their ministries. The sanctification (and purity) of the Body of Christ may be such a focus there's little attention paid to loving the unloved and needy in the world or influencing the world around us for the common good. In these churches "Word-focused" ministry prevails over development of "helps" types of ministries.

Other churches may have a zeal for evangelism and community outreach (Matthew 28:19-20; 22:39) but lack depth in understanding the opportunity for a broader application of biblical truth while fulfilling the salt and light role (Matthew 5:13-16).[212] More often than not, any church related interest in government and politics is weak at best, and non-existent or discouraged at worst. In fact, it's the rare church that is willing to speak out publically and firmly against the egregious actions of government and elected leaders that continually fight against our religious freedoms.

### Understanding or Judging?

The debate over the role of the church can be healthy or divisive, depending on how it's handled. We know the Bible is the Christian's authoritative source (Romans 15:4) to be equipped for every good work (2 Timothy 3:16-17), but the practical outworking always requires wisdom and discernment. Because of this we need to show charity and grace to others whose perspective may differ from ours no matter how sure we are of our position.

---

[212] There are a variety of names used to describe these types of ministries, such as Salt & Light; Christian Citizenship; Biblical Citizens; Contemporary Issues; and the like. The specific name isn't important as long as it isn't easily confused with unrelated ministries usually found in churches.

A good rule of thumb to remember is: when Scripture's clear – strive for unity; when Scripture's unclear – be charitable to one another; and when Scripture's silent – be very careful and patient with each other.[213]

Although justification for a church's political ministry was argued in Chapter 2, this chapter presents core reasons why conflicts may exist when members want their church to be active politically, yet there's strong resistance. For a member to make any difference, the reason for rejecting political ministries needs to be understood.

Is it just an oversight or is there something much more fundamental and serious? Answering that question will go a long way toward understanding what a member will ultimately need to do.

### Some Warnings

In assessing your church, don't be so narrow minded that your personal ministry "agenda" clouds appreciation for other valuable ministries. This attitude could be dishonoring to the Lord and may even create ungodly divisiveness (1 Corinthians 12:12, 14, 20).

Another warning is to not question the spiritual worth or maturity of others who aren't as sensitive to your ministry passion, particularly if they're ministry leaders. Pastors are entrusted with the spiritual care and nurture of your soul and need you to be submissive to their authority; not frustrated by it (Hebrews 13:17).

Finally, submit to the biblical command to strive for unity within the fellowship of believers, only then can the Lord be expected to bless your labors (1 Peter 3:8).

---

[213] This is obviously a loose paraphrase of the classic: "In essentials unity, in non-essentials liberty, in all things charity" which has uncertain authorship but can be traced back to the early 1600's.

## *Assessment Approach*

The following provides categories of how churches relate to the world beyond the chapel walls and is patterned after insights by Richard Niebur.[214] Niebur labeled the Kingdom of God and the kingdom of man as "Christ" and "Culture", respectfully. The following uses a similar grouping but uses the contrast of church and state.

It should be noted that the following are generalizations only, and that no individual church will fit conveniently into just one category. Also, the term "state" is intended to include politics and all that's implied by it.

Finally, in comparing the following church types with your own church it should become clearer what the starting point (if any) would be in to creating a Christ honoring salt and light activism ministry.

## *Separatist: Church Isolated from the State*

This category can also be called isolationist.[215] Monasteries and Nunneries are good examples of distancing oneself from a world viewed as an overwhelmingly corrupt influence on the soul. For our application any interaction or engagement with government is minimized or rejected as much as possible. With this conviction, church and state are two entirely different spheres of authority that have virtually no direct relationship to each other.

---

[214] Christ and Culture; by Richard Niebur, 1951

[215] Other common pejoratives include: holy huddle; holy cocoon; frozen chosen; and the like.

A diagram illustrating this follows:

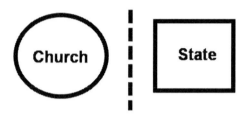

Extreme pietism can also fall into this category, where one's personal relationship to God is the driving force in a person's life and any involvement in other activities is limited to obligation or need. It's also common in churches that foster this environment to not find evangelism or any significant priority given to mercy/compassion ministry. A pejorative way to summarize this philosophy is that the church strives to become a heaven on earth and anything that detracts from that aim needs to be avoided.

### Dualism: Church and State in Paradox

This category identifies the situation where a person's spiritual life is separate from their secular life. In other words, faith is personal and not directly applicable to our activities outside of church. Pragmatism could easily trump scriptural principles when secular issues are considered. In effect, the same person can live and function with and under different life rules when operating in either the church or political spheres.

This situational type of values is particularly common with politicians who claim to be Christians, have exemplary personal family and church lives, but in the political realm compromise on values in order to gain advantage or represent the people or corporations that elected them. Basically, pragmatism rules the public debate; what constitutes the greatest good for the greatest number carries the day independent of God's revealed truth. Churches that foster this attitude are weak in submitting to the authority of Scripture; are unjustifiably pragmatic in biblical applications; and don't emphasize a Christian life being accountable to Christ everywhere and all the time. Diagrammatically, it looks like the following:

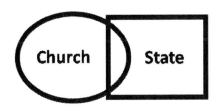

### Theocracy: Church Over the State

Though there are variations and nuances, a general term describing this biblical construct is Theonomy, which was discussed at length in Chapter 1. In effect, Christ, through the church, rules over all of society, all institutions, all governments, and very literally all of mankind. God's perfect Word is to be the law of the land and govern all criminal, civil, business, and societal activities.

This view results from the understanding that Christ is Lord over all of creation; therefore all of creation is to submit to His will and Word. Church and state become one and the same in this paradigm, with doctrinal purity and conformance to the revealed Word of God the standard for everyone.

Needless to say, political involvement is an important means to this end since governmental power is key to implement the heavenly Kingdom here on earth. A simple representation is as follows:

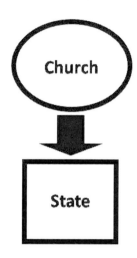

Two historic examples of this include the emergence of the Holy Roman Empire under Roman Catholic rule, and in modern times by the Theonomic movement. Though only a minority of the Christian community currently subscribes to a Theonomic order, it's the favorite example used by politicians and the liberal media to equate Christians with Islamic theocracies as practiced in Sharia governed Muslim nations.[216]

### Liberalism: Church a Promoter of the State

Unfortunately, very large segments of our national Christian community have gravitated to a liberal viewpoint, supporting a virtually unrestrained scope of authority for government. Churches of this nature are effectively cheerleaders for promoting government power to be used for virtually any cause deemed noble under the guise of social justice. The visual representation of this relationship is intended to show the two entities have the same goals and are mutually supportive:

---

[216]  True theocracies existed in the Garden of Eden before the Fall and with ancient Israel when the Lord governed directly in their midst. Muslim countries governed by Sharia are theocracies since there is no distinction between religion and the government. They are one and the same.

For many liberal churches the Bible is a moral guideline, with clear scriptural truths relegated to an optional status with no absolute or authoritative clarity. Good works become the measure of one's standing and merit before God, with mercy and compassion outreach into the community a priority for the church and particularly for the government. Unfortunately, the need for the redemptive work of Christ is downplayed or completely ignored as mankind is seen to be inherently good.

The most devastating aspect from a Christian activism standpoint is that the belief in a benevolent government as an extension of the goodness of man becomes the order of the day. In fact, the larger the aggregate of church denominations and government agencies that are working side by side to meet people's needs, the nobler the work in spite of the wickedness that's aided and abetted by misjudging the sinful nature of man.

### *Preservation: Church the Restrainer of the State*

In this relationship the church pursues a strong political salt-and-light mandate consistent with a robust understanding of Matthew 5:13-16. In doing so, the church recognizes that the ability to fulfill its mandate to love the unlovable (Matthew 22:39; 5:44) depends on the government not co-opting this role.

Ultimately, only the church is salt and light in this world, and only it is able to correctly point others to Jesus Christ as their only hope. Government is incapable and unwilling to do this, and in fact will do everything it can to prevent the truth of the gospel from even being considered.

With this understanding, these churches work to restrain government to their proper biblical roles and preserve the purposes for which they exist: to be a blessing and not a curse; to execute justice; and to encourage the growth of good. When government goes far beyond its biblical role and becomes an adversary to the Body of Christ and ultimately the proclamation of the gospel these churches see their role as transformational: that is, to restore government to its proper realm of authority. This paradigm can be illustrated by the following diagram:

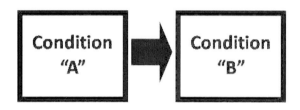

Churches that fall into this category influence the world and the government for the common good and the glory of God. The balancing act that must be constantly evaluated is how to make sure they continue to live "in" the world, yet not become part "of" the world[217] and compromised as a result.

One of the underlying themes of this book is that the preservation perspective is the closest to our biblical mandate. In the class mentioned at the start of this chapter, I asked which of the above examples best represented their church. Virtually everyone said the Separatist. Then I asked which represented what they thought should characterize their church and was closest to the

---

[217] Though there are a number of ways to support this statement, there's no one verse that clearly contains both thoughts. The closest is the High Priestly Prayer of our Lord in John 17:11, 16: "And I am no longer in the world, but they are in the world, and I am coming to you." "They are not of the world, just as I am not of the world, so I have sent them into the world". This is amplified in numerous places, including: Matthew 22:39; Romans 12:2; John 15:19; Galatians 6:10; and 1 Corinthians 9:19-23.

biblical mandate. To a person they said transformational since the culture, the government and the nation was in such decline.

Among the congregations with which I've worked, this dichotomy exists in church after church. It's emblematic of how far removed the general Christian community has drifted from the duty to be effective salt and light to the darkness around us. Though there are many individuals faithfully working to control and limit government to its proper responsibilities, there are few churches that have embraced any responsibility to equip and encourage their members to do so.

If the Christian community continues to be fragmented and ill-equipped then the sixth and last church-state relationship will be just a matter of time.

### *Persecuted: Church Suppressed by the State*

The hostility of the government to the expression of Christian faith in government realms didn't happen overnight. It was an accumulation of misguided court decisions and the heavy influence of antagonistic, anti-faith worldviews permeating governmental leadership at many levels. If the Christian community continues to ignore or fight among itself over the merits of united, legal, Christ-honoring political involvement its clear where the future is heading.[218] Not only will Christian truth continue to become irrelevant to the issues of the day, but ultimately the gospel itself will also be relegated to a private matter with no legal protection to be openly proclaimed against the vileness of the world.

When the Body of Christ removes itself from aggressively pursuing Kingdom work and influence in all legitimate activities (including politics); or compromises it's witness by conforming to the world instead of being a light

---

[218] Examples of the purging of Christian influence in the public square are sprinkled throughout this book. They're indicative of a continual erosion of our constitutionally guaranteed right of freedom of religion, religious practice and religious conscience whether in government, public schools, private business or church practices.

to it, darkness will have free reign. To deny this is to be childishly naive about the nature of spiritual warfare (1 Peter 5:8) which has no desire to allow any light to remain in its presence.

Obviously Jesus Christ is Lord of lords and King of kings (Revelation 19:16), and our nation is in His hands to do with as He sees fit (Daniel 2:20-21; Acts 17:26). But He has given us the incredible privilege and challenge to be the steward of a nation allowing the greatest amount of religious freedom in history. When that freedom is taken for granted and not defended consistently and fervently by exercising our citizenship rights and duties then we've become complicit in allowing a hostile environment to be created by government that limits our ability to fulfill our biblical mandates.[219]

Diagrammatically, the persecuted church paradigm looks like the following:

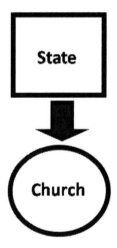

---

[219]   See Chapter 2: Do We Have a Political Mandate? for a fuller discussion of the three main mandates: the Great Commission (Matthew 28:19-20); the Great Commandment (Matthew 22:39); and the Great Challenge (Matthew 5:13-16).

### *Why Do a Church Assessment?*

The reason for evaluating the kind of church you minister in isn't to be critical of its leadership, or its priorities, or how well it strives to bring glory to God. It's to better understand what's needed to gain acceptability for political activism ministries that are biblically based.

If your church leadership embraces a *Preservation* paradigm, then Chapter 5, "How to Approach Your Pastor" should be very helpful. The key is working with pastoral leadership to build mutual trust and create a ministry that leadership is comfortable with. Demonstrating a submissive attitude (Hebrews 13:17) will go a long ways to making sure controversial ministries of this nature will not just be allowed, but openly supported by pastors as they face the inevitable questions that other members will raise.

If your church openly or indirectly subscribes to the *Dualism* characterization, there's a fundamental problem in understanding what the life of a Christian is all about: giving honor and glory to Christ every waking moment of every day in every situation and activity (Romans 12:1-2; 1 Corinthians 10:31). Until a proper biblical foundation is laid for a consistent Christian life and witness in this darkened world, then ministry efforts may be ineffective at best, and counterproductive at worst, in trying to influence government to fulfill its rightful role.[220]

If the *Separatist* paradigm is most evident in your church, it may require developing a long-term, close relationship with your pastor or someone in formal leadership to better understand what conditions must exist before any type of ministry would be sanctioned. It may have to start extremely small, with modest goals such as encouraging members to fulfill their minimum level of citizenship duties by voting. In this environment the biblical basis for

---

[220]   For a more detailed discussion of this topic, see Chapter 6: Separation of State *from* Church?

engagement will need to be promoted as more of a wisdom issue than direct biblical imperative.

The most difficult category to deal with is the *Liberalism* type. Historically, these churches have shown themselves to be compromised concerning the authority of Scripture and the nature of spiritual warfare.[221] It's doubtful that any major change can be brought about, particularly one that results in a Christ-honoring, biblical, uncompromising way that desires to hold government within its rightful role, and recognizes sin for what it is.

For these churches a major change in pastoral leadership may be necessary in order to lay a firm foundation of biblical truth before high-risk activism ministries could ever be attempted. For members that find themselves in this situation, I encourage them to be good Bereans and compare what's preached and taught to the entire counsel of God's Word and strive to bring the authority of Scripture to bear gently and faithfully.

Finally, remember that whether your church becomes active or not, you as an individual can invest your time, treasure and talents as the Lord grants opportunity and ability.

---

[221]   When this compromise becomes endemic throughout a denominational hierarchy, it becomes self-perpetuating and antagonistic towards any individual church leadership that may try to restore the authority of Scripture to its rightful, historical place

# Chapter 12

# When Problem Solving Giftedness Creates Conflict

*"The one who states his case first seems right, until the other comes and examines him"*
**– Proverbs 18:17**

*"Remind them of these things, and charge them before God not to quarrel about words, which does no good, but only ruins the hearers."*
**– 2 Timothy 2:14**

### Decision-Making Realities

Ever met someone that strongly believed in standing on principle, no matter what the personal consequences or how unreasonable it may appear to others? It can be maddening at times, but also convicting when it causes us to honestly look at our own commitment to stand on God's truths. In the political realm, however, an absolute, take it or leave it position without regard or consideration of possible compromise solutions can be devastating in trying to accomplish a wider good beyond a personal impact.

Take the example of making promises. We're taught that if we make a promise we're to keep it no matter what the consequence,[222] even if the circumstances have changed or we didn't understand the full implications initially.[223]

Yet even though this principled approach is clearly taught in Scripture, there can be extenuating circumstances that allow some flexibility.[224]

We also know that lying is ungodly, but is lying to prevent a greater evil from occurring always wrong? A principled pastor friend of mine stated in a sermon that lying is a sin, unless there's a greater good involved like protecting life. Though I understand the clear commands concerning lying, I also appreciate the reasoning that justifies when lying (or in some cases deception) is tolerated.[225]

I have to admit, however, that this slippery slope of relative good can become problematic to implement in any consistent, rationale. The same types of issues can occur in making political decisions: whether determining a candidate, tactics to use to influence someone else's decisions, or approaches to use in complex political battles.

Obviously all decisions, even the most mundane, have some moral aspect to them[226].

---

[222] Several good references to study include Ecclesiastes 5:1-7, Psalm 15:4 and Joshua 9:16-20.

[223] There are incredible examples of Christians who have gone through bankruptcy because of a major economic downturn, and then methodically paid back their debtors years later as their fortunes improved. This demonstrates both a practical and principled approach to real-life financial difficulties.

[224] Exceptions include asking to be relieved from the obligation; or if the commitment was an ungodly one to begin with then it needs to be repented of, whatever the personal consequences that follow.

[225] Proponents of this view use the examples of the midwives in Exodus 1:15-22 and Rahab the harlot in Joshua 2:1-7. However, Scripture clearly and consistently condemns lying (e.g. Exodus 20:16; Proverbs 6:16-17) and never condones or encourages it. Hypothetical examples

[226] A little reflection will show this to be true. Consider our accountability for every careless word we speak (Matthew 12:36); every careless thought we entertain (James 1:13-15); and every careless action we take (1 Corinthians 10:31)

But for our purposes the focus will be on the types of decision making behaviors that have the potential for conflict between Christians who operate from two different sets of decision-making or problem-solving principles.

These two types of people will be referred to as "principlists" and "pragmatists".

### *The Shaky Path from Biblical Truth to Politics*

In politics, it's sometimes the wild, wild West in deciding what position to take on a piece of legislation or which candidate to support when all fall short of acceptability. In fact, the further away we are from having a specific "Thou shall" or "Thou shall not" biblical command or clear scriptural principle on a matter, the more wisdom, experience and prayer is going to be needed. This practical reality is illustrated in the following diagram.

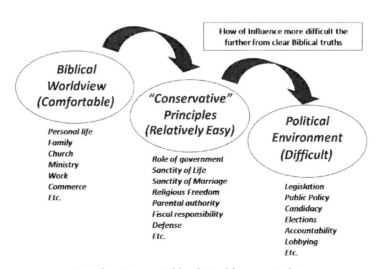

**The Flow From a Biblical Worldview to Politics**

Scripture has an abundance of truths addressing the nature of God and salvation, how to live holy lives, and how to conduct worship and ministry.

The clearer God's Word on a particular topic, the more assurance we have of knowing what to do and what decisions to make. Even the passages of Scripture that are less clear afford us an opportunity to research deeper into God's Word to better equip us to know what to do.

In the above illustration the biblical worldview ellipse represents our comfort zone when Scripture is clear and directly applicable to our lives. When we try to apply biblical principles primarily interested in holy living to the local and national political issues of our day we begin to run into some difficulties. In like manner, when God's Word gives clear lines of responsibility for our relationship to the state[227], or the state's biblical role in God's plan[228], most sincere believers will readily agree until it comes to the practical outworking of those verses. Historically, the general result of that application has been a set of principles commonly known as "conservative" in our popular political jargon.[229]

Even at this level there's more than ample opportunity for controversy among Christians. Like so many things in life, what may be crystal clear to one person may be more nuanced to another because of what they have been taught; the depth of their understanding the "whole counsel of God"; or even their personal life experiences that may directly relate to the issue.

When the actual political environment is encountered (the third ellipse), the practical application and implications of biblical principles can quickly become difficult. This is particularly true when thousands of pages of legislative proposals with varying degrees of good and bad parts are being evaluated, or when believers with different levels of maturity in understanding a biblical worldview attempt to work together. Add to the equation a need to enlist support from

---

[227] Honor, respect and submission where it is due (Romans 13:5-7; 1 Peter 2:13,17).

[228] Dispense justice and promote good (Romans 13:3-4; 1 Peter 2:14).

[229] Obviously, what would fall into the category of "conservative" has changed over the years, but in general conservative principles have tended to align with accepted biblical principles relating to all manner of issues. For a methodical treatment of liberal and conservative distinctives from the late 1700's to the early 1980's see Charles W. Dunn's "American Political Theory".

outside the Christian community in order to prevail, or competing legislative proposals appealing to different segments of the Christian community and splitting the vote, and the problems can become overwhelming[230].

### Classic Problem Areas

To illustrate the nature of political conflict among believers, consider the sanctity of life. If a pro-life Christian legislator supports legislation preventing or limiting abortions except for cases of rape, incest and the life of the mother, is he compromising on clear biblical life principles and a traitor to the cause?[231]

On the surface, it looks like he's saying not all pre-born life is precious, and that circumstances make some lives less valuable than others. Those standing solidly on sanctity of life truths may attack him for compromising on a fundamental principle of life and clear biblical truth. Not only that, but he may not be fully trusted from that point on. On the other hand, the political reality is that should this less expansive legislation pass, it will help in reducing 98.5% of abortions that don't result from rape, incest, or impact the life of the mother. Is his decision appropriate, knowing that a complete ban will not be politically acceptable or achievable at this time? Or should he stand on absolute principle and not support any legislation until all unborn life is protected and treated exactly the same?

---

[230]    As a well-meaning example, when California's Proposition 8 was being strategically planned (marriage protection amendment to the state constitution) an alternative proposal was seeking qualification to be voted on that went much further in defining marriage and removing domestic partnership statutes in existing law. Though many, myself included, had sympathy for the stronger, farther reaching initiative, it was doomed in every public opinion poll, and it couldn't muster strong financial or political support. More critically; it split some of the conservative Christian support making it harder to qualify Proposition 8 for the ballot (which was eventually passed by the voters in 2008).

[231]    A similar argument applies to the recent legislative efforts to limit abortions being performed after 20 weeks following conception since this is the time believed to be when the unborn child begins to feel pain.

Another classic example is when there are three candidates for the same elective office: a liberal; a "moderate"; and a strong conservative. If the conservative candidate (many times the sole sincere Christian) mirrors all of your policy positions, what do you do if he has virtually no opportunity to be elected? By this I mean no name recognition; very little financial support; and minimal "boots-on-the-ground" precinct support. If a portion of the Christian community votes for the sole "true conservative" it is common for the non-liberal vote to be split, helping the least acceptable candidate – the liberal – to win.

This example happens over and over again at all levels of elective office. Right or wrong, when the principlist and pragmatist clash the least acceptable candidate often ends up winning while Christians become annoyed or even vindictive toward each other.

The textbook example at the national level was the Bill Clinton campaign against George H. W. Bush in 1992. Without commenting on the beliefs of either candidate, Bush's fate was sealed when Ross Perot entered the race with strong fiscal conservative credentials, yet with virtually no opportunity to win the election.[232] The result was predictable, a moderate incumbent president was defeated and a politically astute, nihilistic man was elected that ultimately brought shame to the office of the presidency and the nation.[233]

What these examples point out is the obvious: that people generally make important decisions in one of two ways. Either they tend to be more practical (pragmatic) by nature, or more principle driven by nature. This doesn't necessarily imply people are consistently one or the other. Everyone is still a sinner and will, at times, rationalize situations, circumstances or decisions to our own

---

[232] Since no candidate received a majority of the national vote, conceivably Bush could have won if sufficient portions of the 19% vote for Perot would have gone to him. The popular vote was: Clinton 43%; Bush 37.5%; Perot 18.9%.

[233] In California this same situation occurred in the 2003 Governor's race between Arnold Schwarzenegger (supposed fiscal conservative but low keyed social liberal); Cruz Bustamante (Lt. Governor and far left liberal); and Tom McClintock (strong conservative). For more on this race see Chapter 7, "The Lesser of Two Evils Conundrum".

advantage. But when it comes to politics, divisiveness, consternation and down-right anger toward fellow Christians can percolate because of an inability to recognize, appreciate and work with another person's problem-solving nature and strengths.

The terms "principlist" and "pragmatist" aren't meant to imply principles aren't being used on both sides; they're only convenient terms to differentiate the two.[234] Also, both types of people can share the same moral imperatives (purpose and goals) relating to an issue at hand. In the pro-life example above, the legislator may share the same desire for eradicating abortion, but his approach to addressing the issue legislatively is different than others may be willing to accept.

One final note. Successfully engaging the wider political battles we face is not the same as approaching difficult problems within a church environment. In a church, God's Word holds supreme and pastoral leadership is as accountable as everyone else to its authority. Biblical truth, principles and wisdom can be brought to bear directly, relative weight can be applied, and the guidance of the Holy Spirit can be sought to assist in understanding. In the broad public domain, however, gaining community-wide support will probably require a different "tactical" approach to solving a problem, while not violating clear biblical principles. Given these realities, it's important to look more closely at the strengths and weaknesses of the two common approaches to decision making.

### The Principlist

For the principlist, God's Word is the gold standard and everything is refined through the lens of Scripture. Not only does this help define issues

---

[234] Alternative terms can be used for both types. For example, the principlist can be called principle-driven; idealist, conscience oriented, absolutist, uncompromising, even pejoratively as legalistic. The pragmatist can be called practical-driven; pragmatic, contextual, realist oriented, incrementalist, even pejoratively as compromising or situational.

clearly, but it provides a needed contrast with principles that would otherwise only emanate from our own experience and reasoning. Over time, core values will become clearly defined and understood, whatever the controversy. This can send a powerful message that can't be easily ignored by the Christian community. Not only that, but principlists help prevent expediency from carrying the day with potentially disastrous results.

We're all familiar with situations where a good outcome occurs for the wrong reasons. The priniciplist helps ensure that no matter what the outcome, it was for the right reasons and participants can have a clear conscience.

On the other hand, principlists can easily come across as legalistic and narrow minded. Some of this obviously has to do with the nature of conflict in making decisions when passionate people begin at different starting points. But the nature of one standing on God's Word is that they're in effect defending God's honor and His truth, so "bending" may not be in their vocabulary. As a result, stridency and harshness are common attributes describing the principlist.

When a staunch principlist digs in, effective cooperative action may come to an end since there's little common ground to continue to work with others. Another way to say this is that the principlist may focus on truth to the exclusion of any potential benefits or possible approaches that could end up with a similar outcome but with a different approach. This, "I'm right, now leave the results up to God" mentality can also appear as a self-righteous, feel-good attitude to others, or even taking the easy way out instead of bending to accommodate working with others. In the worst-case scenario, those who don't agree completely with a principlist may be accused of being ungodly, scripturally ignorant, sinful, or maybe not even a Christian. [235]

---

[235]   I've personally witnessed this "dis-fellowshipping" attitude and also been on the receiving end of it. To become reconciled after such a breach of unity requires true godly repentance and humility that recognizes Christ-honoring fellowship is overwhelmingly more important than unity on some worldly political issue.

The obvious consequence of being inflexible and claiming to be the defender of God's noble, high ground is that significant support may be drawn away from any reasonable possibility of success and applied to a hopeless cause. In effect, the principlist is trying to model God's perfection in a sinful world without recognizing that wisdom and insight are needed to humbly apply God's truth in areas not directly and clearly addressed by Scripture. This stance may salve a conscience but could doom elections, or even a piece of legislation that has "much good" but a "little bad" in it.

### *The Pragmatist*

Now, what about the "pragmatist"? They may share the same moral imperatives and the same objective goal as the principlist. The pro-life legislation mentioned above is a good example of how Christians can agree on the need to protect all life. The pragmatist has an advantage in that they are comfortable to try to accomplish something in the political realm on an incremental basis without perfection being achieved. In effect, they may very well be willing to accomplish "much good" at the expense of tolerating "some bad", yet continue to move toward the ultimate goal.

This was illustrated several years ago in a California proposition that tried to require parental notification (not consent) when a young girl was being taken by the public school to an abortion clinic. This is desperately needed, and would have gone a long way to recognizing parental rights and curbing the arrogance of a public school system that thinks they can make life-and-death decisions with impunity. Unfortunately, there was an inadvertent poison pill embedded in the proposed legislation. In an attempt to correct weaknesses of prior proposed laws, the term "family" was redefined in a much broader way than what exists in current state statutes. If this would have passed, future legal battles could blur the distinctions between parents, family and relatives in a much broader context than the original measures' intent. However, the near-term potential to save lives and protect the authority of parents was deemed a weightier imperative than any longer-term detrimental effects that would be suffered. [236]

The biggest issue with the pragmatist from a principlist perspective is that they tend to have an "ends justify the means" mentality. In effect, they're being accused of compromising fundamental beliefs in order to gain results. Expediency is another pejorative term used against pragmatists, as well as claiming they're trusting in man's wisdom (schemes?) more than they're trusting in God. Since it's well known that political foes have been incrementally encroaching upon our religious rights and promoting values, public policies and judicial decisions contrary to biblical values; principlists tend to see incrementalism by pragmatists as an ungodly stealth approach that rejects boldly and publically proclaiming biblical truth.

In effect, pragmatists are seen as hiding their convictions and appearing to be afraid of exposing them.[237] A more egregious accusation is that pragmatists appear to be unprincipled, and in some manner actually supporting the enemy's side by not being more forceful and direct. In reality, the pragmatist is actually in a much better position to successfully sway public opinion to their side since they don't seem to be as extreme to the common person as the principlist sometimes appears.

When it comes to candidates for office, the classic "lesser of two evils" quandary clearly highlights the differences between the principlist and the pragmatist. It's true the constant selection of the least-bad instead of the wonderfully-good candidate ensures a continual slide toward ungodly leadership in

---

[236] For now, the consequences are unknown since the measure (Proposition 4: Parental Notification for Minor Abortion) did not pass the statewide ballot, being defeated by a 52% to 48% vote in 2008.

[237] The key verse used here is Matthew 10:32-33. "So everyone who acknowledges me before men, I also will acknowledge before my Father who is in heaven, but whoever denies me before men, I also will deny before my Father who is in heaven."

the public arena. The missing component in these trends, however, is practical in nature. If a solid, godly candidate becomes known during the campaign season, yet they haven't been mentored and engaged for years ahead of time, and haven't built up a financial war chest and a solid reputation in the public's eye over a long period of time, the probability of gaining broad public support will be quite small once professional, unethical political animals begin to go after them publically. More often than not, at this point the candidate's fate is sealed since the Christian community will likely end up fragmenting over who to vote for when practical considerations and implications become real.

Remember, the Christian community acting alone will rarely ensure a candidate or a good piece of legislation will be successful. The common public must also be convinced to lend their support to accomplish what needs to be done. That being said, outspoken principlists tend to alienate the public while pragmatists tend to enlist their support.[238]

### *Can There be Common Ground?*

The entire point of this chapter has been to show one significant source of divisiveness and frustration in the Christian community when public policy, legislation, candidates and voting are at stake. By understanding each other's strengths and weaknesses there's hope that some level of respect can be maintained and that creative ways to assist and support each other for the greater good will result.

But what would cooperative engagement look like when agreement can't be reached?

In a recent statewide initiative, I took what I considered a biblical stance on whether it had merit or not, and came down rejecting it. A dear brother hosted

---

[238]   It's a sad commentary on the state of politics in our nation that the open use of biblical truths is thought by many to be illegally bringing religion into purely governmental affairs; or worse yet, trying to promote an unbiblical theocracy.

a panel presentation for their mega-church on all the ballot propositions that November and invited me to present my position and reasoning on each one. It turned out he was passionately on the opposite side for this one issue. The format of the evening allowed me to make my arguments, then he made his, then it was opened up for the membership to ask questions and make comments.[239] Throughout the "debate" there was obvious respect between us, and respect for the audience and their concerns about how they should vote. This small example illustrated that sincere believers could differ on an important decision, and yet continue to minister together. Would it have been better to be in agreement and not split the vote – yes it would. But given that wasn't going to happen for this one item, it was much more fruitful and instructive to demonstrate Christian brotherly love and continued ministry together than to try to win the battle at all costs, or worse yet end up antagonizing each other.[240]

Another point to remember is that we do great harm to a brother or sister in the Lord when we impugn motives just because we don't agree with a particular choice of candidate or public policy. In working with each other we need to constantly remember that we share eternity together if our faith and trust is centered in the Lord and Savior Jesus Christ. In a very real sense we have infinitely more in common through Christ than we'll ever have in the political realm.

Should we ever give up on someone because on a particular matter we just can't seem to agree on? Obviously not!

God doesn't do that with us when we sin, shouldn't we model the same mercy and grace toward each other every opportunity we have? Resenting someone else, speaking ill of them because they didn't agree with us, harboring bitterness because they're too narrow in their conviction, or too accommodating

---

239   "As iron sharpens iron, and one man sharpens another." Proverbs 27:17

240   That particular election (November 2010), there were nine statewide propositions on the ballot. Of those nine, we agreed on eight.

in their approach serves only to divide the Body of Christ. As I've had to remind myself as well as so many others; once a battle is over there'll be plenty more to face in the future. The sooner we can practice 1 Corinthians 13 and strive to always speak well of each other, the better our example will be to the world.

Scripture says we're to be wise as serpents and gentle as doves (Matthew 10:16). The tactics the world uses are often effective, not because they're always unprincipled, but because often times there's a worldly wisdom that understands a debased human nature and how to use it to advantage. We shouldn't be afraid to be clever and creative[241] in fighting political battles while making use of the spiritual weapons at our disposal (2 Corinthians 10:3-6). Even the Israelites used a form of military deception when fighting its enemies, but they didn't conduct war in a way that conflicted with clear scriptural teaching (Joshua 8:1-22; Judges 7:2-23). Obviously we can make use of information, wisdom, insights, experience, and resourcefulness, but we need to be careful that our approach doesn't use ungodly means or resources in ways that would compromise our testimony of faith and defense of righteousness (2 Corinthians 6:14-15). To ensure that doesn't happen, our activities must continually be measured against God's standard and not the standard of winning at all costs.

Obviously, both the principlist and pragmatist are operating on principles in which they believe. Both are probably striving for the same Christ-honoring goal. But because people think differently we all need to strive to creatively work together constructively and not destructively. This takes time and effort, as well as a humble heart that is willing to adapt to circumstances without creating a conscience issue for ourselves.

So how can this happen when candidates can't be agreed upon or there are competing approaches to a morally good legislative goal?

First and foremost, recognize that "compromise" doesn't have to be a dirty word. The nature of politics is that cooperation implies the absence of one

---

[241]  Maybe even a bit cunning at times

side getting everything it wants and the other side giving up. Wisdom seems to imply that for candidates the most effective approach, the one that has the highest opportunity to succeed, is supporting the one that's <u>closest</u> to our most important values and also is the <u>most</u> electable. The "perfect" candidate that's unelectable will only end in discouragement, while the highly electable one that doesn't share our worldview will be a continual offense to our values. Balancing these two factors is recognition that there's a larger community that needs to be recruited to our cause and without them even worse results will continue to occur.

The same principle applies to proposed legislation, where the "perfect" may need to give way to reality in settling for something less for now, but maintaining the principles in play to guide the next steps taken.

As already mentioned, our ultimate political weapons are not of this world, they're powerful because they emanate from an almighty God (2 Corinthians 10:3-5). We have prayer (1 Thessalonians 5:17), we have God's absolute authority – His Word (2 Timothy 3:16-17), we have the leading and illumination of the Holy Spirit (John 14:15-16), and we have each other (John 13:34-35). The battle is the Lord's, and we're His foot soldiers. May we continually strive to obey His leading and not be captives of hearts filled with pride or resentment for not getting our way.

# Part 3

# Fratricide Between Believers and the World

# Chapter 13

# Dealing with Battleground Political Issues

*"We contend that for a nation [or for that matter a state] to try to tax itself into prosperity is like a man standing in a bucket and trying to lift himself up by the handle."* - **Winston Churchill**

*"The budget should be balanced, the Treasury should be refilled, public debt should be reduced, the arrogance of officialdom should be tempered and controlled, and the assistance to foreign lands should be curtailed lest Rome become bankrupt. People must again learn to work, instead of living on public assistance."* - **Marcus Tullius Cicero**

### The Need for Clarity

Ecclesiastes 12:12 says "Of making many books there is no end". This can also be said of the number of issues our nation faces. Every year there's new crises that skillful politicians manipulate to their own advantage, while old ones languish for want of attention.[242] Modernity is seen as so different from the past that only new and unusual insights will save the day. But while political churn continues, more good people are becoming frustrated trying to force government to take care of business. Unfortunately, there're too few talented political leaders (or informed citizens) able to work through an issues' subtleties, complexities, and organized opposition to implement godly decisions.

One of the tactics effectively employed by the political left is obfuscating an issue so much that basic fundamental principles and wisdom are either ignored or denigrated as "old-school" thinking and no longer germane. In reality the truth of the matter is again expressed in Ecclesiastes: "Is there a thing of which it is said, 'See, this is new?' It has been already in the ages before us" (Ecclesiastes 1:10).

The Creator of the universe knows his creatures and what we need. He's also given us his eternal truths in written form (Psalm 19:7; Proverbs 30:5; 2 Timothy 3:16-17). The Bible hasn't only stood the test of time, it's as relevant today just as it was long ago (Matthew 5:18-19). Does that mean wisdom in practical application isn't needed – of course not! But it does mean the Bible should be studied just as methodically as anything else, yet remain the final moral arbiter when values are involved; and all of politics revolves around values.

So how should Christians approach the giant problems of the day?

The same way they'd approach any problem: pray for wisdom (James 1:5); define the fundamental issues at stake (Proverbs 25:2); and build principle upon principle to arrive at an answer (Ecclesiastes 7:27). The specific circumstances may be difficult to account for, and Scripture may not directly address the problem at hand, but there will always be scriptural truth that can be applied.[243]

---

242  Rahm Emanuel as chief of staff for President-elect Obama in 2008 famously said "You never let a serious crises go to waste. And what I mean by that is an opportunity to do things you think you could not do before".

243  For years I have evaluated every Statewide California Proposition (and many local measures) from a biblical perspective to determine if they were worthy to be voted for or not. Sometimes

## What Issues Are We Talking About?

As mentioned earlier, there's no end to the number and variety of problems that face our complicated national, state and local political sphere. Given that any listing will only be a sampling, the following presents some of the more consequential problems we all face and which are ripe for the application of a biblical perspective.

| Selected Political Issues for Biblical Study | | |
|---|---|---|
| Abortion Rights | Support of Israel | Physician-Assisted Suicide |
| Homosexuality | Gun Control | Hate Crimes |
| Same-Sex-Marriage | Government Run Schools | Embryonic Stem Cells |
| Infanticide | Parental Rights | Parental Rights |
| Euthanasia | Deficit Spending | Home Schooling |
| Cloning | Illegal Immigration | States Rights |
| Genetic Engineering | Tort Reform | Jury Nullification |
| Just Wars | Environmental Stewardship | Global Warming |
| Animal Rights | Capitalism | Entitlement Programs |
| Homeless | No Fault Divorce | Women in Combat |
| Gender Identity | Gambling | Church 501(c)3 Status |
| Slavery & Reparations | Capital Punishment | Creation and Evolution |
| Multi-Culturalism | National Health Care | National Defense |
| Racism | Racial & Ethnic Profiling | National Identification |
| Border Control | Voter Identification | Near-Death Experience |
| Prayer in Schools | City Council Invocations | Global War on Terror |
| Women in Politics | Labor Unions | Hate Speech |
| Medical Ethics | Term Limits | Death Tax |
| United Nations | Palestine | Too Big to Fail |
| Domestic Spying | Spanking | Decriminalizing Drug Use |
| Space Exploration | United Nations | Endangered Species |

the analysis was difficult, but in every case biblical insights could be applied to guide a voter's decision.

## *Dealing With Political Issues Within the Christian Community*

The local church is a powerful gift from the Lord. Not only does it have gifted preachers and teachers, there's always a variety of gifted members available to ensure the church fulfills its purposes as a New Testament church (1 Peter 2:9-10; 1 Corinthians 12:4-7). This is why the local church is the best place to study emotional and divisive issues in the world that impact our lives, our families, and eventually our witness to the world.

The reasons why Christians are often fragmented and even argumentative over political concerns have been outlined in other chapters. Suffice to say that without a humble, teachable heart, proper tools to study the Scriptures, and mature leadership to equip and hold accountable, it's no wonder personal opinions tend be our guide instead of truth. Sunday School classes, home fellowship groups, small groups, lecture series and preaching series are all opportunities to educate, inform and equip members with a proper understanding of current issues. When church leadership is either intimately involved in leading or guiding these studies it not only gives credibility to their importance, but also to the need for unity as far as it's possible (Romans 12:18; 14:1).

The following checklist contains a few simple steps to help structure any study of public concerns from a biblical perspective. In fact, when evaluating work done by others (either from inside or outside the church) this list can help determine how much confidence to place in the results.

## *Contemporary Issues Study Checklist*

*First*: Define the issue to be studied as clearly and succinctly as possible. This sounds easy, but topics like gun control or evolution have many facets that could lead to never-ending rabbit trails instead of focusing on the fundamental issue(s) that lays a foundation for everything that follows. Using the gun control example a reasonable starting point would be the question: "Should all guns be outlawed?"

**Second**: Write down the questions you have concerning the topic. There are always questions that come up in conversations or in our own thinking that we've wondered about. In fact, if you have a question, most other people have had the same one at one time or another. Continuing with the gun control example, one leading question would be: "Are guns intrinsically evil?"

**Third**: Identify and study relevant passages of Scripture. Using key words or related terms to identify relevant Scriptures is always fruitful. But many times the technical terms we use today are not found in the Bible. To find Scriptures that provide insight into gun control consider: different weapons that were used in biblical accounts (e.g. swords; stones; tent peg; sling; etc.); examples of home defense (fleeing; fighting; hiding; etc.); reasons for warfare (self-defense, hatred; etc.); insights about soldiers; clear prohibitions concerning harm to others; the role of murderous hearts; the role of government (Romans 13:4); and arming ourselves (spiritually and physically).

**Fourth**: Summarize general principles that are consistent with God's Word. Studying passages that relate to the issue at hand will give insights to generalized statements of principles. These may include: heart issues; justice matters; Old Testament commands and New Testament insights; and even spiritual analogies like the sword of the Spirit (Ephesians 6:17), or the armor of God (Ephesians 6:10-20), or the specific weapons we are to use or shun (1 Corinthians 10:3-5).

**Fifth**: Find trusted sources that addressed the topic from a biblical perspective. With modern access to search tools on the Internet the opinions and research of countless others is at our fingertips. Unfortunately, many times it's like mining low-grade ore.[244] The same is true of published articles, books and even advocacy groups. That's why at this point it's important that you've done some of your own study beforehand so that you can be discerning with what you find from others. Much that's claimed to be written from a biblical viewpoint will turn out to be very selective in approach and hence questionable in results.[245]

***Sixth***: Compare your conclusions with those arrived at by others. When comparing conclusions it's important to understand how others came to theirs if they differ from yours.[246] It's also important to know whether the source is considered credible in the Christian community so the amount of confidence placed in the material is justified. Non-Christian sources can also be very helpful in identifying inconsistencies or giving a reasoned approach that either has merit or needs to be countered. It's also not unusual to find that some conclusions have to be refined or stated more accurately as a result of this step.

***Seventh***: If necessary, consult with experts for specialized information. It's rare that a church has direct access to specialized knowledge required to better understand not just particular technology but also the ethical implications of technology use. Recombinant DNA is not a common topic of discussion around the dinner table, yet the specifics about what it is and how it's being implemented are critical when trying to apply biblical truth (e.g. Genesis 1:21, 24). For the gun control example, it may mean finding experts that can define terms accurately (like what an "assault" weapon is) or what our legal rights

---

[244]  In other words; looking through a lot of useless "stuff" in order to find the little bit that's truly precious.

[245]  For the example of gun control, many use Jesus' words in Matthew 26:52, John 18:11 and Matthew 5:38-42 to draw the conclusion Jesus was against any weapons being used at any time. However, Luke 22:36 provides some balance.

[246]  This is particularly true when statistical analysis is involved, since data selection and how it is processed will drive the results. The same is true for polling results: how the question is framed will have a huge impact on how people will respond to it.

are when constitutional factors come up. Any number of issues could result in consulting with other fellowships that may have the needed expertise, or Christ-honoring organizations that specialize in niche areas.

**Eighth:** The need for an audience. Studying, reading, and researching are all important. But until a subject of broad and volatile interest is taught it won't be clear if it's been covered adequately to equip members to take action. The give and take within a classroom setting or home fellowship group is where real understanding and refinement happens. This will also provide an opportunity to address urban legends[247], emotional arguments and anecdotal information that cannot be supported by scripture, reasoning or even data.

**Ninth**: Identify specific actions that can be taken to make a difference. These could be anything from documenting the study results and posting on the church web-site, contacting other churches to see if they've any use for the information; conducting lecture series with other churches or the community on the topic at hand; and even identifying concerns that could be communicated to elected officials. In many cases the results of these studies can provide articulate arguments, substantiated by real-life examples and thorough statistical analysis to inform salt-and-light groups, public policy groups and even elected officials and their staffs.

### Dealing with Political Issues Outside the Christian community

It's one thing to face friendly fire within a church community, it's quite a different situation when working with the outside world on volatile issues.

---

[247]    There are a number of good web-sites available to verify whether a news item or some other "factoid" is based on fact or fiction. Unfortunately, no matter how widespread and useful some of these sites are, there's no guarantee they have no agenda on subjects that are emotional for them. Another factor to consider is whether the information we pass along would fall into the category of "gossip" or not.

Serving on community planning boards, advising secular groups on which local policy issues need to be confronted and how to go about it, writing to elected officials to convey concerns about a current hot topic, serving on a local school advisory board, working on a government official's staff, or just talking to neighbors and co-workers all provide opportunities to influence others for the common good.

Just like within the church, it's important to see a problem from many perspectives, yet understand the core biblical principles that provide the starting point. The problem we often have is an inability to articulate concerns in a persuasive way that's heard. Many times Christians have a tendency to trivialize an issue and give one-liner responses as if that will be enough to convince someone to change their minds. That may happen, but the odds are against it. In fact, the more that approach is taken the less credibility we'll have to be a trusted advisor in more serious matters that relate to spiritual concerns.

Christians who live in a bubble can also run into the same problem encountered in evangelism; using "Christian" terms and phrases that become a turn off because they're not understood by the wider public, not used in the same way by the world, or already have negative connotations attached to them.

To gain personal credibility with others by talking to the issues of the day with non-believers is a noble ministry that will serve the gospel well. The question is: how to do that? Like anything else in life, to do it well takes effort and thought. The following is a short self-evaluation check-list to help develop credibility with others and be able to bring them around to values that God has given for everyone's good and His glory. The intent is not to discourage, but to help equip so a person is heard by a skeptical world and at least respected for thinking an issue through even if they do not become totally convinced (1 Timothy 3:7).

## Self-Evaluation Checklist

**First:** What do you know about the topic at hand; how well informed are you? Are you only taking the talking points heard on talk radio as your position or have you done at least a little research or reading to understand some background, the major flash points, and the potential consequences?

**Second:** Do you have any relevant facts that apply from authoritative sources? Anecdotal information is very common, but counterproductive with those who are pre-disposed against our convictions. In reality it doesn't take a lot of time to find a few well established facts that support our views instead of relying on hearsay, unbelievable data that sounds too good to be true, or unsubstantiated stories.[248]

**Third:** Can you summarize the other sides' argument accurately? This is like walking in someone else's shoes. Spending time understanding key positions of opponents and what they're based on allows two things: focusing on what you need a position on; and showing the other person you're thoughtful enough to understand their position. Something they may not have ever tried toward you.

**Fourth:** Can you accept the other person may be motivated by noble reasons? God's common grace (Matthew 5:45; Luke 6:32-34) allows many people to have a sincere concern to do what's right. They also have a conscience (Romans 2:14-15). So it's not surprising when they think they're doing what's right even though it's based on wrong assumptions and an incorrect worldview.

---

[248] I've made it a personal goal to not forward anything I receive that cannot be authoritatively sourced to allow verification. When we send out false stories, inaccurate statistics, and urban legends as if they're true our personal credibility is on the line. I'm particularly leery of e-mails that challenge a person's commitment to the Lord if they don't forward to everyone they know. More often than not, these commitment tests demonstrate laziness and not discernment.

Acknowledging instead of challenging their motives may go a long way to winning them over.

*Fifth:* Do you know the emotional arguments of both sides and their limitations? It's easy to resort to accusations concerning a person's true motives, or use heart-wrenching personal examples to try to shut down any debate. But Christians of all people know the sinfulness of the human heart and shouldn't be surprised by examples of depravity and its devastating consequences. Acknowledging the effects of sin is one thing, but allowing their use to distract from the core problem needs to be avoided.

*Sixth:* Can you articulate the biblical principles that apply? This is where an understanding of a biblical worldview and relevant passages of Scripture comes into play. The use of Scripture in a manner that's heard, or better yet well received by others takes maturity and practice.[249]

*Seven:* Can you detect any false logic or inconsistent reasoning being used? If a person is allowed to talk long enough there'll be a point where they'll begin to contradict themselves (James 1:19). This is because most people do not have a consistent worldview since they've not taken the time to think it thoroughly through and consider the implications on many of the important issues of the day. Typically, people will pick and choose what they feel comfortable with instead of going back to basics to understand the fundamental principles at stake (Acts 17:18-21).

*Eighth:* Is there a common goal on both sides? Most people become pretty good at recognizing a problem, however, the difficulty is identifying the true

---

[249] I've often used the Book of Proverbs in discussions with non-believers about political matters. It gives insights that most people will be warm to and subtly allows the authority of Scripture to not be so alien to the hearers.

cause of the problem. Without a biblical worldview the underlying reasons will be very difficult to correctly identify, much less correct. But if the end result, or goal, of political action can be understood and agreed to there's a possibility that some real progress can be made (see next case).

*Ninth:* If there's a common goal, are there creative ways to work together? In essence, this is the heart of politics – identifying common problems and working together to provide solutions on which both sides can agree. Ultimately, most of our nation's difficulties are the result of the sinful nature of man. No real solutions will ever exist without a changed heart; however, God's imperative for us to be salt and light to the world implies that the common good and our own benefit are served by standing for righteousness and diligently being a blessing to those around us. That includes working with others in a Christ-honoring and knowledgeable way. The alternative is to be confrontational and create even stronger enemies that will demonize truth at every opportunity and make the gospel difficult to ever be shared.

### Final thoughts

This may seem like an overwhelming demand on our time and energies to be adequately equipped to impact the political (and community) issues we all face. But how much time do we invest in hobbies, watching TV, playing Candy Crush or using social media to keep in touch with hundreds of our closest friends?

It's important we take the time to re-claim the importance of a church environment to grapple with political concerns and the role of government from God's perspective. Whenever this is done, it's not surprising that many Scripture verses, clear principles and godly biblical examples of faith start to become the common "go to" truth to influence contemporary issues of the day.

This is true in marriage counseling, personal finances, and every other facet of our lives – God's Truth applies to all of life. Why would we not expect the same result for so-called political matters? This not only demonstrates the wonderful coherence of the Bible but also its timeless and unique ability to shed light on man's troubles – whether political or personal.

Secondly, the Self-Evaluation Check-list above is intended to give awareness of unnecessary stumbling blocks that prevent us from being effective in working with the unbelieving world. These types of skills can be taught, but they'll be honed and matured when applied to a hostile audience and after absorbing the lessons learned that come from experience. Unfortunately, for many reasons the Christian community seems to have lost how to be winsome in our role of being a conscience to and a good steward of this nation, and as a result don't engage with those that need to be offered a different and truer perspective.

In becoming pro-active, we can have confidence from Scripture that God's Word will not come back void (Isaiah 55:10-11). While in this life we're God's means to proclaim His complete Word to this dying world. This mandate isn't just for the world's sake, it's for our nation's sake, our own sake, and ultimately for the sake of the gospel.

# Chapter 14

# Using The Bible Against Us

*"There are some things in them that are hard to understand, which the ignorant and unstable twist to their own destruction, as they do the other Scriptures"*
*– 2 Peter 3:16*

*"A text without a context is a pretext"*
*– Dr. Donald Carson (quoting his minister father)*

### Bumper-Sticker Theology

Have you ever had someone give an argument that sounded authoritative, even biblical, in order to prove a point but on closer examination something just didn't seem right? In the world of politics there's a lot of fractured biblical wisdom that well-meaning people use to support positions on emotional issues. Many times it's a portion of scriptural truth combined with a fragment of worldly wisdom that makes sense at some level, but won't stand up under closer biblical scrutiny. The following are just a few I've heard over the years:[250]

---

[250]  We can all add to this list. The point is that catch phrases that serve to justify some stance or belief can be repeated so often that they become modern-day Proverbs with just as much

- "Jesus never called anyone a sinner"
- "Sodom and Gomorrah were destroyed because they didn't practice hospitality."
- "God made me this way, how could He hate me for it?"
- "Obey government unless it clearly demands us to disobey a biblical command"
- "God helps those who help themselves"
- "Have enough faith in God and he'll perform a miracle in the coming election"
- "This is a Christian nation, and we need to reclaim it"
- "Jesus wouldn't vote for that"
- "That's a political issue, not a biblical issue"

The use of the Bible as a weapon has roots going back to Eve being deceived by the serpent when he twisted, then added to God's Word (Genesis 3:1). The same tactic is used today to confuse and intimidate sincere believers who are ill equipped to counter noble-sounding arguments that are only meant to destroy and not illuminate. Like Satan, modern-day protagonists are tacitly using the authority of Scripture but denying its authoritative power.

Interestingly, of the two major spiritual and political battles of the last generation, only homosexual advocates have methodically and boldly used Scripture to justify their perversion. Abortion promoters and apologists, on the other hand, have never been able to produce a convincing argument from Scripture that a mother is justified in destroying the life God has entrusted to her protection. Clearly, however, some similar tactics are used by both to justify their causes, such as: false research; emotional arguments; imaginary legal rights; denial of obvious biological truths; personal attacks; demonizing

---

authority. If not corrected, eventually they become self-evident truths to the unwary and those who are tender towards biblical truths but ignorant of them.

of opponents; and the trivializing or outright denying of the consequences of sinful decisions and behaviors.

The uniquely aggressive characteristics of the activist homosexual community drive it to eradicate any and all moral opposition by any means possible. And since biblical authority is the strongest opponent they face, twisting of Scripture has become a major tactic in their arsenal to force acceptance of their aberrant behavior.

As the unbelieving world becomes more adept at using our historical tools against us a large portion of the believing community is now finding itself unable or unwilling to defend truth. In fact, many weak Christians found themselves buying into these false arguments and ending up rejecting scriptural authority. Not only is this a sad commentary about the level of ignorance among many believers, but it also speaks to the lack of engagement by pastoral leadership in equipping their flocks to publically defend truth and not be intimidated into silence.

Even further, by allowing the political environment to frame the issue in ways supportive of "gay rights" the legal basis is being established to eventually silence virtually any statement or action that's in opposition, whether by the public or from the pulpit[251]. For that reason, it's instructive to look at a few of the most common abuses of the use of the Bible against Christians, particularly since the same tactics will eventually be used in future moral conflict.

From my viewpoint, there's at least five ways Scripture is wrongly applied to the issue of homosexuality.[252]

---

[251] Although this may sound farfetched, all someone needs to do is see the extent of government actions in Europe and Canada (and even in states where same-sex marriage is legal) to punish businesses and even religious organizations that reject the legitimacy of homosexuality and accept the biblical truth that homosexuality is sinful.

[252] An excellent treatment of this subject is a little known book entitled "Triumph of the Mockers – The Confessions of a Gay Rights Activist" by F. Connor Cason. It recounts the tactics developed by homosexual activists to change the wider culture's view of homosexuality as well as the blatant "re-interpretation" of Scripture to provide a plausible biblical cover for the sin.

### *Jesus Never Condemned Homosexuality*

*First,* claiming that homosexuality is never condemned in Scripture is demonstrably a lie. The entire Bible is God's Word, not just the passages about loving our neighbor (Matthew 22:39) or our enemy (Luke 6:35), as if this meant that all other passages of Scripture are trumped and hence null and void. Homosexuality is clearly described (Leviticus 18:22, 24-25; Romans 1:24-27; 1 Corinthians 6:9) and consistently condemned (Romans 1:18-32; Genesis 19; 1 Timothy 1:9-10, etc.). In fact, this particular sin is mentioned in such descriptive terms that there's no confusion as to the intent of the writer. Conversely, there are no passages anywhere in the Bible that speak well of homosexuality, or even come close to accepting the behavior for other than what it is – sin, and an affront to God.

A classic example of trivializing truth is when President-elect Obama said homosexuality is only addressed in "an obscure passage in Romans". His dismissive attitude not only demonstrated an ignorance of the Bible, but also a willingness to misrepresent God's Word for political ambition. In one short statement the occupier of the highest office in the land invoked biblical authority, gave the impression he's something of a scholar concerning its content, then dismissed any truth that relates to the question at hand. Unfortunately, because so few people have studied the Bible carefully, and have heard many times that the Bible only condemns lust and not homosexual acts; the president's statement helped to further divide the Christian community and embolden gay-rights activists.

The principle that must not be lost in this example is that the entire counsel of God's Word must be looked at to understand important moral issues. Using only selected verses, then using a novel interpretation that flies in the face of traditional scholarship and a clear reading of the text should be questioned quickly, clearly and firmly. To use Scripture as authority, then to place oneself as the authority over that Scripture is presumptuous at best, and wicked at worst.

As far as Jesus never personally condemning homosexuality, all of God's Word is explicitly equated to, and one with the person of Christ himself (John 1:1). The authoritative parts aren't just those in red letters in the gospels[253]. All of Scripture is authoritative and given to us by our Lord (John 16:12-15). The fact that Christ is never quoted as condemning homosexuality, the same goes for pedophilia, bestiality and human trafficking – it doesn't mean those vile sins are then somehow acceptable.

### All Old Testament Laws are Equivalent

*Second*, it's in vogue to quote Old Testament laws whose violation demands the death penalty (e.g. stoning a rebellious son, stoning anyone that curses his father or mother or works on the Sabbath; describing certain activities during menstruation as an abomination),[254] and lumping them with the Old Testament scriptural punishment for homosexuality. Doing so attempts to trivialize and mock any seriousness concerning sexual behavior. What's ignored, however, is that Old Testament Israel was a true theocracy – the LORD actually dwelled and ruled in their midst.

God's physical presence with the Israelites demanded holiness in all aspects of Jewish life, as well as distinctive practices to separate them from the rest of the world. Ungodliness and sinfulness could not be tolerated in the presence of a mighty, holy, pure and just God. With the coming of Christ and the new covenant a theocracy is no longer needed, God dwells in his people individually

---

253    And for purists, Jesus' words are also quoted in the Book of Acts; 1st and 2nd Corinthians; and the Book of Revelation.

254    See Deuteronomy 21:18-21; Leviticus 20:9; Exodus 31:15; Leviticus 18:22,24-26

(2 Corinthians 6:16; Ephesians 1:13-14), and God's people are distinctive by how they treat each other and the world (John 13:35; Matthew 5:44; 22:39).

Our future dwelling place will be with God in heaven, and at that time we'll be clothed with the righteousness of Christ, and not dependent upon earthly obedience to a code of conduct. Until then, however, in this world the moral code and the condemnation of sexual depravity and perversion have never changed and have been consistent throughout the Bible, both in the Old and New Testaments. The perversion of the natural and normal sexual function and desire that is intended for heterosexuals in a loving marriage commitment is an affront on the God-created design for mankind. The very picture of sexual sin in the form of adultery, prostitution and homosexuality is a deviation from God's design and cannot receive God's blessing. Though the punishment for sin is different in the New Testament since there's no physical, holy theocracy in existence, the ultimate punishment for unforgiven sin is the same – eternal death (Romans 3:23; 6:23).

### God Has Changed

*Third*, the same mentality and worldview that has encouraged activist judges to re-interpret the Constitution to mean anything they think it should is the same mentality used by people who believe God changes. His Word is believed to be fungible, with Scripture conveniently stretched to justify anything if it's looked at with modern, insightful eyes and a compassionate heart, while over-looking what are claimed to be "culturally prejudiced" verses that are deemed to no longer apply. A classic example is focusing on the love nature of God (1 John 4:8) while overlooking God's righteous standard concerning sexual purity and personal accountability (1 Corinthians 6:8, 18; Galatians 5:19; Colossians 5:6; 1 Peter 4:3-5).

A specific example is the common liberal belief that Sodom and Gomorrah were destroyed because of a lack of hospitality and not the obvious sexual perversion that the text so clearly recounts. This rationalizing carries over into the New Testament book of Romans where Paul's vivid description of homosexuality (and lesbianism) is claimed to be only condemnation of lustful sexual exploits, not homosexual acts between two committed people who love each other (Romans 1:28-32). In effect, the harsh, judgmental God of the Old Testament who will destroy cities for slight misdeeds is not the same loving God of the New Testament, who is willing to overlook sin because He loves everyone.

This type of progressive reinterpretation is not new and has destroyed many lives over the millennia as any number of sins are justified by a deceived heart willing to believe the lie and any alternative explanation, no matter how remote, in order to justify a personal or a loved one's sinful behavior.

Biblically, however, God's holy and righteous nature has never changed and never will change (Malachi 3:6; Hebrews 13:8; Revelation 22:13). His Word and righteous standard also remains the same, even until heaven and earth pass away (Matthew 5:17-20).

### *What Would Jesus Do?*

*Fourth*, many are fond of using the "What would Jesus do?" question. The implication is that since Jesus was gentle, loving, and kind, he would never condemn those who were in a loving, meaningful relationship since that's what God wants for everyone. In addition, since same-sex attraction is a natural condition, it must be a gift from God that is to be enjoyed and not condemned.

Clearly it's a little presumptuous to speak for Jesus, particularly when one's life is in open rebellion to God's Word. In fact, since Christ himself is the Word incarnate (John 1:1, 14), and the entire Bible is God's revelation to us, Jesus has already spoken on the issue of homosexuality in numerous places – both in the Old and New Testament.

Context, literary genre, and consistent interpretive hermeneutical principles are the keys to understanding the direct and clear statements of Scripture. The entire Bible is easily understandable in what is says; the problem arises when someone doesn't agree with what is being said. Interpreting it in false and tortured ways to justify sin, and at the same time ignore other relevant passages reveals a self-deceived heart that needs to be called out for what it is – arrogant and self-righteous.

The application of the WWJD question is subtle in one respect; it implies that the question under consideration is a situation that didn't exist in Jesus' time or experience. The clearly intended result is to condition the answer on Jesus' known character and loving heart, not on God's righteous standard that demands justice and punishment for sin. For all intents and purposes, the loving nature of Christ is emphasized without regard to the fact that He will return in glory to judge the living and the dead (2 Timothy 4:1).

If the New Testament Pharisees, teachers of the law, scribes and even the disciples couldn't predict what Jesus was going to say or do at any given time, and they spent years watching and learning from him, how could anyone say with certainty today what He would say on moral matters beyond what He's already clearly revealed in His Word?

Using a hypothetical Jesus as a tactic to win an argument or promote misplaced passion and acceptance of unacceptable sin is just what it sounds like – manipulation and false testimony. We're to look to Jesus as the source of truth to understand the depths of our sin and our desperate need for a Savior, not as a tool to work on someone's sympathies to overlook what Scripture clearly and firmly condemns.

## *God Made Us the Way We Are*

*Fifth*, the abuse of God's truth in claiming He created homosexuals the way they are. Scripture itself repudiates this (1 Corinthians 6:9-11)[255], showing they can repent, turn from a life of sin and be received into the Kingdom of God through the saving work of Jesus Christ. This is just as true for murders, thieves, slanderers and others. But it doesn't stop there. The Scripture is clear that those who turn to Christ are regenerated, sanctified and new creatures with a new nature that's no longer in bondage to these sins.

The only conclusion that can be drawn from these verses is that either the Scripture is wrong (God made a mistake or is a liar), or His Word is true and homosexuality can be overcome through the power of the Holy Spirit in a person's life. In addition, 1 Corinthians 10:13 gives assurance that God is faithful and will not let His sheep be tempted beyond their ability, but will either provide a way of escape or the strength to endure it.

One final note is important to make. Homosexual sin is no worse than any other before an almighty, holy God, but it does carry with it incredible implications relating to its destructiveness to the person and its impact on other people as Romans 1:24-27 so clearly describes.

## *The Bible is for Those That Need a Crutch*

There's one remaining way that the Bible is used against us, and it's a common tactic to be expected from the unregenerate in the world. They claim that the Bible provides some moral teaching that's useful for those that need

---

[255]    These are such key verses that they are included here: "Do you not know that the unrighteous will not inherit the kingdom of God? Do not be deceived: neither the sexually immoral, nor idolaters, nor adulterers, nor men who practice homosexuality, nor thieves, nor the greedy, nor drunkards, nor revilers, nor swindlers will inherit the kingdom of God. <u>And such were some of you</u>. But you were washed, you were sanctified, you were justified in the name of the lord Jesus Christ and by the Spirit of our God" (1 Corinthians 6:9-11) (Emphasis added)

a crutch, or have to have simple guidelines to live their lives by, but that it is obviously for those who are uneducated, unsophisticated, and incapable of attaining any position of rationale prominence. In effect, if you believe the Bible, you're the equivalent of a weak, uneducated, intolerant simpleton who could just as easily be worshipping crystals or lightening.

This turns out to be more powerful of a tactic than we care to admit. It drives many Christians to try to rely upon facts and reasoning to carry the day in convincing others of the merit of our values and principles to govern life and government, instead of standing openly and winsomely for the truths God has entrusted into our care.

Nobody likes to be marginalized or laughed at, but the world has, and will continue to do so; if not to our faces, then definitely behind our backs. If we think we can win friends and support by appeasing their views of us, then we've compromised ourselves to the point of being ineffective. God's Word is clear, He wants us to stand for truth, be faithful to do so, and not to be self conscience about what the world thinks of us (1 Corinthians 1:26-29).

As Christians we need to rightly divide the Word of truth. Coming to Scripture with our mind made up about what we want to find there will only result in foolish and stupid arguments (2 Timothy 2:23-24). Remember this as we continue to contend for the truth, loving those who are lost, and condemning unjustified manipulation of God's perfect and timeless Word.

We can't have it both ways. To tear down the authority and clear teaching of the Bible on the one hand, then use it in a twisted manner as an authoritative source to bolster acceptance of sin (Matthew 4:1-11; Genesis 3:1) is arrogant, hypocritical and destructive. Scripture warns against such people – whether clergy or laity – and we're not to be lead astray by them (2 Peter 3:14-18).

For all the good intentions Christians may have to exhibit compassion on the lost, and to do what seems right in the public arena, it's God's absolute truth that must be turned to as the standard to guide and undergird our understanding. We are not authorized to artificially extent God's Word to areas it does not address, in effect going beyond what has been written (1 Corinthians 4:6). That is a dangerous temptation. It's also tempting to minimize and ignore clear biblical truth concerning moral matters, which only feeds itching ears and fuels divisiveness and disunity among God's people.

# Chapter 15

# Practical Steps

*"Or what king, going out to encounter another king in war, will not sit down first and deliberate whether he is able to with ten thousand to meet him who comes against him with twenty thousand?"* – **Luke 14:31**

*"Unless the LORD builds the house, those who build it labor in vain."* – **Psalm 127:1**

*Leverage Your Church's Strengths*

It's one thing to be concerned about the moral free fall our nation is experiencing, or the growing public hostility toward Christianity, but it's quite another to take active steps to make a difference without creating enemies within your own church.

We all have a duty to be godly citizens, to be good neighbors, to work hard and to respect and pray for the authority God has placed over us. We also have a clear biblical mandate to labor in the political realm for the common good (Jeremiah 29:4-7), to be salt and light (Matthew 5:13-16), and to share the gospel (Matthew 28:19-20). While all of these duties and privileges apply individually, I believe the Lord has gifted each church with the needed talent and understanding (2 Timothy 3:16-17) to equip us in our corporate political outreach. But for many reasons, most churches shy away from anything that smacks of being political and have all but ignored how to hold our government and our elected leaders accountable.[256]

To reclaim our moral imperative to be counselors to the nation and to uphold God's righteous moral standard throughout our nation for God's glory and the sake of the gospel, we need to begin in our own fellowships and leverage what God has already provided.

If your pastor has become convinced there's a citizenship role to be nurtured and he's willing to consider the creation of a citizenship ministry – your job is to help him where ever you can. If there's nothing even related to this type of ministry the following steps should be helpful to begin formalizing one. However, there are a few key warnings that need to be prayerfully considered.

First, every church is different.[257] You may know of other churches that have a significant political engagement and want to follow that pattern in your fellowship. Be careful, though, as each church has its own uniqueness, leadership personality, and understanding of their purpose to exist. Most churches also reflect the strengths of their pastoral leadership. If the primacy is preaching and teaching (word ministries) and the creation of other teaching ministries, then outreach-oriented ministries may not be as easy to form.

If its strength is primarily community oriented with mercy, compassion, and evangelism (deed ministries) then lengthy Bible preaching series and deep theological study on the issues of the day may be uncomfortable. No church can do everything, but all churches have both members and the necessary gifted

---

[256]    The entire first section of this book outlines why this is the case.

[257]    Differences can be in doctrine, ecclesiology, eschatology, philosophy of ministry, demographics, size, financial resources, or any number of other factors. It the Bible is your authority then you have a mandate to create citizenship types of ministries in balance with other ministries and scaled to the resources available.

teachers to equip them for every good work – and this includes influencing the political realm (2 Timothy 3:16-17).

Second, whatever you do, be submissive to pastoral authority. They're focus is to shepherd and care for you. You're not to be a burden for them, or to create division or unnecessary controversy in your church.[258] Instead, you're to help them grapple with what would be appropriate within your church at this point in its spiritual development. This requires prayer, preparation, and patience. But whatever you do, realize it may take much longer than you think it should to establish a vibrant salt-and-light ministry.

Good foundations take a lot of hard work and care; this is true for construction of a building as well as establishing a mature, effective ministry. Remember, this change is for the long haul and not just to respond to the current inane legislative action of the day by your state or Congress, or decisions by the your local municipality.

Given these cautions, the following "10-Step Program" should be useful in guiding your planning and also in tracking progress.

### Ten Steps to Create a Ministry

*Step 1:* For large churches the sheer extent and variety of ministries can make it challenging to find if there's an existing ministry vaguely similar or related to what you want to do. If there is, join it and help grow and mature it.

Unfortunately, for the great majority of churches, citizenship types of activities don't fall easily into traditional outreach or adult oriented ministries. To expand an existing ministry to encompass political engagement it may be necessary for that leadership to re-assess what constitutes being salt and light,

---

[258]    For a detailed treatment of how to pitch your pastor, see Chapter 7: How to Approach Your Pastor.

what it means to do good to everyone, and how citizenship related labors actually promote the gospel[259]

*Step 2:* If a citizenship type of ministry doesn't exist, find several people in your church who share your passion. You know they're out there – because you talk with them about your concern for what's going on in our country and what should be done that will glorify God in making a difference. If you don't know anyone like that, begin to ask others if they have interest in becoming more involved, or at least discussing what would be of interest and fruitful to do, no matter how small the initial steps.

*Step 3:* Meet together to discuss what you would like to see happen within your church. This isn't a time to pile on the pastor (it's never good to do that!), or gripe about what isn't being done. It's a time to discuss what types of activities could make a difference in educating, equipping, and energizing Christians to make a difference in a Christ-honoring way. Fortunately, there are lots of outstanding materials available to read and use as templates to stimulate your thinking and be a source of encouragement, just remember to be realistic.[260]

*Step 4:* Every ministry needs to have someone who leads or guides it. For citizenship types of ministries it's important to make absolutely certain the leader is a mature, well-rounded believer with a broad base of interests, and good

---

[259] Salt-and-light types of ministries are a good example. Until recently, the understanding of what salt and light seemed to encompass was limited to our personal example in the work environment or answering for the hope within us when questioned about our faith. These are obviously important and good, but narrow in application when the full potential of Matthew 5:13-16 is considered.

[260] For a summary of representative sources of information and resources, see Chapter 18 Resources.

people-skills[261]. The challenge for someone that is passionate about this ministry area is to not take it personally if leadership decides you aren't the perfect fit to actually lead it.[262] Remember, the goal is to begin fruitful labor in a hostile and controversial area, so maturity is absolutely critical, as is the understanding that this isn't your ministry, it's the Lord's and it must honor him.

*Step 5:* Find those church leaders (pastor, elder, ministry leader, etc.) who are sympathetic to your passion. For small churches this may be a short list. But even so, there will be someone serving in a leadership capacity who will know how the pastors (or elders) think, how they make decisions, and what their concerns are for the health of the church[263]. This type of insight is invaluable as you develop your plans and eventually approach leadership.

For larger churches, the probability of finding a pastoral staff member that's sympathetic to your cause is probably much higher, but the labyrinth of decision making will probably be much more complex. But large or small, having someone in the leadership circle to help coach you and your little group is important.

*Step 6:* With this leader, strategize an approach to defining, developing and implementing a citizenship ministry given your particular church environment. Make sure you're flexible in approach, and willing to start small if necessary.

---

[261] By this I mean someone that can handle a wide range of personality types with finesse, discernment, grace, kindness, discernment and at the same time be teachable. Not that someone has to be perfect, but because of the volatile nature of politics and personal opinions it's important to be able to defuse potential conflict and focus others on what's important and Christ-honoring.

[262] It's unfortunate but true, that those who are the most passionate about getting Christians involved politically are sometimes the very ones that prevent it from happening within their own church. If you don't think so, read Chapter 6 What About Zealots? and do a self-assessment. I've personally witnessed this phenomenon in churches, with the person eventually leaving for unjustifiable reasons.

[263] I affectionately call this person the "trusted agent" because they are in a unique position to help work "the system" and eventually gain ministry approval in a manner that doesn't compromise the church in any way that the wider leadership cannot support.

Also, be careful to not just pass this ministry off to your confidant unless they personally want to run with it. They're counselors for you and may not want to be the doers, especially with all that they are undoubtedly doing already.

*Step 7:* Formulate a clear, crisp purpose statement; the goals to be accomplished (both near term and long term)[264]; a general approach to accomplishing those goals; resource needs (particularly if there is a financial impact); and how this ministry will ensure pastoral oversight is maintained.

This step is extremely important since having a straightforward, concise statement of what the ministry is intended to do, what it will take to accomplish it, and how issues or problems that may be encountered will be handled, will go a long ways to demonstrating you've thought through the implications and are up for the task. Also remember, you can't do everything yourself, but there's a lot that can be easily done with just a handful of helpers.

*Step 8:* Present your plan to wider church leadership (if needed) for approval and oversight. Be receptive to their concerns and remain flexible in adapting your plans to accommodate any issues they have. Again, it's important to have the longer view in mind – the equipping and encouraging of the flock to engage the political realm (government and elected representatives specifically) for the common good, to protect our religious freedoms, and for the sake of the gospel. Showing explicitly how these relate to each other will help give church leadership assurance that the purpose is justifiable and biblical.

---

[264] In industry, the military, and most organizations the terms "tactical" and "strategic" are useful to represent short-term and long-term perspectives. These terms have the illusion of warfare, which is reasonable considering it is spiritual warfare. Of necessity, the near-term goals should be better defined than the long-term ones, and your purpose needs to be well thought out. Another factor that can be extremely helpful is the definition and use of metrics to gauge effectiveness, such as number of members newly registered to vote, number of times the ministry is promoted publicly, etc.

*Step 9:* Be patient. If this type of ministry doesn't already exist in some form, it may take quite some time to create and expand one. Not only is this important in order to gain needed volunteers and resources, but also to build up a solid foundation of trust and support from your pastors. Welcome shepherding oversight; welcome the opportunity to inform and confer with your pastor before you do anything; and ensure any burdens or needs placed on them are few and light.

*Step 10:* If approved, establish a standard meeting time and place for your ministry, advertise widely to gain additional volunteers, and create an agenda to focus the meeting and to be a good steward of other people's time. Make sure the ministry purpose is well understood by those who want to participate, and be careful in whom you entrust responsibility. Also, it's important to take good notes and make sure any action items that are developed have someone willing to follow up on them and that there is a date when they are to be done.

A little warning – there's an old saying that if the only tool you have is a hammer, then everything will look like a nail. Aggressive political activists are passionate, engaged, and focused on their particular hot button issues. There's a time and place for their energy, but it has to be in balance with the overall purpose of enlisting as many Christians as possible in the right battles, in the right way, at the right time.

### Practical Activities

The citizenship-oriented activities that are legal within a church environment are virtually endless. Truly, we're only limited by our imagination and the confines of Scripture to pursue our rightful role as citizens of this nation.

To stimulate some of that imagination, the following lists provide samples for possible use. Decide what impact you want to have and pick something that's acceptable for your church situation. As a general rule, concentrate on high-interest activities at the start and always ensure biblical truth and worldview is the foundation. Also, if there's any doubt about the legality of what you're doing, numerous legal organizations provide free advice, and even defense if needed.[265]

Finally, deal only with facts and not emotional hyperbola when attacking some issue of public concern. There's a right time and place for indignation toward the deeds of darkness around us (Ephesians 5:11), but being patient and charitable toward each other is what builds the Christ-honoring unity and focus we need to be effective.

### *Education and Awareness Examples:*

- Bulletin boards (post current issue education events; relevant classes available; local activities or lectures; published letters to the editor)
- Bulletin inserts (citizenship group meeting times; special classes offered; national founders quotes; national Christian events (e.g. National Day of Prayer; Pro-Life Sunday; traditional marriage Sunday; Pulpit Sunday)
- Information tables (publications; brochures; reference material; voter registration information; pending legislation; church policies on current issues)
- Resource library (books; DVD's; magazines; election district maps; issue papers; pamphlets; periodicals; etc.)
- Contact information (phone numbers; web sites; e-mail addresses) on all elected officials at the city, county, state and national levels
- Community/regional maps of legislative district boundaries
- Legislative district numbers listed in church family phone directories to identify elected representatives

---

[265]    For a partial list of available resources see Chapter 18.

- Yearly calendar of Christian; legislative; national events of interest
- Legal referral information for family, faith and freedom protections, whether at home, school, work or in the community[266]
- Periodic public/pulpit recognition of the citizenship ministry to increase visibility
- Compile a list of issue-oriented information web sites of known character, balance, and research
- Ministry page on church web-site
- Reading program for the Declaration of Independence, the Constitution, the Federalist Papers, and other early documents
- Offer classes, seminars and information objectively addressing the Christian history of the United State
- Communicate issue topics through a social media platform like Facebook, Twitter or E-mail distributions of current issue alerts requesting comment from the public

### Internal Church Examples:

- Conduct routine prayer for elected officials, judges, etc. during worship services, in small groups and in prayer meetings
- Host a biblical worldview lecture series, invite guest speakers to speak on current issues of the day
- Conduct a Sunday School class on hot topics of the day from a biblical perspective and provide useful, factual background information
- Generate short, biblical position papers on issues of the day for wide use by church members
- Conduct a hands-on letter-writing Sunday school class to express opinions on pending legislation or current issues

---

[266]  For a partial list of available resources see Chapter 18.

- Conduct periodic voter registration drives
- Create, or make use of available, non-partisan voter guides
- Prepare for, and conduct an Election Pre-View Evening
- Conduct candidate forums (invite all viable candidates, and treat equally). Solicit all candidates' personal testimony and positions on moral matters of concern
- Encourage members to sign up for legislative alerts from reputable organizations, and have available for general use
- Provide family subscriptions to "World" magazine or encourage subscription to CitizenLink, a public policy partner of Focus on the Family
- Host legal seminars on current issues of interest
- Gather signatures for petition drives that are for issues clearly within a Christian's interest and concern
- Encourage topical sermons several times a year on a current socio-political issue
- Identify available subject matter experts within your church to speak at church forums or in Sunday School on issues of current interest

### External Examples:

- Identify local groups and support them financially and with volunteers (e.g. adopt a Crisis Pregnancy Clinic)
- Develop compassion ministries not dependent on government control and keep up on related legislation (pro-life; homosexual (Truth in Love); homeless; obscenity; illegal immigrants; human trafficking)
- Adopt a legislator to meet with, express support and concerns for (as appropriate), and to pray with
- Build a relationship with city council members, mayors, state legislators
- Routinely write/call/e-mail elected officials (concerns, encouragement)

- Coordinate letters to the editor on issues of common concern
- Encourage individual involvement in the campaigns of godly candidates (precinct walking; phone banks; get-out-the-vote; etc.)
- Review public school curriculum, inform parents of opt-out opportunities
- Represent church at city council and local school board meetings[267]
- Provide church representation at local/regional secular, business and political seminars, luncheons, open political party meetings, etc.
- Equip retired church members to attend superior courts in the area to monitor and document the activities, decisions and temperament of questionable judges
- Equip retired church members to attend public school classes, to monitor what's said and encouraged by teachers, and document any inappropriate indoctrination

### Long-Term Activity Examples:

- Mentor future pastoral leadership in the implications of a biblical worldview
- Mentor young men and women for future public leadership, including potential elected office
- Encourage qualified men/women to run for elective office or to provide direct staff support to elected officials
- Identify collaborative activities and approaches with other like-minded churches on key legislative opportunities

---

[267] A sad note, in a large city near my home, there is an opportunity for pastors to provide a moment of reflection (prayer) before each city council meeting. It's difficult to fill the opportunities with evangelical pastors, however, Muslims, wiccans, and new age adherents seem to be readily available.

- Establish a recurring, biblical worldview curriculum to train and equip all church members on a routine basis
- Organize a regional pastor's roundtable on issues of common concern
- Encourage collaborative church projects such as pro-life billboards

One particularly effective way to engage members is through a Sunday school class. Where better to grapple with national or local concerns rather than relying on news media as the source of information and insight? It may take a little more preparation for the leader to select the topic, mine biblical principles that apply, and think through how to handle the presentation and discussion in order to ensure a good understanding; but the investment will be well worth it. Not only will the teacher develop a good grasp of the issue but you'll gain more than just opinion when talking to neighbors, co-workers, or even other family members as the relevance of Scripture is brought to bear.

A newspaper, a newscast, an informative e-mail, any source can be used as the starting point. For that matter, even the prior week's sermon can be a springboard to discussing how the content can be applied to the contemporary issues of the day from the principles preached and any related texts used.

For the leader: don't be concerned about becoming the expert on a given issue. Sometimes the reasoning and discussion during the class brings out the best principles and understanding.

### Now For a Reality Check

It's common for Christians engaging our irresponsible government to be discouraged by a lack of co-workers. Experience has shown, however, that managing expectations is the key to preventing your own unnecessary "burn-out" or frustration.

Right or wrong, although most Christians are concerned about the direction of our nation and the open attacks on our faith and religious liberties, few will take any action to correct it.

Experience also shows that with any size church and an important issue of the day, if 10% of the membership is willing to make a call, write a letter, talk to neighbors, or take action of any kind to influence others (including personal, committed prayer), a substantial impact for good can occur. Remember, you'll never get 100% participation, and compared to the common public 10% demonstrates overwhelming interest and concern.

Would I give up trying to motivate many more to uplift righteousness in the public square – absolutely not! But a dose of realism along with our zeal will help keep us enthusiastic and encouraging to others. It will also prevent undue frustration with others that could result in destructive contention.

What's appropriate for you particular church must be worked out with your pastoral leadership, committed to prayer, and patiently pursued in a Christ-honoring, humble manner. It may take only a few weeks to begin, or it may take several years[268], but the labor in this Kingdom work will be worth it.

---

[268]    In my own home church, it took approximately six years to establish a Christian Citizenship Ministry. In the area, one mega church took more than five years, while another took less than a year. Much of the difference will depend on the current moral imperative driving the interest.

# Chapter 16

# Government Legislation Checklist

"*Government's view of the economy could be summed up in a few short phrases: If it moves, tax it. If it keeps moving, regulate it. If it stops moving, subsidize it*" – **Ronald Reagan**

"*Nothing is so permanent as a temporary government program.*" – **Milton Friedman**

### Government Gone Awry

Government is not our friend when it throws off restraint. The recent federal takeover of the mortgage, banking and auto industries; and astronomical deficit spending has placed our nation on a road to democratic-socialism and bankruptcy. Add the nationalization of the health care industry with business-crushing cap-and-trade legislation and it's no wonder confidence in our federal government is at an all time low.

But the financial problems don't stop there. Most states are in fiscal crisis, as are large numbers of cities across the country. It's painfully obvious that decisions are being made at every level of government without regard for the unavoidable consequences on society, businesses, and ultimately our families.

Not surprisingly, the same worldview that brings financial ruin has also brought us social ruin. Government-sponsored welfare programs are creating generational dependency on handouts; abortion-on-demand and physician-assisted suicide has cheapened life; promotion of same-sex marriages has legitimatized sexual perversion and immorality; hate crime laws have institutionalized injustice for entire classes of people; and anything resembling Christian values and faith has been removed from public schools and government functions.[269]

There's a commonality in many of these trends: the belief that biblical values and principles are outmoded and even dangerous. In fact, when the rightful, biblically focused role of government is ignored it's just a matter of time before government will reflect the worst of mankind's nature and become an aggressive enemy of any opposition to its growth.

Government's addiction to power (1 John 2:16), our money (1 Timothy 6:10), and an arrogant "we-know-better-than-you" attitude is putting our nation into a financial and moral death spiral that's the logical result of a defective worldview that is as blinded to reality as a druggie is to his own addiction.

Can anything realistically be done to stop the inevitable collapse? Historically, when people of faith decide "enough is enough" and demand accountability their elected representatives begin to change. This was true with the Immigration Reform Act under President George W. Bush; the massive rejection of Congressional incumbents in the elections of 2010 and 2014, and is slowly playing out through public disgust for the current nationalization of healthcare[270].

---

[269]  The list of trends that are demonstrably destructive is very long. The ones mentioned are only intended to be representative of some of the more egregious, far-ranging ones.

[270]  Or better known as Obamacare; or technically the Patient Protection and Affordable Care Act.

The rest of this chapter summarizes reasonable questions our elected representatives should be able to answer before supporting any new legislation or government proposed programs. Each is intended to draw on relevant biblical principles and force some needed reflection both in the Christian community and on our representatives before enacting legislation that could prove to be destructive and not within proper governmental responsibilities.

But ultimately to hold leaders accountable we need two things. The first is a much broader understanding and acceptance across the Christian community of the biblical principles that apply to today's issues;[271] and the second is spiritual leadership who is willing to energize their flocks to demand accountability from our elected leaders.[272]

## *The Function of Government*

***Constitutional Merit.*** Even in Paul's day there were those who would go beyond the bounds set for them (1 Corinthians 4:6), and create major difficulties for others. Applying this principle to the federal government, it's appropriate to ask if proposed legislation or a new program is clearly included within the enumerated constitutional powers of the government. If so, can the specific Article and Section be referenced that unambiguously authorizes the legislation? The same question applies at the state and local levels, with the requirement that the legislation, program or policy clearly be an inherently governmental function with no other option to perform it, and that the consequences of not taking action would be demonstrably serious.

---

[271]   Clearly, the issues in our nation are not new to humanity. Many are found in the Old Testament accounts of Israel and other nations. Specific details will vary, but the underlying principles never change.

[272]   The first four chapters of this book develop these two factors in greater depth. The reader is directed there for a more thorough analysis and the biblical reasoning behind it.

***The Founders Intent.*** Just as Paul laid a foundation on the person of Jesus Christ and others profitably built upon it; some with gold, silver and precious stones; others build with wood, hay and straw to their own loss (1 Corinthians 3:10-15). Our founders were learned men who created a unique governmental system by combining the best of western political thought with timeless biblical truths warning about man's nature. Since the original construct served us well, it's appropriate to question what new universal principles or biblical insights justify expansion of government responsibilities instead of seeking solutions that can be accomplished in a more godly and effective way by the people themselves?

New principles must be historically representative of, and consistent with the powers and limitations defined in the nation's founding documents[273] and not spurious opinions unrepresentative of our founding fathers' original intent.

***Uniquely Governmental Functions.*** Just as you wouldn't ask an auto mechanic to repair your hernia, a compelling argument must exist to justify why government is the only entity that has the insight, expertise and experience to accomplish what's proposed. In addition, it must be shown that private industry or the faith community can't accomplish the same thing faster, cheaper or more effectively. The biblical equivalent is asking someone with the gift of administration to perform mercy ministries, or a foot to perform as a heart (1 Corinthians 12:14-26)[274]. There may be some benefit but taking on roles not within an entities nature can only lead to frustration and waste.

---

[273]  Basically, these are the Declaration of Independence and the Constitution of the United States. Founding principles have been well argued in the Federalist Papers and extracted and summarized in "The 5000 Year Leap" by W. Cleon Skousen, 1981.

[274]  The biblical analogy obviously breaks down quite rapidly because the intent is for the body of Christ to minister together with its variety of giftedness in harmony to the glory of God. The government can provide necessary functions that can work effectively with its citizens for the common good, but being secular and power hungry, the tendency is to abuse that power and overreach as often as possible, thus, wrecking havoc on those who can more effectively do the work.

## Fiscal Responsibility

*Feasibility.* Scripture teaches the need to plan properly – whether to conduct war or accomplish some great project (Proverbs 15:22; 24:3-6; 24:27; Luke 14:28-30; 31-32). To ensure success, the proper expertise and counsel is always necessary. It's no different when considering a new government program.

It's appropriate to ask what prior government programs of similar size and complexity convincingly demonstrate that this new program will be successful in accomplishing its intent while being cost effective. Can this legislation be implemented and enforced within existing resources without degrading the effectiveness of any other existing government function?

*Fiscal Impact.* In 1 Timothy 6:10 we read "For the love of money is a root of all kinds of evils." No truer description exists of the fiscal irresponsibility we find in so much of government budgeting.[275] These evils don't necessarily imply personal financial gain; they may solely be to increase one's prominence, power base, sense of importance, or feed one's pride. Even if the program motivation is sincere, it doesn't imply there's competence to understand the unintended consequences in other areas.[276]

Therefore, what assurance is there that this legislation or government program will be fiscally responsible and not require additional tax revenue to fund it? Can it be shown to be revenue neutral throughout its intended life? How will the implementation of this program decrease the costs in other related programs or legislative requirements currently in place? Will the government

---

[275]   Clearly there are exceptions, particularly with those individuals who are dedicated to doing a good job and serve us all well. However, I challenge the reader to come up with a few unambiguous examples that show otherwise.

[276]   For a classic, excellent treatment of this effect, I encourage the reading of "Economics in One Lesson" by Henry Hazlitt; 1946

go into debt or borrow funds to pay for this program; if so, why? How will this decision decrease the national debt, the budget deficit, or federal borrowing?

*Taxes.* How will this legislation decrease the overall tax burden? On what legal basis is it justifiable to disproportionately tax certain classes of individuals or activities while protecting others? How does this legislation decrease the complexity of the current tax code? When will this tax change proposal end, under what conditions will it end, and what conditions must be met before it will be considered necessary to extend?

*Economy.* What definitive analysis has shown that this legislation or program will have a positive fiscal impact upon the general economy? What wider economic impacts are expected beyond the immediate focus of this legislation or program? How will indirect effects on the economy be measured as this legislation or program progresses? What historical examples prove this type of legislation or program will benefit the economy? Are there counter examples for comparison, if not, why not?

*Necessity*

*Performance.* How will the effectiveness of this legislation or program be measured, continually monitored and independently verified by outside authorities not directly impacted by it (Proverbs 18:17)? What criteria will be used to decide if this program or legislation should be cancelled or not? What comparable programs demonstrate conclusively that this legislation or program will accomplish the goals set for it?

*Experience.* Even a king with little experience can be successful in war if he relies on those that understand conflict (Proverbs 20:18). For most issues legislators will have virtually no extensive, direct life experience in the matter. They rely on others to adequately inform them on the matter at hand and the implications of taking action. It's appropriate, therefore, to ask what experts are being used and if they're only knowledgeable in narrow areas of expertise or well acquainted with potential complications in other areas. Are there a variety of experts representing a number of perspectives and do they know how to measure success or failure?

**Interference.** How will this legislation reduce government encroachment in our lives, the economy, or the free enterprise system? How will it reduce the burden on businesses and personal lives and allow them to be more productive and successful in their pursuits? How will this legislation increase the freedom to exercise our fundamental rights as documented in the Bill of Rights?

**Transition.** How will this legislation or program lead to a smaller role for government in the out years? How will it encourage and ensure greater private and faith-based involvement and less government involvement in the years ahead? What metrics will be used to ensure these goals are met?

**Sundown Requirement.** If prophecies, knowledge and tongues will cease, (1 Corinthians 13:8), shouldn't government programs be even more perishable? When was the last time a government program or a piece of legislation was eliminated? It's only reasonable to demand built-in features to automatically end legislation and programs when no longer required. In fact, what mechanism will be used to constantly monitor effectiveness to determine whether it should be terminated prior to the end of its authorization? How will a determination be made at the end of the authorization period to determine if it was successful in meeting its goals? What exceptional performance must be demonstrated before any re-authorization for continuation?

**Redundancy.** With thousands of new laws, regulations and program modifications each year a valid question is whether there's redundancy between what is being proposed and what is already being done. Has a thorough survey been conducted to find if other programs already exist, and if so, why a new one will have any different result? If similar programs or legislation do exist, why aren't they cancelled if this new approach is implemented? Does this new legislation replace other laws so that the intent is now clearer and easier to understand?

**Exceptions.** Much has been made over the years about legislators at the national and state levels exempting themselves from the very rules and regulations they impose on others, whether its retirement benefits, medical benefits, staff hiring practices, pay equality or even investment decisions that would be considered insider trading in the private sector. A valid question, therefore is why there's any preferential treatment in this legislation in any way (Proverbs 22:16)?

### Selected Enduring Issues[277]

**Family Integrity.** The family is an institution created by God and is the basic foundation to our society (Genesis 2:18-22). Protecting it is critical to the success of all other social endeavors. The obvious question to ask, therefore, is how will this program or legislation strengthen the traditional family? What measures will ensure there's no weakening of the traditional family structure as an institution? Does this legislation or program directly or indirectly incentivize the formation of alternative family structures, and if so what safeguards are included to reduce and eliminate these affects measurably over time?

---

[277]     There are many other enduring issues of consequence, such as education, war, parental authority, etc. These are given as representative examples only.

***Justice.*** A fundamental purpose for government is to dispense justice (Leviticus 19:15; Proverbs 18:5; 21:15; Romans 13:3-4). When this is corrupted, the legitimacy of government authority is rightfully questioned. Anything that differentiates one person from another and treats them differently, regardless of social or material standing (Proverbs 28:21) is intrinsically biased and unjust. This doesn't mean mercy can't be given in unusual circumstances, but this should be uncommon.

In that light, what injustice is this legislation intended to correct that is constitutionally warranted? Does it recognize the basic equality of every person before the law, or does it treat a category of victim or perpetrator differently because of some unrelated circumstances or characteristic? Is the same crime treated differently depending on anything other than the crime itself? If so, how is this justified?

***Life.*** The sanctity of life is another foundational truth government must be required to recognize and protect (Genesis 9:5-6). If government fails in this regard then all other freedoms are at risk. Accordingly, does this legislation or program in any way impact the protection of life from conception to natural death? If so, what fundamental principle or need (such as capital punishment for murder) justifies government imposing this decision on the life or health decisions of a person?

***Environment.*** With the potential for the climate change (global warming) controversy to have on our economy and our lives, it's reasonable to ask what definitive analysis proves beyond a shadow of a doubt that legislation to control emissions is critical.[278] Has credible and verifiable research been performed to prove that any actions taken will actually improve the situation and not make

---

[278] The "shadow of a doubt" criterion isn't used arbitrarily. The case for manmade climate change and the need to radically change the entire economic and social order of the nation and indeed the world should withstand objective scrutiny consistent with the most life-death criminal cases.

matters worse? Are the models used to make predictions robust enough to accurately predict historic changes in climate over the last several thousand years – including the appearance and disappearance of multiple ice ages?[279]

## Due Diligence

It used to be that legislators would be familiar with the content of any proposed bill, or at least have read it. With late night "gut-and-amend" tactics[280], extremely long and complex legislation, and "crisis" voting this is now rarely true.[281] The fact of the matter is that there are literally thousands of pages of legislative bills proposed each year at the federal level and even in large states such as California.[282] These bills are subject to continuous modification as they work their way through subcommittees, full committees, then each legislative house, followed by reconciliation meetings, and then for final chamber votes prior to executive decisions.

To expect our legislators to be aware of every nuance of every bill that will ultimately be voted on is probably unreasonable – particularly when eleventh-hour tactics are used to make substantial changes prior to an artificially

---

[279] In Matthew 16:2-3 Jesus condemned the Pharisees and Sadducees for being able to interpret the weather day to day, but the signs of the times are beyond them. It is similar in our day that weather is difficult to predict, particularly on a global scale, yet the ideological underpinnings of the environmentalist movement to worship mother earth and remove human influence are not recognized.

[280] According to the state of California Legislature Glossary of Legislative Terms "Gut and Amend" is "when amendments to a bill removes the current content in their entirety and replace them with different provisions". These different provisions, incidentally, may have no relationship to the original intent of the bill or its title.

[281] The recent Federal Health Care Reform legislation is a clear example of this tactic. Comprised of over 2,700 pages, no known legislator was able to read the entire bill prior to voting on it. In a classic demonstration of the level of contempt held toward deliberative government, then-Speaker of the House Nanci Pelosi stated: "We had to pass the bill before we could read what's in it."

[282] In recent reports by John Stossel of Fox News, it was reported that there are 170,000 pages of federal regulations, with about 80,000 pages of new and proposed regulations created each year. If these were stacked on top of each other, the pile would be about 23 feet high.

created time limit. If having awareness of what's in a bill isn't hard enough, to be able to fully comprehend it as well as anticipate the unintended[283] consequences can become a nightmare. Although staffs provide incredible support to ferret out what is important and what isn't, the sheer magnitude of the task is oftentimes intentionally overwhelming to prevent adequate scrutiny.

The representative questions provided in this chapter can also be applied to existing laws that have been destructive to families, our freedoms, or have resulted in the promotion of values contrary to what's in the best interests of a moral society. In fact, placing sundown clauses for even good legislation is also reasonable. This allows a continual reminder of the justification for the original decisions and helps to weed out legislators that tend to become compromised over time. This process won't be easy, but it should become routine as we influence leaders to do what's right and not what's expedient.

### Don't Despair

In this dismal situation, there are two bright spots!

Conservative legislators claim that the vast majority of proposed legislation, at least at the state level[284], is concerned with routine governance matters and not related to social issues or programs with significant fiscal impacts. Although a moral argument can be made to put close scrutiny onto even the most trivial action (Proverbs 16:4)[285], as a practical matter it may be a poor use of limited

---

[283]   I use the term "unintended" very mercifully. There are numerous examples of what is thought to be innocuous text placed in proposed legislation that is specifically intended for a certain impact. This is manipulation of the process for vested interests and, many times, ideological advancement.

[284]   At the federal level there's a similar phenomenon, such as the naming of buildings and resolutions acknowledging supposedly worthy causes.

[285]   It's not my intent here to argue whether there are any decisions or actions that could be considered morally neutral. Since the Lord is sovereign in all things and has foreordained everything in the entire universe, there's an intent and plan behind each thought or action, be it godly or ungodly.

time and resources even though there is risk involved. That being said, the most controversial types of legislation are those that touch on moral issues such as abortion, homosexual rights, parental authority, and our basic freedoms. These decisions for conservative legislators who claim a biblical worldview are for the most part easy, unless they're personally compromised in one way or another.

The second bright spot is that there are many watchdog organizations representing our values that are combing through proposed legislation to find those that substantively support or degrade the representation of our values. These organizations provide a tremendous service not only to their constituents, who are encouraged to call and write their representatives, but also to legislators and their staffs who may not have been able to adequately review or assess any particular piece of legislation. These organizations are not only concerned about Congressional actions, but they're also found in every state[286]

Our representatives need to be accountable for their decisions and know that we're carefully watching what they say and do. There may be nuances in any given piece of legislation, but at the end of the day will it support or detract from furthering the values, principles and freedoms we hold dear? The most powerful way we can influence those in leadership is to routinely communicate with them, whether in public forums, through letters or e-mails, phone calls, or personal appointments. If the response is wrong, problematic, or unclear then the classic intervention by vote remains the last weapon of choice.

---

[286] Examples include Concerned Women for America; Family Resource Council; etc. A resource listing of like-minded organizations is provided in Chapter 18.

# Chapter 17

# Final Thoughts – What's at Stake?

*"And let us not grow weary of doing good, for in due season we will reap, if we do not give up. So then, as we have opportunity, let us do good to everyone, and especially to those who are of the household of faith"* – **Galatians 6:9-10**

*"It does not require a majority to prevail, but rather an irate, tireless minority keen to set brush fires in people's minds."* – ***Samuel Adams***

### *You Do Not Have, Because You Do Not Ask*

Prayer is a powerful tool in our spiritual arsenal (James 5:16). Our prayer life is refined and motivated when we or someone close to us are going through severe trials. When we share the gospel with someone; our prayer life is energized for that person as we humbly remember the Lord is sovereign in their life (John 6:44). But are we just as committed to pray for our nation, its leaders (1 Timothy 2:1-3), and our own hearts (Proverbs 4:23) as we figure out how to preserve our fragile freedoms by being salt and light (Matthew 5:13-16)? If we don't pray for this nation, who will? If we're not concerned about the growing hostility of government toward our faith and the need to restrain and properly focus governmental power, who is?

This book outlines sources of friction in the Christian community that currently weaken and demoralize any united biblical voice in politics. It also attempts to clarify the reasons why involvement's so important for the sake of the gospel. Are there solutions to our current Christian fratricide in all things political? There are, but they'll take time and diligent effort to accomplish.

All kinds of things can be done, but to seek God's blessing on our labors we must first know our own hearts. Too often political activity becomes an end in itself. Like any human endeavor, politics can become addictive because of the power, influence, and attention it creates. Because it can be a snare for pastors and church members, it's critical to seek the Lord's will with proper motives and to learn how to work together instead of against our fellow brothers and sisters.

That journey must begin with and be sustained and refreshed by prayer. Without prayer cover, Christians will continue to be susceptible to the same prideful traps that many politicians fall into. Without consistent prayer the battle can easily become just a goal to win instead of doing what's right for the glory of God. And finally, without prayer we'll forget that it's the Lord that sustains, protects and brings about the unity we must have in order to stand strong against the evil one (Matthew 16:18), and to do everything we can to bring honor to the name of the Lord (1 Corinthians 10:31).

### Are Christians at Fault?

The question can legitimately be asked, "Are Christians at fault for our out-of-control government?" I personally don't believe the current condition of government can be directly and completely blamed on a complacent church.

We know biblically and by experience that there will always be those seeking to punish the Christian faith because they're offended by it (2 Corinthians 2:15-16). These haters are willing to go to any extent and use any tool to denigrate, marginalize, and eventually destroy the Truth we represent (1 Peter 5:8-9). Even with our national Christian legacy, governmental means has become a much more direct and powerful way for darkness to accomplish the same goal. Whether or not the Christian community tries to engage and prevail in these battles, spiritual combat will continue until the Lord's triumphant return (1 Thessalonians 4:16-18). In that day the ungodly will be judged for their thirst to call evil good and good evil (Isaiah 5:20) and their hatred of Christ and His people.

Where the weak and factious body of Christ is at fault is being apathetic to the extreme dangers a hostile government can quickly become toward Truth. This has been the case throughout history, and our nation isn't immune. Large portions of spiritual leadership as well as many church members have also bought the lie that faith has no place in the affairs of the nation or political matters. But this non-engagement isn't taught in Scripture. In fact the exact opposite is true. Christians are to work diligently for the good of everyone (Jeremiah 29:7; Matthew 22:39); knowing, except for the grace of God, where ever Christian influence is removed whatever remains will quickly rot and become our adversary.

Christians aren't the cause of an evil government, but they're responsible for ignoring the good they know they ought to do when it's within their power to be wise counselors to the nation to which we're called to be good stewards. Also, many times when Christians do engage it becomes a "fire-and-forget" activity that sees voting as all that's needed to be a good citizen. As important as voting is, it's naive to think that a trifling amount of effort (casting a vote) should be rewarded by God with long lasting, godly benefit. Everywhere else in our lives hard work is required, so why would we expect it to be different with matters of such immense importance?

### *Why We Do What We Do*

Since the beginning, Christianity has been characterized by an evangelistic zeal. The Great Commission (Matthew 28:18-20) clearly wants us to give the gospel of Christ to those without hope in this world. In fact, this command is one of the major reasons why God keeps us in this world after we've come to faith.

Besides the Great Commission, we have the Great Challenge of the salt-and-light passages (Matthew 5:13-16). These show we have a duty to influence community, culture and even the government for the common good. Doing so brings benefits to our families, to our nation, and especially protection for the Kingdom work the church is called to accomplish. In fact, with every legitimate activity Christians take on the relevancy of God's truths and the credibility of our personal testimony is affirmed.

Unfortunately the world has convinced many believers that politics is the one area that's not a legitimate pursuit for anyone with a biblical worldview. This tactic shouldn't surprise us. What secular humanists (liberals) can't accomplish through fair competition or objective examination they'll try to accomplish through legislative or judicial means. Removing us from politics makes the way clear for the most powerful institution on the planet to be used for man-centered not biblical purposes. In reality, Christians are the only group that stands in their way.

The ultimate goals of darkness are to first legitimize evil, gather as much support as possible for credibility, and then push anything having to do with biblical faith and the proclamation of the gospel into a closet and lock the door. There's no happy middle ground with evil, no peaceful co-existence. If our influence continues to become marginalized to the point of irrelevance, we can be assured we'll eventually be looked upon as the source of societies' problems and persecuted accordingly. At that point our freedom to openly proclaim the gospel will become orders of magnitude harder.

This spiritual struggle will ultimately show whether the great power and prosperity of this nation will be used to fulfill noble purposes or to crush the unlimited opportunities we have as Christians to influence the conditions and events here and around the world for the glory of Christ through Kingdom work and the gospel.

### Why I'm Still Optimistic

In my personal ministry to equip churches and individuals to become more biblically informed in political activism I've had times of severe discouragement. It's during those times that I needed to be reminded of some timeless truths that have become a real source of encouragement:

*First*, we serve a sovereign God who will accomplish all of His purposes for this nation as He sees fit (Acts 17:26-27). His plan is perfect; He makes no mistakes; He places whomever He wants in governmental leadership positions to meet our needs and to grant us what we deserve.

*Second*, as a family of God we're only called to be faithful, not to guarantee results. We can't predict the future with any certainty. All we can do is make decisions we believe are honoring to the Lord while knowing the ultimate fruit of our labors is only what God will grant to us. If our joy was based on winning elections instead of centered on our Lord and Savior, then our labors are of no more value than those of the ungodly.

*Third*, even with the visible and pronounced influence of evil throughout our nation, "good" still thrives (Matthew 5:45). God's common grace will always provide for us and those around us in remarkable ways. He also gives us favor with non-believers and even uses them to fulfill His purposes for our own good.

*Fourth*, even an unbeliever can still be pierced with facts, logic and sound reasoning (Romans 2:14-16). Although the corrupt nature is incapable of understanding spiritual truths (1 Corinthians 2:14), God has still given them a conscience that can resonate with moral truths.

*Fifth*, unlike the war on smoking, coal mining, or even plastic bags, our war is an ongoing spiritual battle with the fallen world to bring glory to God, and never to ourselves (Isaiah 55:9-11).

And *Sixth*, God's Word (truths, principles, wisdom) will not return void (Isaiah 55:11) if we faithfully live it and proclaim it. In fact, if the gates of hell can't prevail against God's Kingdom, then man's institutions and schemes will also crumble (Matthew 16:18).

May the Lord bless our labors as we strive to do everything for His glory.

# Chapter 18

# Resources

*"Or what king, going out to encounter another king in war, will not sit down first and deliberate whether he is able to with ten thousand to meet him who comes against him with twenty thousand?"* – **Luke 14:31**

*"Unless the LORD builds the house, those who build it labor in vain."*
– **Psalm 127:1**

### *Only as Good as Our Tools*

Any resource listing for politically concerned Christians can only be a small sampling. With that caveat the following provides a short list of organizations that have a good track record and typically a nationwide reach. There is no attempt to try and characterize each groups mission or purpose statements, or the extent to which newsletters, e-mail alerts, electronic and hardcopy publications, on-line materials or lectures, specific services, or other forms of help are provided since this information is readily available on their web sites. In addition, most, but not all, are typically 501(c)3 organizations.

## Legal Groups

**Alliance Defending Freedom (ADF):**
http://www.adflegal.org

**Liberty Council (LC):**
https://www.lc.org

**National Center for Law and Policy (NCLP):**
http://www.nclplaw.org

**Pacific Justice Institute (PJI):**
http://www.pacificjustice.org

## Legislative Watchdogs

**Concerned Women for America (CWA):**
http://www.cwfa.org

**Family Research Council (FRC):**
http://www.frc.org

**FreedomWorks:**
http://www.freedomworks.org

## Current Events

**Family Research Council (FRC): Washington Update (E-Mail):**
http://www.frc.org

**Focus on the Family:**
http://www.citizenlink.com/about-us; http://www.focusonthefamily.com/socialissues/; http://www.thetruthproject.org; https://www.citizenlink.com/state-groups

**Media Research Center:**
http://www.mrc.org

**Townhall.com:**
http://townhall.com

**World Magazine:**
http://www.worldmag.com

## United States History

**Hillsdale College: On-Line Constitution Courses:**
http://www.hillsdale.edu

**Patrick Henry College:**
http://www.phc.edu

**WallBuilders:**
http://www.wallbuilders.com

## Worldview Training

**Summit Ministries:**
http://www.summit.org

**Colson Center for Worldview Training:**
http://www.colsoncenter.org

## Mobilizing

**Family Research Council (iVoteValues):**
http://www.ivotevalues.org

**Faith & Freedom Coalition:**
http://www.ffcoalition.com

**Eagle Forum:**
http://www.eagleforum.org

**Ethics & Religious Liberty Commission:**
http://erlc.com

## Conservative Research

**The Heritage Foundation:**
http://www.heritage.org

**LifeWay Research:**
http://www.lifewayresearch.com

# About the Author

Frank Kacer has been a Christian worldview activist in the political realm for almost twenty years. Besides authoring over 160 columns and commentaries on Biblical politics for *Good News Etc*, the *Christian Examiner*, and on-line with the *Washington Times "Communities"* and *Communities Digital News*, he has also produced his unique *"Kacer's Call"* biblical perspective on every California statewide Proposition since 2002.

A frequent guest speaker and lecturer at churches, Para-church and partisan organizations on current political issues from a Biblical worldview perspective, Frank has been instrumental in organizing and advising many individual church salt & light ministries. As Founder and Executive Director of the Christian Citizenship Council (C3), and creator of the Christian Statesman Internship Program (CSIP), Frank has a long history of mentoring Christians and churches to engage the public realm in a biblically balanced, Christ-honoring and legal manner. In the political realm, Frank has been elected to county Central Committee political office, been a state party delegate, and been actively engaged in numerous aspects of political campaigns, including strategic planning, candidate recruitment and assessment, get-out-the-vote, precinct operations and volunteer training.

Frank was a physicist in the Department of Defense Intelligence Community for over 35 years, and a senior systems engineer with Science Applications International Corporation (SAIC) for over 12 years. He has a

B.A. in Physics from Western Washington State College (now University) and a M.S. from U.C.L.A. in Engineering/Operations Research.

Frank and Lynn have been married for 42 years, reside in San Diego California, and have three adult children and two granddaughters. He has served on the Elder Board of Grace Bible Church since its founding in 1990 and is responsible for Outreach ministries.